Cromwell was Framed

Ireland 1649

Cromwell was Framed

Ireland 1649

Tom Reilly

CHRONOS BOOKS
Winchester, UK
Washington, USA

First published by Chronos Books, 2014
Chronos Books is an imprint of John Hunt Publishing Ltd., Laurel House, Station Approach,
Alresford, Hants, SO24 9JH, UK
office1@jhpbooks.net
www.johnhuntpublishing.com

For distributor details and how to order please visit the 'Ordering' section on our website.

ISBN: 978 1 78279 516 2

A CIP catalogue record for this book is available from the British Library.

Design: Stuart Davies

Printed and bound by CPI Group (UK) Ltd, Croydon, CR0 4YY

CONTENTS

To Noeleen, Cathy & Eoin

Acknowledgements

While I am indebted to the following people in a myriad of ways, their mention here in no way aligns any of their opinions to the ones I have expressed in this work. This is simply my way of acknowledging engagement I have had with them during its compilation and may not be perceived as endorsement. Some remain to be convinced by my arguments. Michael Hall was my chief inspiration and to him I am eternally grateful. Comments by Terry Connell and Dr Alan Marshall concerning early drafts were reassuring. Nick Poyntz deserves special mention for his advice and attention to detail concerning Drogheda. Jane Mills performed Trojan research for me on Wexford. Prof. Joad Raymond, Prof. Raymond Gillespie and Dr. Sarah Barber all agreed to read my final text. Hubert Murphy found the time to evaluate the manuscript and was very supportive. Elizabeth Finnegan's analysis of the text was exemplary. Mary and Munich Reilly (the mother and the brother respectively) gave me uplifting feedback.

I am also profoundly beholden to Marilyn Meeker, Permissions Manager at Proquest, whose efforts to ensure that the newsbook images were appropriately published here went way above the call of duty and then some.

Most appreciably however, it is the published rationale of Prof. Micheál Ó'Siochrú, Dr Jason McElligott, Prof John Morrill and Prof Padraig Lenehan that provided me with the impetus to return to this topic.

Preface

This is not an academic book. Nor has any history academic given it their seal of approval. I do not have a degree in history. In fact, I failed second level history (Leaving Certificate) at school. My first published book on the subject, *Cromwell, An Honourable Enemy* caused a storm of controversy when it came out on the 350th anniversary of the massacres of Drogheda and Wexford in 1999. It was my first ever attempt at constructing a historical narrative. Many historians exposed the obvious flaws in the methodology, the integrity of some of the sources, the clumsy endnote configuration, the disorganised principles of interpretation, and the underlying theoretical thought process I used to reach conclusions. They were absolutely right. For instance, in *Kingdoms in Crisis* (Page 11) Early Modern historian, Prof Micheál O'Siochrú has described Cromwell, An Honourable Enemy as an 'unconvincing effort' and that it is 'littered with factual errors, makes no use of manuscript sources, and fails to incorporate the findings of any recent research of the period.' Also in *Rewriting Cromwell: A Case of Deafening Silences,* by historian and President of the Cromwell Association, Prof John Morrill, opined that my work constituted a 'major attempt at rehabilitation was attempted by Tom Reilly ... but this has been largely rejected by other scholars'. This may well all be true but in this new book I will use these opinions of the experts to highlight their hostility to my suggestion that they might be mistaken. It is important to do this in order to show where the roadblocks to interpretational balance lie. However, while I don't have any educational qualifications to support my assertions I do have the necessary scepticism, and while the reviewers might have been right about the flawed methodology – it turns out they were wrong to dismiss the theory.

Astonishingly, despite all the criticism of my work from some quarters, in the fifteen intervening years, no historian has ever made a serious challenge to the thesis contained in the *Honourable Enemy*. Even more significantly, the counter-arguments of those academics who ventured into print with rebuttals, and those who continue to expound the traditional version of events, are singularly unimpressive. When it comes to our modern-day understanding of Cromwell in Ireland, with their contributions to articles, books, TV documentaries, etc. these historians have undoubtedly set us back years. For this reason, and many others, this new book is necessary because it implicitly challenges their work further, and it will go a long way to redressing the balance. History tells us that Cromwell mercilessly slaughtered whole communities in Drogheda and Wexford. Change that and you change every subsequent interpretation of his character by present and future generations. This book changes that.

My main aim here was to print as many of the primary source documents as possible. Readers can then make up their own minds about what the contemporary documents actually tell us. There is really no great mystery about the popular sources concerning Drogheda and Wexford. They primarily consist of the newspapers (newsbooks) of the day and they are essentially available at the click of a mouse. So instead of exhaustive footnotes to support a point, I have included most of the actual primary documents themselves. So where *Honourable Enemy* contained copious footnotes (however inadequate), *Cromwell was Framed* takes a different approach.

Also unusually for this genre, this book is mostly written in the first person singular. I have selected the refutations of the most prominent history academics to address here. Most people think Cromwell is guilty of murdering civilians. Because of the problematic nature of the surviving evidence however, at the very least there should be balance when it comes to this debate. Unfortunately some well-respected historians still do not see it that way.

As a native of Drogheda I understand only too well the legacy that Cromwell left in Ireland after his visit to my hometown. Since *Honourable Enemy*, few have ventured into print who wholeheartedly embrace the possibility that the academics got it wrong. Accepted wisdom that Cromwell was a war criminal prevails. The numbers of dead unarmed civilians vary. This book presents a further stiff challenge to the verdict of history and is another attempt to introduce balance to the debate. For some it will finally dismiss any lingering myths, for others it might be totally unconvincing. That is the joy of interpreting history. There might also be those who will see this as a score-settling exercise, but any such crass analysis would be predicated on the playing field being level, which of course it can never be.

But something happened at Drogheda and Wexford. And looking back from this distance to establish exactly what that was, all we can do is evaluate the surviving evidence. To me Cromwell was framed and I believe that this book proves it. Therefore, I have a moral obligation, indeed I am duty bound by history, to play my part in an attempt to overturn one of the greatest historical miscarriages of justice ever. Only history can be the winner.

List of Illustrations

1. *Mercurius Elencticus,* Number 24, Monday, Oct 8 to Monday, October 15, 1649
   Thomason / E.575 [19], reel position: Thomason / 88:E.575 [19]
2. *Mercurius Elencticus,* Number 25, Monday, 15 October to Monday, 22 October, 1649
   Thomason / E.575 [27], reel position: Thomason / 88:E.575 [27]
3. *The Man in the Moon,* Number 26, Wednesday, October 17 to Wednesday, October 24, 1649
   Thomason / E.575 [32], reel position: Thomason / 88:E.575 [32]

4. Hugh Peters, *A Letter from Ireland read in the House of Commons on Friday September 28, 1649 from Mr Hugh Peters, Minister of God's word and chaplain to the Lord Lieutenant Cromwell* (1649) Wing (2nd ed.) / P1709, reel position: Thomason / 88:E.574 [28]
5. Anonymous, *Two great Fights in Ireland on Sunday, Monday, Tuesday and Wednesday last between the forces commanded by the marquis of Ormond and the Lord Lieutenant Cromwell* (1649) Wing (2nd ed.) / T3448, reel position: Thomason / 88:E.574 [3]
6. Anonymous, *Two Letters, one from Dublin in Ireland, and the other from Liverpoole of a Bloody Fight in Ireland at the taking of Drogheda by the Lord Lieutenant Cromwell* (1649) Wing (2nd ed.) / T3469, reel position: Thomason / 88:E.574 [18]
7. *Perfect Occurrences of every Daie Journall of the Parliaments Armies Proceedings,* Number 144, Friday, September 28 to Friday, October 4, 1649 Thomason / E.533 [15], reel position: Thomason / 83:E.533 [15]
8. England and Wales. Privy Council, *At the Councel of State at Whitehal, Die Saturni, 19 September 1649, Whereas it hath pleased God to bless the endeavors of the forces of this Commonwealth . . .* Wing (2nd ed.) / E794B, reel position: Wing / 1668:33
9. Bernard Alsop, *The Perfect Weekly Account . . .* Wednesday, September 26 to Wednesday, 3 October, 1649 Thomason / E.575 [8], reel position: Thomason / 88:E.575 [8]
10. *The Kingdomes Faithfull and impartial Scout,* Number 36, Friday, 28 September to Saturday, 5 October, 1649 Thomason / E.533 [16], reel position: Thomason / 83:E.533 [16]
11. Robert Ibbitson, *Severall Proceedings in Parliament. . .* Number 1, Tuesday 25, September to Tuesday, 9 October, 1649 Thomason / E.575 [14], reel position: Thomason / 88:E.575 [14]

12. *The Kingdomes Weekly Intelligencer,* Number 331, Tuesday, September 25 to Tuesday, October 2, 1649
Thomason / E.575 [5], reel position: Thomason / 88:E.575 [5]
13. Samuel Pecke, *A Perfect Diurnall of Some Passages in Parliament* Number 322, Monday September 24 to Monday October 1, 1649
Thomason / E.533 [13], reel position: Thomason / 83:E.533 [13]
14. Samuel Peck, *A Perfect Diurnall of Some passages in Parliament* Number 323, Monday October 1 to Monday October 8, 1649
Thomason / E.533 [17], reel position: Thomason / 83:E.533 [17]
15. John Dillingham, *The Moderate Intelligencer* Number 237, Thursday September 27 to Thursday October 4, 1649
Thomason / E.575 [10], reel position: Thomason / 88:E.575 [10]
16. *Letters from Ireland, relating the Several great successes it hath pleased God to give unto the Parliaments Forces there in the taking of Drogheda, Trym, Dundalk, Carlingford, and the Nury. Together with a list of the chief commanders, and the number of the officers and soldiers slain in Drogheda. . . .* (1649)
Wing (2nd ed.) / L1778, reel position: Thomason / 88:E.575 [7]
17. *The Taking of Wexford, A letter from an Eminent Officer in the Army under the command of the lord Lieutenant of Ireland* 1649, Wing (2nd ed.) / L56B, reel position: Thomason / 88:E.575 [35]
18. *A Perfect and Particuler Relation of the severall marches and proceedings of the Armie in Ireland from the taking of Drogheda to this present . . .* London, 1649
Wing (2nd ed.) / P1471, reel position: Thomason / 88:E.575 [39]
19. *A Letter from The Lord Lieutenant of Ireland to the Honorable William Lenthal Esq; Speaker of the Parliament of England giving*

an account of the proceedings of the army there under his Lordships command, and several transactions between his lordship and the Governor of Wexford . . . London, 1649

Wing (2nd ed., 1994) / C7101A, reel position: Thomason / 88:E.576 [2]

20. *A very full and particular Relation of the great progresse and happy proceedings of the Army of the Common-wealth of England toward the reducing of Ireland under the command of his Excellency, the Lord Lieutenant of Ireland . . . ,* Number 6, 31 October 1649

    Thomason / E.576 [6], reel position: Thomason / 88: E.576 [6]
21. *Mercurius Elencticus,* Number 27, 29 October to 5 November, 1649

    Thomason / E.578 [3], reel position: Thomason / 89: E.578 [3]
22. *The Man in the Moon* Number 28, 31 October to 7 November 1649

    Thomason / E.578 [9], reel position: Thomason / 89:E.578 [9]
23. *A Briefe Relation of Some affairs and transactions, civill and military, both forraigne and domestique* Number 9, 13 November to 20 November, pp. 3-8

    Thomason / E.581 [4], reel position: Thomason / 89:E.581 [4]
24. James Heath, Flagellum, or, *The life and death, birth and burial of O. Cromwell,* . . . London, 1669 Wing / H1331, reel position: Wing / 420:11

All images produced by ProQuest as part of *Early English Books Online* www.proquest.com

Reproduction permissions for all images has been granted by The British Library Board. Ref: A651 (24)

Chapter One

As the crow of antiquity flies, the early modern period is not really that far away in terms of distance in time, especially in Ireland where history has an irritating habit of not going away. This is something that we Irish know to our cost. History and myth have always been close companions; indeed, one is frequently mistaken for the other. Myth is a powerful tool that has been used to shape nations. The axiom that truth is the first casualty of war has rarely been in sharper focus than in seventeenth century Ireland. Irish history is strewn with colourful myths, many of which are associated with Oliver Cromwell. Often given credit for being personally responsible for founding the British Empire, Cromwell is full of contradiction; a country squire who became an outstanding military commander; a king-killer who was offered the crown and refused it; a champion of religious toleration who was terrified of the power of Catholicism; a party reveller who danced late into the night and who banned Christmas; a practical joker who became an enduring symbol of everything Puritanical.

Such is his murderous legacy, Cromwell features in a modern-day cult card game called Terror Top Chumps, a 'politically charged version' of the children's card game Top Trumps (created by Fear Trade Ltd.) alongside Genghis Khan, Attila the Hun, Hitler, Mussolini, Pol Pot, Ivan the Terrible, Vlad the Impaler, Sadam Hussein, Osama Bin Laden; a total of thirty-two terrorists and dictators in all – and has a body count of 600,000 attributed to him. Not by coincidence, this figure has often been used as the entire number of people who died due to famine, pestilence and war during the Cromwellian period in Ireland.

John A. Murphy, emeritus professor of Irish history at NUI Cork agrees that few historical figures have made such a deep impact on Irish tradition as Cromwell. Yet he says: 'Much of the history that the present generation of Irish adults was given was palpably untrue. What they were taught up to 20 or 30 years ago was propaganda.' Die-hard Irish nationalists will never give up their basic tenets such as the Black and Tans, the Great Famine, Bloody Sunday (1972) or Oliver Cromwell. But as Prof John Morrill has recently declared, 'Paradoxically, by blaming Cromwell for the much more lasting horrors of the Commonwealth period in Ireland, we let those really responsible off the hook.'

After Ireland Cromwell, king-killer and the darling of his soldiers, became the chief actor on the mid-seventeenth century stage when he assumed the role of Protector of the Commonwealth. The documented evidence for the period is fraught with inconsistencies as contemporary writers sought to convince with motives that were either genuine or ulterior. This reached a peak after the failure of the Commonwealth when the ensuing Restoration propaganda directed at the Interregnum began to queer an already muddy pitch. Much later, at the end of the nineteenth century, the abundant anti-British sentiment from the pens of Irish nationalists helped to further endorse contemporary propaganda, and as a result, embed the facts in an indecipherable historical morass. When the revamped and triumphalist Catholic Church took centre stage in Irish life at this time one of its first manifestations was a thorough revision of Irish history to emphasise the indestructible age-old bond between Catholicism and the Irish nation. In this narrative Cromwell was a vital character. New books like *Cromwell in Ireland* by Fr Denis Murphy (1883) created a politically correct Catholic version of Cromwell, one that was accepted universally and without reservation. Today Murphy's analysis largely stands firm as an accurate version of events.

When I published *Cromwell, An Honourable Enemy* on the 350th anniversary of Cromwell's storming of Drogheda in 1999, an atmosphere was created in that town that would see public displays of outrage and a mini media blitz. A subsequent exhibition of Cromwell's death mask in Drogheda caused the then deputy mayor, Councillor Frank Godfrey, to be quoted in the *Irish Daily Mirror* as saying: 'The people in this town are in no doubt that he (Cromwell) was responsible for putting thousands of innocent civilians to the sword, no matter what some authors might say.' The lowest ebb of the affair was when the walls of the exhibition centre were daubed with tomato juice to represent the blood of Cromwell's innocent victims.

In Irish history it is more difficult than in the story of most other countries to reverse traditional views, and although there have been many investigators of this period at first hand, few have concluded that Cromwell was not a war criminal. The idea that the massacre of the unarmed civilian populations of both Drogheda and Wexford by Oliver Cromwell's New Model Army did indeed take place has survived through the centuries almost perfectly intact. Indeed, it is so well constructed that it is virtually indestructible. The years bristle with the names of erudite academics who have studied Cromwell's Irish campaign and who have produced hundreds of articles and books on the subject. Even the most ardent Cromwell enthusiasts who have studied the period forensically have conceded that large-scale massacres of defenceless civilians occurred in September (Drogheda) and October (Wexford) 1649. Done deal. Case closed. The result of their labour is captured in short sound bytes in both past and present Irish school textbooks. In 2004, Folens published *Earthlink 5th Class*. On page 87 the following words are printed: 'Cromwell captured Drogheda. About 3,000 men, women and children were killed.' The Educational Company of Ireland released *Timeline* in 2008. A paragraph on page 223 reads, 'He [Cromwell] first laid siege to Drogheda. He was determined to make an example of the town. When he captured it he slaughtered the entire population.' There is no ambiguity there.

However, we now know both of these statements to be

inaccurate. No contemporary historian worth their salt would stand over either of them today. So generations of historians got it wrong. The evidence to support both statements is simply not there. The entire population of Drogheda was not killed, nor is it any way plausible that 3,000 men, women and children lost their lives. And still, present day generations of primary school children all over Ireland continue to be exposed to this erroneous version of events. But like many historical certainties in Ireland, if you tug at the loose ends the whole thing begins to unravel.

Back in 1999 this thesis was generally received with a mixture of bemusement and ambivalence among the Irish public. But its appearance does mean that many people are at least coming around to the idea that the evidence is at least inconclusive. The premise simply hones in on the deaths of defenceless civilians. Did it happen on any scale, or did it not? Is Cromwell guilty of genocide or is he not? Among seventeenth century experts *Honourable Enemy* was met almost universally with either dismissal or derision, a scenario that was predictable given the provenance of their professionally thought-out conclusions. I expected the book to be criticised in the usual way, in book reviews for example, and by vested historical interests that were implicitly challenged by its thesis. In Britain the book's reception was much warmer as the academic fraternity there were generally more willing to accept that Cromwell's reputation in Ireland was unlikely to be the one that became the ultimate verdict of Irish history. This British versus Irish theme of Cromwell's Irish campaign had been long established along these very lines. While on one level Ireland seems to be coming to terms with the dying embers of centuries of anti-British sentiment, below the surface it is a different story. The name 'Cromwell' is so talismanic that its very invocation still causes Irish hearts to stir. Oliver Cromwell is easily Irish history's most resistant figure to a favourable re-evaluation.

The general controversy surrounding the thesis focussed not

so much on the fact that an amateur historian had the temerity to claim the discovery of a fundamental flaw in the teaching of Irish history, but more on the plausibility of the case that was put forward in Cromwell's defence. As reviewers, and indeed some academics, gleefully began to reject the latter point, the former was simply the icing on the cake. Even a cursory glance by a trained eye at the methodology used to construct the thesis rendered it completely useless to many.

When it came to reviews, at one extreme *The Irish Times* said, 'There is an interesting book to be written about Cromwell in Ireland, this is not it...none of this is convincing.' At the other extreme the UK edition of *The Sunday Times* said, 'This book humbles us all...this is an important book.' Perhaps predictably in a scathing review the republican publication *Saoirse* wrote that the book 'masquerades as history.' The *Irish Independent* concluded 'Tom Reilly has done a terrific job of research to make a case for Cromwell against the verdict of history.' *The Sunday Business Post* said, 'If Reilly is right, and he appears to make a strong case...if he succeeds in de-demonising our collective image of the man (Cromwell), he could help us to focus instead on the long-term political developments in which Cromwell was a leading player.' *The Examiner* wrote, '...all of which seems to drive a coach and four through Reilly's central thesis...in other words we are being offered Hitler instead of Stalin. It's a bit like saying that if Hitler had only sanctioned Auschwitz and not Belsen as well then he would be less monstrous...' The *Sunday Tribune* asserted, 'Make no mistake, this is a very important re-appraisal of Cromwell's nine month tour of Leinster and Munster.' Such is an example of the spectrum of reaction from the newspapers at the time of publication.

During an exchange of letters in the *Drogheda Independent* in June 1999, Prof Padraig Lenihan, an early modern expert then at NUI Limerick was clear about his argument:

> I must say I do not agree with Tom Reilly's interpretation of what happened in Drogheda in September 1649. Thomas Wood, a Cromwellian soldier who participated in this massacre testifies quite clearly as to what he saw and did. Tom Reilly devotes three pages of his book to attempt to discredit this account. Space does not permit a point by point rebuttal but Tom's objections do not stand up and, indeed, some betray an inadequate knowledge of contemporary practices and idiom. So innocent civilians were killed. Having said that it is dangerous to speculate. I would tentatively suggest about a thousand civilian fatalities, some of whom as Tom Reilly suggests elsewhere, may have been armed.

The book's impact on periodicals, documentaries, and general history books has also been diverse, with the British versus Irish theme constantly prevalent. In *History Ireland*, Eugene Coyle was sceptical, 'Reilly's treatment of the massacre at Drogheda is disingenuous, and he ignores the conclusion, long recognised by generations of historians that Cromwell lost his self-control at Drogheda. The historical evidence presented by Reilly is not convincing. The book adds little to our understanding of Cromwell's actions at Drogheda and Wexford.'

Cromwell in Ireland (2008) and *The Story of Ireland* (2010) were major RTE documentaries and both conclude that Cromwell was guilty of civilian atrocities. Conversely, Simon Schama's BBC TV's series, *A History of Britain* (2000-02), takes a different view. His book of the series states, 'Only recently have Irish historians like Tom Reilly had the scholarly integrity to get the story right.' A Channel 4 documentary, *Cromwell, New Model Englishman* (2002) also introduced balance to the debate by highlighting the non-massacre theory. Perhaps most surprisingly, also in 2002 the BBC conducted a poll of the 100 Greatest Britons, a list that featured Oliver Cromwell at number ten. The resultant documentary that was broadcast on Cromwell was presented by military historian

Richard Holmes, who fully embraced the arguments presented here. Indeed both the renowned historian himself and the documentary makers sought me out and spent a few days with me in the Drogheda area to get the balance for the programme right. In his *Civil War: The Wars of the Three Kingdom's 1638-60* (2004) the historian Trevor Royle embraces my thesis, and author of *Cromwellian Ireland,* (2000) Toby Barnard says: 'He brings to the subject an enviable familiarity with the terrain and a shrewd way with the sources....Reilly knows how tainted are most accounts on which the history of the Cromwellian war rests.'

Then in 2008 Phillip McKeiver's *A New History of Cromwell's Irish Campaign* was published. Following my lead the English historian analyses the civilian massacre theory and comes to the conclusion that:

> The allegation that New Model soldiers killed unarmed citizens at Drogheda must be treated as a myth, because in reality this has never been supported by evidence...It must also be emphasised that the evidence of Cromwell himself supports the fact that no unarmed citizens were killed...Although it is possible that some unarmed inhabitants were accidentally killed there is actually no evidence of this from an eyewitness but only rumours and reports at second hand. One such report was the fictional account of a massacre of women and children made by Thomas á Wood to his brother Anthony...it must be remembered if New model soldiers had killed any unarmed inhabitants at Drogheda they would have disobeyed Cromwell's orders.

A third impression of my book appeared in paperback in 2008 and this spawned a new raft of reviews, the most vitriolic of which came from the pen of Marc Coleman whose appraisal appeared in the *Irish Independent* in 2008 (21 September):

> Had Reilly stuck to his story, he might have written something worth reading. Like someone telling a victim of child abuse that they should try to understand the motives of their abuser, there is something deeply disturbing about Reilly's book. Its very title *Cromwell, An Honourable Enemy* is a sweeping statement that the incomplete facts gathered in the remainder of the book fail to validate. Cromwell was not "honourable" as he claims (massacring tens of thousands of innocent people never is). Like Elizabeth, Cromwell denied knowledge of the worst atrocities committed by his generals in Ireland. But the atrocities committed under his nose in Drogheda, together with his inaction against generals guilty of mass killings and evictions, testify to the ultimate truth of Cromwell's intentions and actions. Reilly's interpretation of Cromwell's motives here is gullible beyond belief... So much did the English hate Cromwell that after his death they threw his corpse on a dump. Once the chore of reading it was over, that's what I did with this book.

Coleman's attitude to Cromwell is representative of the opinion of the majority of Irish people. But, as John Morrill has said, there were members of the Long Parliament who were much more anti-Irish and anti-Catholic than Cromwell. There is a distinct absence from Cromwell's voluminous written correspondence of sentiments that would support the religious hatred allegations that have so easily attached themselves to his reputation.

Many writers have given a detailed chronology of Cromwell's Irish campaign so there is no necessity to return to old, well-trodden ground here. However, before approaching the wider implications of this subject, it would be prudent to provide a brief outline of the circumstances that dominated his visit to Ireland.

By the 1640s King Charles I had fallen out with his Parliament. The English Civil War began on 22 August 1642. In Ireland, following the Plantation of Ulster and the Flight of the Earls, the native Catholic population became more unsettled as their native properties, that once belonged to the clans, were skilfully whisked away by the land-hungry English and Scottish settlers. This aggressive colonisation policy had culminated in the rebellion of the Irish on 23rd October 1641. That day, the Ulster nobleman Sir Phelim O'Neill, a loyal servant of the King, issued a proclamation declaring that he and his associates had taken up arms for the defence and liberty of both the Old English and native Irish Catholics. Owen Roe O'Neill (Sir Phelim's cousin) had left Ireland as a young boy at the Flight of the Earls. He had served in an Irish regiment of a Spanish army and he now returned to Ulster in 1642 to take part in the Rising. The situation rapidly escalated into a Confederate war where the dividing line for some of the chief protagonists was prone to change, especially when Charles Stuart would lose his head. Also around this time, the Adventurer's Act (1642) was passed by Parliament giving any entrepreneurially minded oligarchs in England an opportunity to procure cheap land in Ireland. All they had to do was to contribute money to Parliament's Irish mission, and when the time came and Ireland was conquered, they would cash in handsomely.

James Butler, the Earl of Ormond, a resolute Protestant, was obsessively loyal to the English throne, and it was he who would emerge as Cromwell's main adversary in Ireland as the commander-in-chief of the Irish forces. Butler's family seat was Kilkenny, where the Confederation of Irish Catholics was set up in 1642 to achieve national unity against the Protestant invaders. Both Old English and native Irish Catholics swore to restore Catholicism to a united Ireland. In these early days it would be Ormond who would open deep divisions within the Confederacy, and it would be Ormond who would eventually form an alliance between the Confederacy and the Royalists, where religious allegiances took second place, when Charles was executed. In one fell swoop, the prospect of a Royalist army possibly 20,000-30,000 strong coming from Ireland to fight for the young Prince Charles against Parliament was becoming a real possibility. The problem was that Ormond's forces were dysfunctional, poorly equipped and discord between the comprising factions was always simmering just below the surface.

Following the execution of King Charles I on 31 January 1649, Parliament had the task of attempting to govern the three Kingdoms of England, Ireland and Scotland. It was an unprecedented position of power in which any body of Englishmen had ever found themselves. Champion of the New Model Army, Oliver Cromwell was bestowed with the title of Lord Lieutenant of Ireland and the responsibility of subjecting that nation to the control of Parliament. Having proved himself an exceptional military tactician, Cromwell had excelled himself in the Civil War where he had not lost a significant military engagement up to that point. In July 1649 he made his way to Milford Haven and waited there patiently until the funds arrived from London that would enable him to conduct an effective military campaign. Ireland had never invited the sword of the conqueror, but it would come just the same. While moored there, he heard the news of Colonel Michael Jones' defeat of Ormond's forces at Rathmines, with the significant acquisition of guns, ammunition and provisions. Surrounding a Parliament-held city of Dublin, Ormond's army had been completely taken by surprise by an attack from the city under Jones and his army was routed. This cleared the way for Cromwell to head for Dublin where he could now land easily and without being attacked by the coalition forces.

Arriving (seasick) at Ringsend on 15 August, Cromwell was warmly welcomed by both the civilian and military populations of Dublin. That fact is well-documented by hundreds of historians in this well-mined historical terrain. And yet few scholars draw a comparison between the inhabitants of Dublin and the inhabitants of Drogheda in the 'civilian massacre' context. Politically, theologically and economically both Dublin and Drogheda were mirrors of each other where the Old English Catholic lords had dominated for centuries. Both were within the Pale and both were substantially shaped by the Anglo-Normans from the time of the Conquest. Dublin became the centre of English power in Ireland and Drogheda also held parliaments. Poyning's Law was passed there in 1494 in an effort to make Ireland obedient to the English monarchy. In 1641 the Irish insurgents planned to take both urban centres but were foiled in both cases, as the entire Pale community held fast and remained hostile to the native Irish. The plan to take Dublin was scuppered by deception and the fortress of Drogheda kept O'Neill's forces at bay for five months. For the most part Catholics proliferated in Dublin, but during the Confederate wars of the 1640s Protestants from all over the country flocked to Dublin and this resulted in the majority adhering to that faith. Of course Parliament had a ban in place that Catholic men were prohibited from living in the city and Colonel Michael Jones had driven them out in 1647 with the result (at least in theory) that no Catholic male adults were living within the city walls. Their wives and children, however, were allowed to stay. So under these circumstances the question must be asked: why would the New Model Army cut the civilian population of Drogheda down in cold blood and at the same time have such cordial relations with the civilian population of Dublin?

We have now arrived at one of the seminal moments of this entire episode. Cromwell was in Dublin. The military campaign was about to begin. Because of the several marauding armies that had traversed the Irish countryside pillaging supplies and provisions, often wantonly killing civilians as they went, Oliver Cromwell was at pains to let the common people of Ireland know that they could not expect the same from his forces. His orders to his troops in this regard have survived to this day:

This declaration is appointed to be printed and published throughout all Ireland: by special direction from – Oliver Cromwell.

Whereas I am informed that, upon the marching out of the Armies heretofore, or of parties from Garrisons, a liberty hath been taken by the Soldiery to abuse, rob and pillage, and too often to execute cruelties upon the Country People: being resolved, by the grace of God, diligently and strictly to restrain such wickedness for the future.

I do hereby warn and require all Officers, Soldiers and others under my command, henceforth to forebear all such evil practices as aforesaid; and not to do any wrong or violence toward Country People, or persons whatsoever, unless they be actually in arms or office with the Enemy; and not to meddle with the goods of such, without special order.

And I do further declare, That it shall be free and lawful to and for all manner of persons dwelling in the country, as well as gentlemen and soldiers, as farmers and other people (such as are in arms or office with or for the Enemy only excepted), to make their repair, and bring any provisions unto the Army (while in march or camp), or unto any Garrison under my command: Hereby assuring all such, that they shall not be troubled or molested in their persons or goods; but shall have the benefit of a free market, and receive ready money for goods or commodities they shall so bring and sell: and that they, behaving themselves peaceably and quietly; and paying such Contributions, proportionably with their neighbours, as have been, are, or shall be duly and orderly imposed upon them, for maintenance of the Parliaments forces and other public uses, shall have free leave and liberty to live at home

> with their families and goods; and shall be protected in their persons and estates by virtue thereof, until the 1st day of January next: by or before which time, all such of them as are minded to reside, and plough and sow, in the quarters, are to make their addresses, for now and further protections, to the Attorney-General, residing at Dublin, and to such other persons as shall be authorised for that purpose.
>
> And hereof I require all Soldiers, and others under my command, diligently to take notice and observe the same: as they shall answer to the contrary at their utmost perils. Strictly charging and commanding all Officers and others, in their several places, carefully to see to it that no wrong or violence be done to any such person as aforesaid, contrary to the effect of the premises. Being resolved, through the grace of God to punish all that shall offend contrary hereunto, very severely, according to Law or Articles of War; to displace and otherwise punish, all such Officers as shall be found negligent in their places, and not see the due observance hereof, or not to punish the offenders under their respective commands. Given at Dublin, the 24th of August 1649. Oliver Cromwell

This declaration is Cromwell's *modus operandi* for the upcoming engagement. He explicitly forbids any of his army to do any 'wrong or violence towards country people, *or persons whatsoever*, unless they be in arms or office with the enemy' or they shall 'answer to the contrary at their utmost perils'. Ten days later the New Model Army were camped outside the walls of Drogheda. On the march to the town, two of his men dared to steal some hens from an old woman, and when Cromwell discovered the culprits, he had them hanged as an example to the rest.

Due to adverse weather conditions, a week then passed before the large cannon pieces could be landed on the Boyne. On Monday 10 September, Cromwell summoned Arthur Aston, the recently appointed governor of Drogheda, to hand over the town. The rules of war then pertaining were very clear. A long siege was expected by the royalist defenders. That being the case, the attacking army would be exposed to inclement conditions and it was quite common for dysentery and disease to afflict those camped in the squalid outdoor conditions, where lives would inevitably be lost. By refusing to surrender, which Aston duly did, he had (in theory) condemned many of the Ironsides to death by sickness. With this action he also exposed his entire garrison to the risk of death, should the attackers prevail. According to military convention, now Cromwell was within his rights to kill the entire garrison. This prerogative had not yet been taken by a commanding officer in this conflict. Prisoners would usually be captured and traded while others often took the opportunity to change sides. But a plan was hatching in Oliver Cromwell's head that week, the consequences of which would echo through the centuries. And nobody saw it coming.

Breaches in the wall were soon made assailable and thanks to a charge led by an impatient Cromwell in person, the New Model Army were soon masters of the town walls. Almost immediately, the entire town fell with the attackers swarming through the narrow streets with orders from their commanding officer not to spare any that were in arms. At this point, many witnesses testify that the majority of the defenders flung down their weapons and surrendered. But most of them were summarily killed where they stood. Certainly Arthur Aston and his men, who had taken a further stand on a medieval motte and bailey within the walls (called Millmount) the defensive bulwark of the town, were all brutally slain after they had been disarmed. In an effort to get away, some of the defending soldiers scaled the belfry tower of St Peter's Church on the north side of the town but Cromwell gave the order for the church pews to be assembled underneath and set ablaze. All of those in the tower were either burned alive or fell to their deaths. Others locked themselves into various towers that were set into the town's defensive curtain wall and began to snipe at the Ironsides from within.

The slaughter of those poor royalist soldiers who failed to escape may have been over in a matter of hours. Meanwhile, of course, we know that hundreds of them managed to get out and run for their lives. The next day the men who had occupied the towers surrendered and every tenth man as well as every officer and a Catholic priest who pretended to be a soldier were 'knocked on the head promiscuously', as Cromwell so succinctly put it. The rest of the towers' occupants were spared their lives and were all sent to Barbados. These were lives that, according to military convention, Cromwell had every right to take, but didn't. The number of lives that were lost that night has been variously estimated at being between 2,500 and 3,000, a figure usually attributable to the number of the garrison with all the accompanying difficulties; the hundreds of escapees, and the others who were spared by both Cromwell (in the towers) and his men throughout various parts of the town.

The gateway to the north was now open. Cromwell left a garrison of men at Drogheda, headed back to Dublin and then turned his attention towards the rest of the east coast, south of Dublin. Mopping up all of the minor towns and fortifications on his journey south, by 2 October both he and his army were camped outside the walls of Wexford. Cromwell's intelligence officers would have told him that Wexford was a den of iniquity, a haven for pirates and a hotbed of native Irish activity. While camped before its walls he learned, firsthand, of the alleged cruelty of some of the Catholic natives towards their Protestant neighbours during the preceding years. The following week was spent with both Colonel David Sinnott and Cromwell exchanging cordial messages in an effort to agree terms. For some unknown reason the royalist troops abandoned the fort of Rosslare, thus facilitating the easy entry of the Parliamentarian ships to the harbour. The townsmen of Wexford were willing to discuss the surrender of the town; indeed relations were so convivial that they despatched a cart load of gifts addressed to Cromwell containing 'sack, strong waters, and strong beer' for his pleasure while he waited in the inclement conditions. Ormond himself appeared before the town with 3,000 men – quite disinclined to get involved in a field engagement with Cromwell – and requested the evacuation of all of the 'auld men, women and children' from the town.

Despite Cromwell's preconceptions about the defending troops, he was very keen to display restraint, and both men fully expected an agreement to be made on paper. However, just when Cromwell was preparing a response to Sinnott, Captain James Stafford, the governor of the castle, which lay adjacent to the town walls surrendered his position. It wasn't long before the flood gates opened, and the New Model Army were pouring into the town, without the order to storm. Another massacre ensued. This time around 1,500 lives were lost, again roughly the same number that made up the garrison.

There is no getting away from the fact that the composition of the royalist defensive forces at Wexford included local inhabitants. There are several eye witness testimonies that corroborate this, including Cromwell himself. Furthermore, it is not really surprising that locals got involved, given the circumstances of the siege of Wexford, the structure of the garrison and both the political and theological inclinations of those who lived in the town. They were no friends of that Protestant Ormond, and for a long time they refused the reinforcements he offered them in the run-up to the siege. Sinnott, an Ormond appointee (via Lord Castlehaven), had reluctantly been allowed through the town gates at the intimidating prospect of the Parliamentarian ships in Wexford harbour. This was a town that had declared for the Confederacy and many of the local men took up arms in defence of their town, their properties and their goods. Ironically, there are fewer allegations of an unarmed civilian massacre at

Wexford; on the contrary there are actually more eye witness accounts that suggest many of the defenders were privately saved by the Parliamentarian soldiers. The total of the defending forces was around 1,500 – 2,000, made up of an assortment of townsmen and the regiments of Castlehaven, Lord Iveagh and Sinnott himself. The myth that 300 local women were massacred at the cross in the town square is without eye-witness attestation and has no basis in truth.

Despite the fact that the backgrounds to Drogheda and Wexford were two entirely different entities culturally, ethnically and politically, the two towns have become inextricably linked in the historiography of Ireland as the places where Cromwell carried out heinous massacres. Wherever the histories of both towns appear in print, the headlines usually feature the unarmed civilian massacre stories, and invariably the myths prevail.

Meanwhile, Owen Roe O'Neill departed from Ulster after finally agreeing to serve under Ormond and left the northern part of the country unprotected. It was at this stage that the Parliamentarian Colonel Venables advanced north and secured most of Ulster for Parliament with O'Neill and his men heading south. It was at the town of Ross (New Ross) that Cromwell again highlighted his attitude to Irish civilians, an attitude that he maintained throughout the entire campaign that is consistent with the surviving evidence. While responding to a request from Sir Lucas Taaffe, the then governor of the town, Cromwell emphasised that his opposition to Catholicism was political rather than personal. The celebration of mass was an indictable offence as the ceremony had been banned in Ireland for some time. Cromwell writes:

> For that which you mention concerning liberty of conscience, I meddle not with any man's conscience. But if by liberty of conscience you mean the liberty to exercise the mass, I judge it best to use plain dealing, and to let you know where the

> parliament of England have power, that you will not be allowed of. As for such of the townsmen who desire to depart and carry away themselves and their goods, as you express, I engage myself, they shall have three months time to do; and in the meantime shall be protected from violence in their persons and goods, as others under the obedience of the Parliament.

The law was the law and the mass was prohibited. Cromwell did not make the law but he was certainly in favour of it, and he was not prepared to allow any open displays of the Roman faith, a view he expressed often in Ireland. It was also at Ross that Cromwell showed consistency with regard to his policy towards the ordinary Irish people. As various Parliamentarian troops joined his main army he had to remind the newcomers of his proclamation to protect the Irish citizenry and in particular their goods and their property. On 27 October he issued a further proclamation:

> Whereas there are divers complaints made by the inhabitants in and near the town of Ross that the soldiers under my command do daily take away their garrons and plough horses and their seed corn, and do hinder them from threshing their seed corn and from following their business of husbandry, whereby the land is unmanured and unsown, which doth manifestly tend to the prejudice of the public and may prove to be of very ill consequence if not timely prevented. These are strictly to charge and command all officers and soldiers under my command that they do not presume to take away any plough horses or garrons or any seed corn from any persons whatsoever residing and inhabiting within our quarters, nor in any wise to hinder them from threshing out their corn, ploughing their lands or following their business of husbandry upon pain of the severest punishment that may be inflicted on them.

Always conscious of protecting the Irish public, when Cromwell arrived before the walls of Waterford he sent a letter to the mayor and aldermen of that city since they had refused entry to Ormond's troops, in which he wrote: 'Being come into these parts, not to destroy people and places, but to save them that men may live comfortably and happily by their trade.' With the winter approaching Cromwell spent the weeks after Wexford taking the rest of Munster including its capital Cork, which revolted with the Parliamentarians now close by. The English garrison and inhabitants there turned the Irish troops out and welcomed Cromwell's troops gratefully. Kinsale and Youghal quickly followed by renouncing Ormond's authority and declaring for Parliament. Also around this time, Cromwell's foremost Celtic adversary, whom he never got to meet in battle, Owen Roe O'Neill, died in Cavan from gout. Cromwell also lost a comrade of his own when Colonel Michael Jones succumbed to sickness just before the winter break. By 5 December, Cromwell had reached Youghal. Control of the northern, eastern and southern coasts from Belfast to Cork was interrupted only by the city of Waterford and small fort of Duncannon, both of which would eventually surrender in August 1650. Cromwell had been complaining of feeling 'the infirmities of old age' (he was 50 years-old) and no doubt welcomed the chance to recuperate for a few weeks with the winter now fully set in. On 8 December he had to act in the defence of the local populace when, yet again, some of his recently acquired troops began to step out of line by plundering the area:

> Whereas I am informed that the horse under my command (since their being quartered within the Black-water) have and do in their several quarters take away and waste wheat and barley for their horses and do behave themselves outrageously towards the inhabitants, not consenting themselves

> with such provisions as they are able to afford them, but do kill their sheep and other cattle within and as often as they please. I do hereby straightly charge and command all soldiers to forbear such like practices upon pain of death...And I do farther will and require all officers and soldiery within the limits aforesaid, that they do not break down any stacks of barley or wheat in their respective quarters, to give the same to their horses; but that they content themselves with peas, oats, hay and others such forage, as the country affords, paying or giving tickets, at such reasonable rates for the same, as they were usually sold for, before their coming into the said quarters.

These proclamations have often been used as evidence that Cromwell had no control over his troops and that they simply did as they pleased whether in battle or in their downtime. They could also be interpreted to mean that Cromwell went to enormous lengths to behave honourably towards the Irish people and he himself has left us a written legacy from his own hand to prove this. One of his biggest concerns was to treat the local populace with the utmost respect by buying their produce, unlike every other raggle-taggle army - including Parliamentarian soldiers before his arrival - that had arbitrarily plundered their way across the entire country since the wars began in 1641.

Following the winter break, Cromwell soon advanced on the former confederate capital of Kilkenny and on 22 March 1650, he summoned the town to surrender. For five days the garrison, under the command of Sir Walter Butler, assisted by many townsmen repulsed a series of attacks from the New Model Army. On 27 March, Butler sought terms for the defenders and Kilkenny was now in Cromwell's hands. Throughout the Munster campaign Cromwell's troops were being reduced with every garrison he took, but despite the numerical advantage that Ormond often had he never once engaged the New Model in the field and proved to be a most unworthy opponent as the Parliamentarians marched relentlessly on with victory after victory. Clonmel was the final battle of Cromwell's Irish crusade. Things were not good in London and he had ignored several pleas from Parliament to return, focussing instead on mopping up Irish towns with clinical efficiency. Hugh Dubh O'Neill, a veteran of the Spanish wars, was defending Clonmel and stepped up to the plate where Ormond didn't. He cleverly allowed the New Model Army easy access to the breach they had made in the town's defensive walls and watched them file into a long channel of rubble which he had fashioned into a cul-de-sac. When the channel was full of attacking soldiers O'Neill gave the order to attack. Hundreds of Roundheads were hacked to death. The attackers retreated but came again a second time and a second time they were ripped to shreds in O'Neill's trap. Estimates of the total of attacking soldiers range from 1,500 to 2,000, easily the biggest loss that Cromwell, indeed the entire New Model Army, ever suffered. A week later Cromwell returned to England where he was feted with a hero's welcome.

One of the most important pieces of evidence/information that we have concerning these events is the exchange of documents that occurred between the Irish Catholic clergy and Cromwell during the winter break. With hostilities ceased for the foreseeable future, concerned at Cromwell's relentless march through Ireland, the Catholic prelates met at Clonmacnoise on 4 December to see what could possibly be done to halt the Parliamentarians' rapid advance since Rathmines. The result of their deliberations was a written plea to the various disparate groups all over Ireland that opposed Parliament, to forget their past disagreements and fuse into one coherent force that would stop the mighty conqueror. The Clonmacnoise Decrees were printed in pamphlet form and circulated around the country. The bishops claimed that the parliamentarian objective was to wipe out the Catholic faith in Ireland; 'many of our flock are misled with a vain opinion of hopes that the Commander-in-Chief of the rebel forces, commonly called parliamentarians, would afford them good conditions...to undeceive them in this their ungrounded expectation, we do hereby declare as a most certain truth that the enemies' resolution is to extirpate the Catholic religion out of all his Majesties' dominions...And in effect this banishment and other destructions of the common people must follow the resolution of extirpating the Catholic religion, which is not be effected without the massacring or banishment of the Catholic inhabitants.'

When Cromwell saw the decrees of the bishops, his ire suitably aroused, he drafted a written response. We have arrived now at another seminal piece of evidence concerning the civilian massacre theory. When Cromwell's Irish campaign is being discussed it is vital to see this exchange of documents in sharp focus. Here we have an insight into Cromwell's mind that fits with the surviving evidence. There is no need to look any further to appreciate his attitude to Catholicism than here. And yet, throughout the centuries, and still today many historians strangely treat Cromwell's reply to the bishops, his own words, with suspicion. In the document Cromwell denies killing unarmed civilians.

To those millions of Irish people who have experienced the pre-1980s Irish educational system and who were exposed to large doses of Nationalistic Irish history the general rule of thumb regarding this era would be Irish = good, English = bad. The history of the horrors of the Catholic Church throughout history was well-known in the seventeenth century. The Roman Church had a lot to answer for. During the Middle Ages the persecution of nonconformists was rife. For instance, it is impossible not to feel sympathy for the Cathars in Southern France who were wiped out (slaughtered in cold blood, men, women and children) during the Albegensian Crusade on the orders of Pope Innocent III simply because they did not conform to the Roman

Church. Indulgences didn't help the Church's case. Many bishops saw them as an easy way to get rich as they extorted money in exchange for the promise of eternal life or the release of loved ones from Purgatory. The legacy of the inquisitions where you either converted or were executed is another horror invented and ruthlessly implemented by the Catholic Church. It is difficult also to imagine that Oliver Cromwell was unaware of the exploits of Johann Tserclaes, the Catholic Count of Tilly fighting for the Holy Roman Empire, who was responsible for the deaths of 25,000 Protestant civilians at Magdeburg on May 20, 1631 during the Thirty Years' War. Cromwell was also of the opinion that it was the Catholic clergy – and no other entity – who stirred the impressionable native Irish into the rebellion of 1641, and it was they who were directly responsible for the 'horrid massacres' (his words) of innocent Protestants that ensued. He is very clear on this point. Given the history of the Church, it is easy to see why Cromwell would have thought his was the high moral ground in his response to the bishops. Theologically, his world did not have room for a religious hierarchy. Like Luther, he could find no passage in the Bible that could justify the existence of the Pope. God was his only authority figure in these matters and access to Him was not interrupted by a plethora of ecclesiastical administrators. In the real world of the seventeenth century this was a time in which all things religious totally dominated the everyday lives of every man, woman and child on these islands. Stories have come down to us of people being afraid to put on their shoes because they were possessed by the Devil. Ordinary folk were consumed by religious convictions. Like many of his parliamentarian peers, Cromwell was in direct communion with the Almighty, and that was enough for him. Parliament dreaded the prospect of Roman Catholicism and the prospect of such a despotic regime again finding a significant foothold in England. To them, this was a political entity that duped people into joining them, whose motives were more avaricious than spiritual. These factors were uppermost in his mind when he sat down to write his response to the prelates:

> A declaration of the Lord Lieutenant of Ireland, for the Undeceiving of Deluded and Seduced People: which may be satisfactory to all who do not shut willfully their eyes against the light: In answer to certain late Declarations and Acts framed by the Irish Popish Prelates and Clergy in a Conventicle at Clonmacnoise.
> Having lately perused a book printed at Kilkenny in the year 1649, containing divers Declarations and Acts of the Popish Prelates and Clergy framed in a late Conventicle at Clonmacnoise the 4th day of December, in the year aforesaid, I thought fit to give a brief answer unto the same.
>
> And first to the first; which is a Declaration wherein (having premised the reconciliation of some differences among themselves), they come to state their War, upon the interest of their Church, of his Majesty and the Nation, and their resolution to prosecute the same with unity. All which will deserve a particular survey.
>
> The meeting of the Archbishops, Bishops and other Prelates at Clonmacnoise is by them said to be 'proprio motu.' By which term they would have the world believe that the secular power hath nothing to do to appoint or superintend their spiritual conventions (as they call them) although in the said meetings they take upon them to intermeddle in all secular affairs; as by the sequel appears.
>
> And first for their union they so much boast of. If any wise man should seriously consider what they pretend the grounds of the differences to have been, and the way and course they

have taken to reconcile the same; and their expressions thereabout, and the ends for which, and their resolutions how to carry on their great design declared for; he must needs think slightly of it. And also for this, that they resolve all other men's consents into their own, without consulting them at all.

The subject of this reconciliation was (as they say) the Clergy and Laity. The discontent and the division itself was grounded on the late difference of opinion, happening amongst the prelates and laity, I wonder not at differences in opinion, discontents and divisions, where so Antichristian and dividing a term as Clergy and Laity is given and received; a term unknown to any save the Antichristian Church, and such as derive themselves from her, 'ab initio non fuit sic'. The most pure and primitive times, as they best knew what true Union was, so in all addresses to the several Churches they wrote unto, not one word of this. The members of the Churches are styled Brethren and Saints of the same household of Faith, although they had orders and distinctions amongst them for the administration of ordinances (of a far different use and character with yours), yet it nowhere occasioned them to say, 'contemptim', and by way of lessening in contra distinguishing Laity to Clergy. *It was your pride that begat this expression, and it is for filthy lucre's sake that you keep it up, that by making the people believe that they are not so holy as yourselves, they might for the penny purchase some sanctity from you and that you might bridle, saddle and ride them at your pleasure; and do (which is most true of you) as the Scribes and Pharisees of old did (by their Laity), keep the knowledge of the Law from them, and then be able in their pride to say 'this people that know not the Law are cursed'.*

And no wonder (to speak more nearly to your differences and union) if it lie in the Prelate power to make the Clergy and the

Laity go together by the ears when they please, but that they may as easily make a simple and senseless reconciliation which will last until the next Nuncio comes from Rome with supermandatory advices; and then this Gordian knot must be cut, and the poor Laity forced to dance a new tune. I say not this as being troubled at it; much good may do you with it, *By the grace of God, we fear not, we care not for your union. Your covenant is with death and Hell, your union is like that of Simeon and Levi. Associate yourselves, and you shall be broken in pieces; take council together, and it shall come to naught. For though it becomes us to be humble in respect of ourselves, yet we can say to you, God is not with you. You say your union is against a common enemy; and to this, if you will be talking of union, I will give you some wormwood to bite on, by which it will appear God is not with you.*

Who is it that created the common enemy? I suppose you mean Englishmen. The English! Remember ye hypocrites, Ireland was once united to England. Englishmen had good inheritances which many of them purchased with their money; they or their ancestors, from many of you and your ancestors. They had good leases from Irishmen for a long time to come; great stocks thereupon; houses and plantations erected at their cost and charge. They lived peaceably and honestly amongst you. You had generally equal benefit of the protection of England with them, and equal justice from the laws, saving what was necessary for the State (out of reasons of State) to put upon some few people apt to rebel upon the instigation of such as you. You broke this union. You, unprovoked, put the English to the most unheard-of and most barbarous massacre (without respect of sex or age) that ever the sun beheld. And at a time when Ireland was in perfect peace, and when through the example of the English industry, through commerce and traffic, that which was in the natives' hands was better to them than if all Ireland had been in their possession and not an Englishman in it. And yet, then I say, was this unheard-of villainy perpetrated by your instigation, who boast of peacemaking and union against this common enemy. What think you by this time, is not my assertion true? Is God, will God be with you? I am confident He will not!

And though you would comprehend old English, new English, Scotch, or who else you will, in the bosom of your Catholic charity, yet shall not this save you from breaking. I tell you and them, you will fare the worse for their sakes, because I cannot but believe some of them go against, some stifle their consciences. And it is not the figleaf of pretence that they fight for their King, will serve their turn, when really they fight in protection of men of so much prodigious blood; and with men who have declared the ground of their union and fighting (as you have stated in your Declaration) to be 'Bellum Prelaticum et Religiosum', in the first and primary intention of it; especially when they shall consider your principles: That, except what fear makes you comply with – viz. that alone without their concurrence you are not able to carry on your work-you are ready, whenever you shall get the power into your hands, to kick them off too, as some late experiences have sufficiently manifested. And, thus we come to the design, you being thus wholesomely united intended to be prosecuted by you.

Your words are these: 'That all and every of us, the above Archbishops, Bishops and Prelates, are now by the blessing of God, as one body united. And that we will as becometh charity and our pastoral charge, stand all of us as one entire body for the interests and immunities of the Church, and of every the Prelates and Bishops thereof; and for the honour, dignity, estate, right and possessions of all and every of the said Archbishops, Bishops and other Prelates. And we will as one entire and united body, forward by our councils, actions, and devices, the advancements of his Majesty's rights, and the good of this nation in general, and in particular occasions to our power. And that none of us, in any occasion whatsoever concerning the Catholic religion, or the good of this Kingdom of Ireland, will in any respect single himself, or be or seem opposite to the rest of us, but will hold firm and entire in one sense, as aforesaid &c.

And if there were no other quarrel against you but this, which you make to be the principle and the first ground of your quarrel:- to wit, as so standing for the rights of your Church (falsely so called) and for the rights of your Archbishops, Bishops and Prelates, as to engage people and nations into blood therefore. This alone would be your confusion. I ask you, is it for the Lay-fee (as you call it), or revenue belonging to your Church, that you will after this manner contend? Or is it your jurisdiction, or the exercise of your ecclesiastical authority? Or is it the Faith of your Church? Let me tell you, not for all or any of these is it lawful for the ministers of Christ, as you would be thought to be, thus to contend. And therefore we will consider them apart.

For the first, if it were St. Peter's Patrimony, as you term it that is somewhat that you lawfully came by, although I must tell you, your predecessors cheated poor seduced men in their weakness on their deathbeds; or otherwise unlawfully came by most of this you pretend to. Yet Peter, Though he was somewhat too forward to draw the sword in a better cause, if that weapon, not being proper to the business in hand, was to be put up in that case, he must not, nor would he, have drawn it in this. And that blessed Apostle Paul, who said the labourer was worthy of his hire, chose rather to make tents than be burdensome to the Churches. I would you had either of those men's spirits on the conditions your revenues were doubled to what the best times ever made them to your predecessors.

The same answer may be given to that of your power and jurisdiction, and to that preeminency of prelacy you so dearly love. Only consider what the Master of the same Apostles said to them; 'So it shall not be amongst you. Whoever will be chief will be servant of all'. For He himself came not to be ministered unto, but to minister. And by this he that runs may read of what tribe you are. And surely, if these, that are outward things, may not thus be contended for, how much less may the doctrines of Faith (which are the works of Grace and the Spirit) be endeavoured by unsuitable means! *He that bids us contend for the Faith once delivered to the Saints tells us that we should do it by avoiding the spirit of Cain, Corah, and Balaam; and by building up ourselves on the most holy Faith, not pinning it upon other men's sleeves, praying in the holy Ghost, not mumbling over Matins; keeping ourselves in the love of God, not destroying men because they will not be of our Faith; waiting for the mercy of Jesus Christ; not cruel, but merciful! But, alas, why is this said? Why are these pearls cast before you? You are resolved not to be changed from using the instrument of a foolish shepherd! You are a part of Anti-Christ, whose Kingdom the Scripture so expressly speaks should be laid in blood; yea in the blood of the Saints. You have shed great store of it already, and ere it be long, you must, all of you have blood to drink; even the dregs of the cup of the fury and the wrath of God, which will be poured out unto you!*

In the next place, you state the interest of his Majesty, as you say. And this you hope will draw some English and Scots to your party. But what Majesty is it you mean? Is it France or Spain or Scotland? Speak plainly! You have, some of you lately been harping (or else we are misinformed) upon his Majesty of Spain to be your Protector. Was it because his Majesty of Scotland is too little a Majesty for your purpose? We know you love great Majesties. Or is it because he is not fully come over to you in point of religion? If he be short in that, you will quickly find out upon that score, another Majesty. His Father who complied with you too much, you rejected; and now would make the world believe you would make the Son's interest a great part of the state of your quarrel. How can we but think there is some reserve in this, and that the son is agreed to do somewhat more for you than ever his Father did. Or else tell us whence this new zeal is? That the Father did too much for you, in all Protestant's judgements instead of many instances let be considered what one of your own doctors, Dr. Enos of Dublin, who (writing against the agreement made between the Lord of Ormond and the Irish Catholics) finds fault with it, and says that it was nothing so good as the Earl of Glamorgan had warrant from the King to make; But exceeding far short of what the Lord George Digby had warrant to agree with the Pope himself at Rome in favour of the Irish Catholics.

I intend not this to you; but to such Protestants as may incline to you, and join with you upon this single account, which is the only appearing inducement to them, seeing there is no such probability of ill in this abstracted; and so much certainty of ill in fighting for the Romish religion against the Protestant; and fighting with men under the guilt of so horrid a massacre. From participating in which guilt, whilst they take part with them they will never be able to assoil themselves, either before God or good men.

In the last place you are pleased, having after your usual manner remembered yourselves first, and his Majesty (as you call him), next; like a man of your tribe with his 'Ego et Rex meus', you are pleased to take the people into consideration, lest they should seem to be forgotten; or rather you might make me believe they are much in your thoughts. Indeed I think they are! *Alas poor Laity! That you and your King might ride them, and jade them, as your Church hath done, and as your King hath done by your means, almost all ages.* But it would not be hard to prophesy, that the beasts being stung and kicking, this world will not last always. Arbitrary power men begin to weary of, in Kings and Churchmen; their juggle between them mutually to uphold civil and ecclesiastical tyranny begins to be transparent. Some have cast off both and hope by the grace of God to keep so. Others are at it! Many thoughts are laid up about it, which will have their issue and vent. This principle, that people are for Kings and Churches, and Saints for the Pope and Churchmen (as you call them), begins to be exploded; and therefore I wonder not to see the fraternity to be so much enraged. I wish the people wiser than to be troubled at you, or solicitous for what you say or do.

But it seems, notwithstanding all this, you would feign have them believe it is their good you seek. And to cozen them, in deed and in truth, is the scope of your whole Declaration, and of your acts and decrees, in your aforesaid printed book. Therefore to discover and unveil those falsities, and to let them know what they are to trust from me, is the principle end of this my Declaration. That if I be not able to do good upon them, which I most desire (and yet in that I shall not seek to gain them by flattery; but tell them the worst, in plainness, and that which I am sure will not be acceptable to you; and if I cannot gain them), I shall have comfort in this, that I have freed my own soul from the guilt of the evil that shall ensue. And upon this subject I hope to leave nothing unanswered in all your said Declarations and Decrees at Clonmacnoise.

And because you carry on your matter somewhat confusedly, I shall therefore bring all that you have said into some order, that so we may the better discern what everything signifies, and give some answer thereunto.

You forewarn the people of their danger; which you make to consist;

First, in the extirpation of the Catholic religion; secondly in the destruction of their lives; Thirdly in the ruin of their fortunes. To avoid all which evils you forewarn them: First that they be not deceived by the Commander-in-Chief of the Parliament Forces: and in the next place (having stated [the ground of] your war as aforesaid), you give them your positive advice and councel to engage in blood; and lastly bestow on them a small collation in four ecclesiastical Decrees or Orders, which will signify as little, being performed by your spirit, as if you had said nothing. And the obligation to all this you make to be your pastoral relation to them, over your flocks.

To which last a word or two. I wonder how this relation was brought about? If they be flocks, and you ambitious of the relative term, you are pastors: but it is by an antiphrasis – 'a minime pascendo!' You either teach them not at all, or else you do it, as some of you came to this conventicle who were sent by others, 'tanguam Procuratores', or as your manner is, by sending a company of silly ignorant priests who can but say the mass, and scarcely that intelligibly; or with such stuff as these your senseless Declarations and edicts! – But how dare you assume to call these men your flocks, who you have plunged into so horrid a rebellion, by which you have made both them and the country almost a ruinous heap, and whom you have fleeced and polled and peeled hitherto, and make it your business to do so still. You cannot feed them! You poison them with your false abominable and antichristian doctrine and practices. You keep the word of God from them and instead thereof give them your senseless orders and traditions. You teach them implicit belief; he that goes amongst them may find many that do not understand anything in the matters of religion. I have had few better answers from any since I came into Ireland, that are of your flocks than this, that indeed they did not trouble themselves about matters of religion but left that to the Church. Thus are your flocks fed; and such credit have you of them. But they must take heed of losing their religion. Alas poor creatures,

what have they to lose?
Concerning this, is your grand caveat; and to back this, you tell them of Resolutions and Covenants to extirpate the Catholic Religion out of all his Majesty's dominions. And you instance in Cromwell's letter of the 19 of October 1649, to the then Governor of Ross, repeating his words which are as followeth, viz- 'For that which you mention concerning liberty of religion, I meddle not with any man's conscience. But if by liberty of conscience you mean, a liberty to exercise the Mass, I judge it best to use plain dealing, and to let you know where the Parliament of England have power, that will not be allowed of'. And this you call a tyrannical resolution; which you say hath been put in execution in Wexford, Ross and Drogheda.

Now let us consider. First you say that the design is to extirpate the Catholic Religion. Let us see your honesty herein. Your word extirpate is as ill collected from these grounds, and as senseless as the word Catholic, ordinarily used by you when you mention Catholic Roman Church. The word extirpate supposes a thing to be already rooted and established which word made good by the proof of Covenants, your letter which expressed the non-toleration of the Mass wherein, it seems you place all the Catholic Religion (and therein you show some ingenuity) and [by] your instance of what was practised in the three towns aforementioned. Do these prove either considered apart or all together, the extirpation of the Catholic Religion?

By what law was the mass exercised in these places, or in any dominions of England or Ireland, or Kingdom of Scotland? You were intruders, you were herein open violators of the known laws! And yet you will call the Covenant, that in the letter, and these practices, extirpations of the Catholic Religion, thus again set on foot by you, by the advantage of your rebellion, and shaking-off the just authority of the State of England over you. Whereas I dare be confident to say, you durst not own the saying of one mass above these eighty years in Ireland. And through the troubles you made, and the miseries you brought on this nation and the poor people thereof (your numbers which is very ominous, increasing with the wolves through the desolations you made in the Country); you recovered again the public exercises of your mass! And for the maintenance of this, thus gained, you would make the poor people believe that it is ghostly counsel, and given in love to them as your flocks, that they should run into war, and venture lives, and all upon such a ground as this! But if God be pleased to unveil you of your sheep's clothing, that they may see how they have been deluded and by whom I shall exceedingly rejoice; and indeed for their sakes only have I given you these competent characters (if God shall so bless it) for their good.

And now for them, I do particularly declare what they may expect at my hands in this point; wherein you may easily perceive that, as I neither have nor shall flatter you, so shall I neither go about to delude them with specious pretences as you have ever done.

First, therefore, I shall not, where I have the power and the Lord is pleased to bless me, suffer the exercise of the Mass where I can take notice of it, nor suffer you that are Papists, where I can find you seducing the People, or by an overt act violating the Laws established; but if you come into my hands, I shall cause to be inflicted the punishments appointed by the laws (to use your own terms) 'secundum gravitatem delicti', upon you; and to reduce things to their former state on this behalf. As for the people, what thoughts they have in matters of religion in their own breasts I cannot reach; but think it my duty, if they walk honestly and peaceably not to cause them in the least to suffer for the same, but shall endeavour to walk patiently and in love towards them, to see if at any time it shall please God to give them another or a better mind. And all men under the power of England, within this dominion, are hereby required and

enjoined strictly and religiously to do the same.
To the second, which is the destruction of the lives of the Inhabitants of this Nation to make it good that this is designed, they give not one reason. Which is either that they have none to give, or else for that they believe the People will receive everything for truth they say, which they have too well taught them, and God knows the people are too apt, to do. But I will a little help them. They speak indeed of rooting out the Commons; and also by way of consequent, that the extirpating the Catholic Religion is not to be effected without the massacring, destroying or banishing the Catholic Inhabitants. Which how an illogical argument this is, I shall easily make appear by and by.

Alas the generality of the Inhabitants are poor Laity (as you call them) and ignorant of the grounds of the Catholic Religion. Are these then so interwoven with your Church Interest as that the absence of them makes your Catholic Religion fall to the ground? We know you think not so. You reckon yourselves (and yourselves only) the pillars and supporters thereof; and these as far as they have the exercise of club-law, and, like the ass you ride on, obey your commands. But concerning these [in?]relation of your Religion, enough has been spoken in another place, only you love to mix things for your advantage.

But to your logic, here is your argument. The design is to extirpate the Catholic religion. But this is not to be done by the massacring, banishing or otherwise destroying the Catholic inhabitants; ergo it is designed to massacre, banish and destroy the Catholic inhabitants. To prove this no-concluding argument, (but yet well enough agreeing with your learning), I give you this dilemma, by which it will appear that, whether your religion be true or false, this will not follow:
If your religion be the true religion, yet if a nation may degenerate

from the true religion, and apostatise (as too many have done) through the seducements of your Roman Church, then it will not follow that men must be massacred, banished or otherwise destroyed, necessarily, no, not as to the change of the true religion in a nation or country! Only, this argument doth wonderfully well agree with your principles and practice; you have chiefly made use of fire and sword, in all the changes of religion that you have made in the world. If it be change of your Catholic religion so-called, it will not follow: because there may be found another means than massacring, destruction and banishment; to wit the Word of God, which is able to convert (a means that you as little know as practise, which indeed you deprive the people of) together with humanity, good life, equal and honest dealing with men of different opinion, which we desire to exercise towards this poor people, (if you by your wicked counsel, make them not incapable to receive it, by putting them into blood).

And therefore by this also your false and twisted dealing may be a little discovered. But well; your words are, 'massacre, destroy and banish'. Good now: give us an instance of one man, since my coming into Ireland, not in arms, massacred, destroyed or banished, concerning the two first of which justice hath not been done, or endeavoured to be done. But for the other of banishment, I must speak unto the People whom you would delude, and whom this most concerns that they may know in this also what to expect at my hands.

The question is of the destruction of life, or of that which is but little inferior to it, to wit, banishment. I shall not willingly take or suffer to be taken away, the life of any man not in arms, but by the trial to which the people of this nation are subject by law, for offences against the same. *And for the banishment, it hath not hitherto been inflicted on any but such who, being in arms, upon the terms they were taken might justly have been put to death – as those instanced in their Declaration to be sent to the Tobacco Islands. And therefore I do declare, that if the people be ready to run to arms by the instigation of their clergy or otherwise, such as God by his providence shall give into my hands may expect that or worst measure, from me, but not otherwise.*

Thirdly, to that of the ruin of their fortune. You instance in the Act of Subscription, whereby the estates of the inhabitants of this nation are sold, so as there remaineth now no more but to put the purchasers in possession, and that for this cause are the forces drawn out of England. And that you might carry the interest far, to engage the common sort of people with you, you further say to them, that the moderate usage exercised to them, is to no other end but to our private advantage, and for the better support of our army, intending at the close of our conquest (as you term it) to root out the commons also, and to plant the land with colonies to be brought hither out of England. This consisting of divers parts will ask distinct answers.

And first, to the act of Subscription. It's true there is such an Act, and it was a just one. For when by your execrable massacre and rebellion, you had not only raised a bloody war to justify the same, and thereby occasioned the exhausting of the treasure of England in the prosecution of so just a war against you – was it not a wise and just Act in the State to raise money by escheating the lands of those who had a hand in the rebellion? Was it not fit to make their estates to defray the charge, who had caused the trouble? The best therefore that lies in this argument is this (and that only reaching to them who have been in arms, for further it goes not); you have forfeited your estate, and it is likely that they will be escheated to make satisfaction, and therefore you had better fight it out than repent, or give off now, or see what mercy you might find from the State of England. And seeing Holy Church is engaged in it, we will, by one means or another, hook-in the commons, and make them sensible that they are as much concerned as you, though they were never in arms, or came quickly off. And for this cause doubtless are these two coupled together, by which your honest dealing is manifest enough.

But what? Was the English army brought over for this purpose, as you allege? Do you think that the State of England will be at five or six millions charge merely to procure purchasers to be invested in that for which they did disburse little above a quarter of a million? Although there be a justice in that also, which ought, and I trust will be seasonably performed to them. – *No I can give you a better reason for the army's coming over than this. England hath had experience of the blessing of God in prosecuting just and righteous causes, whatever the cost and hazard be. And if ever men were engaged in a righteous cause in the world, this will be scarce a second to it. We are come to ask an account of the innocent blood that hath been shed; and to endeavour to bring them to an account (by the blessing and presence of the Almighty, in whom alone is our hope and strength), who by appearing in arms seek to justify the same. We are come to break the power of a company of lawless rebels, who having cast off the authority of England, live as enemies to human society, whose principles (the world hath experience of) are, to destroy and subjugate all men not complying with them. We come (by the assistance of God) to hold forth and maintain the lustre and glory of English liberty in a nation where we have an undoubted right to it – wherein the people of Ireland (if they listen not to such seducers as you are) may equally participate in all benefits, to use liberty and fortune equally with Englishmen if they keep out of arms.*

And therefore, having said this to you, I have a word to them, that in this point, which concerns them in their estates and fortunes, they may know what to trust to. Such as have been formerly and are not now in arms, may (submitting themselves) have their cases presented to the State of England, where no doubt the State will be ready to take into consideration the nature and quality of their actings, and deal mercifully with them. For those that are now in arms, and shall come in, and submit, and give engagements for their future quiet and honest carriage, and submission to the State of England, I doubt but that they will find like merciful consideration – excepting only the leading persons and principle contrivers of this rebellion, whom I am confident they will reserve to make examples of justice, whatsoever hazards they incur thereby – And for such private soldiers as lay down their arms, and shall live peaceably and honestly at their several homes, they shall be permitted so to do. – And for the first two sorts, I shall humbly and effectually represent their cases to the Parliament, as far as becomes the duty and place I bear. But as for those who, notwithstanding all this, persist and continue in arms, they must expect what the providence of God (in that which is falsely called the chance of war) will cast upon them.

For such of the nobility, gentry and commons of Ireland as have not *been actors in this rebellion, that they shall and may expect the protection in their goods, liberties and lives which the law gives them; and in their husbandry, merchandising, manufactures and other trading whatsoever, the same. They behaving themselves as becomes honest and peaceable men, testifying their good affections, upon all occasions, to the service of the State of England, equal justice shall be done them with the English. They shall bear proportionably with them in taxes. And if the soldiery be insolent upon them, upon complaint and proof, it shall be punished with utmost severity, and they protected equally with Englishmen.*

And having said this and purposing honestly to perform it, if this people shall headily run on after the counsels of their Prelates and Clergy and other leaders, I hope to be free from the misery and desolation, blood and ruin, that shall befall them, and shall rejoice to exercise utmost severity against them.
O. Cromwell.

While the entire document should be read closely by anyone who wants to gain an appreciation of the issues, I have italicised many of the salient points above and the attentive reader will notice several strikingly conspicuous factors concerning Cromwell's attitude to Ireland in these words. This document completely sums up his Irish campaign. It was the Catholic clergy that was the source of Ireland's woes and it was they with whom he had major issues, not the people of Ireland. In this declaration alone, no fewer than TEN times does he emphasise that unarmed folk were not to be harmed, or suffer in any way at the hands of Parliament, indeed on one occasion he explicitly denies that he had deliberately harmed any unarmed civilians whatsoever up to that point. He even refers to the Catholic Church's deplorable past when telling them what he perceives to be God's directives; they should avoid the spirit of Cain, Corah and Balaam, by building the faith, not by forcing it on others, by praying to the Holy ghost, not mumbling over matins, and most tellingly of all, '*not destroying men because they will not be of our Faith.*' This last sentiment perhaps being a reference to the atrocities perpetrated by the Church throughout history.

If we believe Cromwell then everything else begins to fit into place. These are not the words of a mass murderer. He is consistent in his approach to the ordinary Irish people from the moment he lands in Ireland. We will see later that his evidence is also consistent with all of the other primary source evidence. And while many historians dismiss this document and Cromwell's denial of war crimes, there is absolutely no good reason to believe that he was lying, or even being economical with the truth.

Furthermore, massacring innocent men, women and children did not accord with Cromwell's personality. Any study of the man will show that he was tender towards children, he was a family man who had a high moral threshold, and that he was acutely aware of the folly that such action would be dastardly deeds that he clearly abhorred. As soon as he landed in Dublin he was determined to get the population of the entire country on his side. A slaughter of innocents would have been in complete contrast to the way he was resolved to fight the war in Ireland. He persistently accuses the Catholic Clergy of their complicity in 'horrid massacres' in a clear display of his attitude to atrocities. Deliberately killing innocent civilians was anathema to his ethical ideals of which we have plenty of evidence. He did not lose his moral principles in Ireland only to find them again when he returned to England. His thoughts about Irish men and women are encapsulated here: 'As for the people' he writes, 'what thoughts they have in matters of religion in their own breasts I cannot reach; but think it my duty, if they walk honestly and peaceably, not to cause them in the least to suffer for the same.'

Among the many historians who have commented on this document is Professor Micheál O'Siochrú, an early modern expert now at Trinity College Dublin. Regarding Cromwell's various proclamations to his troops against plundering O'Siochrú interprets Cromwell's proclamations to his troops as follows:

> This declaration, along with the subsequent execution of a handful of soldiers for unlicensed pillaging, has been used to suggest that Cromwell did not harbour any hostility towards the ordinary Catholic inhabitants of Ireland. In fact, his actions represented nothing more than prudent military practice, motivated by genuine necessity.

Where perhaps it might have been more balanced to contextualise Cromwell's mindset using the opinions, nuances, and deep-rooted revelations, in particular his clearly outlined attitude towards the Irish people, (above), O'Siochrú instead hones in on a single and oft-quoted excerpt, takes it out of context and speculates. Cromwell writes: 'But well, your words are, massacre, destroy and banish. Good now, give us an instance of one man since my coming into Ireland, not in arms, massacred, destroyed or banished, concerning the two first of which justice hath not been done, or endeavoured to be done.' O'Siochrú italicises the last five words of the statement in his book (*God's Executioner*, of which we will see more later) and says:

> This crucial caveat (*or endeavoured to be done*) not only justified the atrocities committed by his troops since August, but also exposed an unexpected degree of sensitivity to criticism. These comments reflect the self-doubt already apparent in his earlier letters to Lenthall, where he spoke of the need for tough tactics, which otherwise would work "but remorse and regret". Cromwell, unlike some of his subsequent apologists, was clearly troubled by some of what he had seen at Drogheda and Wexford.

What the popular historian could really only be saying here is that Cromwell was aware of the fact that unarmed civilians were massacred (or destroyed) by his troops at Drogheda and Wexford and that Cromwell tried to find the culprits to punish them, but couldn't, and so he simply let it go. Or indeed he didn't bother looking in the first place. O'Siochrú's claim is not supported by the surviving evidence. Mitigating against it are the words of Cromwell himself and all of the other eye witness testimony that survives from the period.

Chapter Two

Aside from the impact of *Honourable Enemy* on the world of popular culture, there were other voices, arrogating the resonance of authority, who had plenty to say about it. Leading the assault team in the early days was seventeenth century expert Jason McElligott. In a carefully-planned pincer attack McElligott had an article published in the historical publication *Bullán* entitled, *Cromwell, Drogheda, and the Abuse of Irish History* which he combined with a review of my book that he posted on Amazon and that has remained there since it first appeared on 20 June 2001. In both articles McElligott attacks the book from almost every angle. Dismissing the thesis outright he writes:

> It is my contention not merely that this book is fatally flawed from beginning to end, but that the praise heaped upon it by certain sections of the media and the historical profession tells us something both interesting and profoundly disturbing about contemporary Irish society and its attitude towards the past....The author exhibits a profound unfamiliarity of the English revolution of the mid-seventeenth century...This is a painfully bad book, and it is tempting to suggest that its main use is to teach students how not to conduct research, assess evidence or write prose...All the evidence suggests that Cromwell slaughtered the garrison and many of the towns-people of Drogheda in September 1649. In doing so, he stepped outside the norms of seventeenth-century warfare. To pretend otherwise is an abuse of Irish history.

As this was the first real academic challenge of the book I approached both of McElligott's pieces with great interest. I had disputed Cromwell's demonic reputation and by definition I had questioned the academic integrity of hundreds of historians;

surely here now was the meticulous dismantling of my thesis by an expert in the field, with many more to follow. Let the cards fall wherever they may, true history demands nothing else. At least the civilian atrocity allegations will now have been thoroughly investigated and we can return to the natural order of things with Cromwell firmly ensconced in Irish history as an inhuman ogre - the killer of thousands of ordinary Irish people, including innocent men, women and children. I was fully prepared to distance myself from my thesis, chalk it up to experience, and let history be the winner.

Predictably, in defence of his profession, McElligott interpreted the examples of contemporary sources that he highlights in his commentary in the way that many of his predecessors and peers would have done. Unfortunately, most of the primary source evidence concerning Cromwell in Ireland is open to interpretation. One of the most contentious issues about Drogheda is the evidence of Cromwell himself. McElligott seems to believe that the three words 'and many inhabitants' that appear at the end of a contemporary document that contains a list of officers and soldiers appended to a transcription of Cromwell's letter (the official parliamentary pamphlet) was virtually irrefutable proof of Cromwell's personal admission that he and his army killed unarmed men, women and children at Drogheda.

Indeed, other contemporary newsbooks transcribed and published the same list but left out these three words. While, up to now, there has been no solid evidence to suggest that any 'inhabitants' took up arms at Drogheda in the defence of their town and were killed in the posture of soldiers, such an occurrence could easily have taken place.

Historian Christopher Firth has suggested that these three words may have been added spuriously by the parliamentary printer, who was actually responsible for the printing of the document. Thomas Carlyle (wrongly) says that the words were not in the original official document. And it was to these possibilities that I clung for an explanation of the conundrum it posed when I was researching *Honourable Enemy*. Elsewhere, in Cromwell's other writings, known to be in his own hand, there is strong contrary evidence that Cromwell could simply not have admitted to large-scale civilian atrocities – at all in the first place, and in such a glib fashion in the second. But it was not necessary for me to rely on Firth's interpretations as we will see. There is no question that this document is open to interpretation, making any statement about it (including mine) speculation and not fact.

But McElligott is in no doubt that my treatment of these three words was wide of the mark: 'Reilly…makes a number of serious blunders, the most important of which concerns Cromwell's letter to the House of Commons after the battle at Drogheda.'

McElligott then cites two other primary source documents, neither of which appeared in my book, and of both he says;

> He is completely unaware of John Evelyn's diary entry of 15 September 1649 which tells that he "received news of Drogheda being taken by the rebels and all being put to the sword." Had Reilly been aware of these sources, he would undoubtedly have found some grounds to dismiss them but when they are read in conjunction with the numerous other accounts of civilian deaths at Drogheda there can be no doubt what happened in that town in September 1649.

Here McElligott is correct. I was completely unaware of this diary entry. But in contrast to the learned academic, I have chosen to interpret the expression 'all being put to the sword' to refer to the military defenders. Indeed the Duke of Ormond (who never mentions civilian deaths in all the letters that he wrote) in a letter to Charles II on 18 September 1649 uses almost the same expression. Referring to Drogheda, Ormond writes, 'the bloody execution of almost all that were in it.' Many accounts of the taking of Drogheda exist and the language used is often in military terms, and even in the context of a seventeenth century diary entry, when Evelyn's quote is set in context it can easily be determined to refer to the defenders and not the local inhabitants. But more importantly, it is quite surprising to see an expert of the period using such vague sources to support an argument. The diary of John Evelyn was first published in 1818 under the title of *Memoirs Illustrative of the Life and Writings of John Evelyn* that was edited by William Bray who was assisted in his undertaking by William Upcott, who had access to the Evelyn family documents. The entries are not daily but were compiled much later from notes and often show the benefit of hindsight. Royalist virtuoso Evelyn was a prolific author who wrote books on such diverse subjects as theology, politics, horticulture, architecture, and vegetarianism and he often travelled with the royal court of Charles II. The diary entry for October 15th (not September 15th as McElligott claims) reads as follows;

> 15th October 1649: Came news of Drogheda being taken by the rebels, and all put to the sword, which made us very sad, forerunning the loss of all Ireland

After Bray's initial editing and selection, other editors worked on the diary in the following century. A revised edition was published in 1827 that was edited by Upcott. It was then reprinted in four volumes in 1879 by Henry Benjamin Wheatly and re-issued in 1966. There was also a four volume edition published by John Forster (1850-52). A later edition was by Austin Dobson (three volumes, 1906). This evidence that McElligott submits appeared in public 169 years after the events. It would be tempting to suggest that since it was edited by several hands it could well have been altered by persons unknown, but there is little point in even doing that because it has nothing whatsoever to add to the civilian massacre theory.

McElligott then goes on to say, 'Neither is he familiar with a report in a newspaper named *Mercurius Elencticus,* dated 15th October 1649, which tells how the Cromwellians at Drogheda "possessed themselves of the towne and used all cruelties imaginable on the besieged, as well inhabitants and others, sparing neither women nor children."

In dealing with this particular statement it would seem appropriate at this juncture to refer to the fact that numerous historians have accused me of selecting evidence to suit an agenda. John Morrill puts it rather succinctly, 'Reilly fails the test of source criticism at almost every turn. He argues a case and unreasonably privileges second-and third-hand evidence that supports his pre-supposition and unreasonably dismisses contrary evidence.'

(185) PP. London. K. with 2. [Numb. 24.] (9)

Mercurius Elencticus.

Communicating the unparralell'd Proceedings of the Rebbels at Weſt-minſter, and the Head-quarters, diſcovering their Deſignes, reproving their Crimes, and adviſing the Kingdome.

From *Monday Octo.* 8. to *Monday, Octob.* 15. 1649.

——Ridentem dicere verum
Quid vetat?

Sure all's *not* loſt : *If ſo*; *not* wonne :
One Iriſh-trick *remaines,*
Which e're the Iriſh Game *bee done*
Sweepes Stake, *and* ſtock *of* Braines.

The Conquering Tyrant *never* winnes
So much by Cruell-deedes,
As gentle-uſage : *nor leſſe* Sinnes
Then when his Foe *leaſt* Bleedes.

If this bee ſo : in what ſweete Caſe
Stand Cromwell *and his* Crew,
Who ſpare nor good *nor* gallant-Face,
Not Chriſtian *more then* Jew?

Oneale! *goe on, 'tis given to thee*
For to Revenge *their* Blood:
Reſtore thy Nations Liberty!
"*God* ſees *and* ſaies *'tis* good.

THE Act (falſely ſo ſtiled) againſt (ſuch as the ſaints are pleaſed to call) ſcandalous and ſeditious Bookes and Pamphlets, hath beene put ſo diligently in exequution, by the States Blood-hounds, that the laſt weeke I had enough to doe in ſecureing my ſelfe from their hungry Jawes, and could not ſo oportunely apeare as formerly ; in which reſpect I chuſe rather not to bee ſeene at all. Which diſcontinuance yet not a little agrieved mee, becauſe a timely ſolution of thoſe Letters of the twentieth and two-and-twentieth of *September* that ſpoke Tredagh

A a in

(186)

in so good a Condition (which was neverthelesse taken before that) till now was wanting which that they may receive, be pleased to peruse a third from the same hand, and I presume 'twill satisfy,

SIR,

I MUST Crave your Pardon for what you received in my two last of the twentieth and two-and-twentieth Wherein I intimated the holding out of Tredagh: For though they bee true in every Particular, as to the Repulsing of Crumwell the taking of three Peeces of his Cannon, and the losse therein mentioned &c. yet this day came certaine newes that the Towne was taken by storme some few daies before; and the Governour (Sir Arthur Aston) with the greatest part of the officers and soldiers put to the Sword: Which yet wee know not how to beleeve, considering the frequent Alarmes brought us of the losse before it, and the Advance of Ormond to it's Reliefe. But though Wee believe their losse exceedes one halfe of their Army since they first sate downe before it; yet wee found it too true that at last they had possessed themselves of the Towne, and used all crueltie imaginable upon the Besieged, as well Inhabitants as others, sparing neither Women nor Children: and after that marched to Trym and Dundalke, Which thereupon were both quited and slighted; yet in all this time no Ormond appeared, to the Wonder and amazement of all the Kings Friends: Whether it Were out of an over-weening confidence in the strength of the place and the gallantry of the men within it, or What other Reason wee know not: But this Wee are sure of, that Oneale and hee are joyned, so that wee can think of no interruption, unlesse occasioned by Inchiqueene, which wee have not the least of ground for; and that they had a Power sufficient to fight Cromwell with, is out of question. Sir, the truth is Affaires are Wrapped up in such Clowdes (and that on both sides) Wee know not how to judge of them. For, is it not strange, that Tredagh, Trim and Dundalke should bee all theirs betwixt the twelfth and fifteenth day, and yet Wee at Dublin have no certainty thereof till eight daies after at the least? And yet this is the least to bee wondered at, considering the strictnesse that is heere used to prevent all Intilligence, but what comes immediately from the hand of Cromwell, not any man being suffered to write to his friend either in England or Ireland, nor to ride or Walke a mile out of Towne without speciall license first obtained from a Committee for Intelligence, which they have here erected, as also another at Chester and Liverpoole, Who have power to examine, let passe, or stay, all Persons and Papers they meete with. Since the taking of Tredagh they are marching Southwards; and aime Principally (as wee heere) at Wexford, which I should feare much, but that themselves tell us the Royallists have re-inforced

(187)

forced it with 3000. *Horſe and Foote; which with thoſe that were in it before will make about* 4500. *And for proviſions they have no want &c. But* Cromwell *relies not altogether upon ſtrength, ſomething on policy; and therefore hath hee ſent abroad Proclamations and Papers, that promiſe Liberty of Conſcience, Propriety, Eaſe and Freedome to all the* Engliſh *(not any* Iriſh*) in Armes, that will come in and ſubmit to him. But wee heare not of any but ſome of their owne run-awaies, and wee hope this will bee a meanes rather to cement then ſeparate the Royalliſts &c.*

Dublin September
24. 1649.

By another Letter from the ſame hand of 2 *Oct.* it is further certified: That Sir *Arthur Aſton*, Sir *Edmund Varney*, and thethe reſt of the prime Officers, who after the Enemy had gained the Towne, retreated into, and maintained the Mount, had all of them Quarter promiſed them for their lives, and upon that condition went all into the Wind-Mill on the top of the Mount, whileſt the Enemie tooke poſſeſſion thereof; which no ſooner they had done, but they diſarmed, and afterwards moſt perfidiouſly Murthered them one by one, in the moſt cruell manner they could invent, cuting off their Members, and peeces of their fleſh, which they wore in their Hats triumphantly two daies after &c. That their Barbarouſneſſe was no leſſe exerciſed upon the reſt of the Souldiers and Inhabitants, eſpecially Religious men, amongſt the reſt the Lord *Taaff's* Brother an *Auguſtine Fryer*, and one *Parſons* (of the ſame Order) whom they kept two daies alive, torturing them by all the cruell waies and meanes they could deviſe, to make them confeſſe what they knew of the Royalliſts Deſignes, and then ended them. That above 1200. were Murthered in St. *Peters Church.* That about two hundred Officers and Souldiers maintained the Tower at the Weſt Gate till the next day, in which time they killed above two hundred of the Enemy, refuſing to ſubmit to mercy; but the Enemy at length conſidering the ſtrength of the place, and how their ſeverall attempts of firing them out had failed, and what loſſe they had already received, offered them conditions of quarter for their lives, upon which they ſurrendered, yet neverthelesſe *Cromwell* afterwards commanded the Officers to bee all Murthered and every tenth man of the Souldiers, which they were accordingly, and the ſurvivers ſold and Shiped away for *Barbadoes*, there to bee made ſlaves of all the daies of their lives &c.

Something elſe concludes this Letter, which I hope by this hath made ſome part of amends for this loſſe; but I am (as yet) command-

Aa 2 ed

In quoting *Mercurius Elencticus* and offering it as a credible primary source McElligott could easily be seen to be capable of the odd serious blunder himself. The 'evidence' of the royalist 'mercuries' is notoriously unreliable as all of the period experts know well, including McElligott, whose area of expertise is the early modern newsbooks. We know who the writers of these publications were and we know exactly what their respective opinions were, as they shouted them from the rooftops loudly and clearly. Thanks to many historians who have studied the printing/newspaper industry of the early modern period (JB Williams, Blair Worden, Joad Raymond, Jason Peacey, Jason McElligott, Nick Poyntz, to name but a few), we have incredible detail about who the authors of each of these publications were. Sir George Wharton was the author of *Mercurius Elencticus*. One historian has recently written extensively about some of these royalist authors:

> All of these men penned propaganda in a variety of formats during their time at Oxford, and they probably knew each other well. It has been noted above that a pamphlet written in 1644 suggested that Birkenhead, Taylor and Wharton met once a week in a tavern in Oxford to muster up whole regiments of lies, slanders and ridiculous quibbles against the Parliament and the city of London.

The most surprising aspect of this quotation is that its author is Jason McElligott, who on one hand wants to submit Wharton's publication as credible primary source evidence, while on the other is acutely aware of the quality of the information contained in the royalist author's publication. The language throughout *Mercurius Elencticus* is inflammatory to the core and is a perfect example of the ongoing propaganda war.

ed; but yet that hee heares not of one man (foote or horse taken on fo
Montrosses *Designe*: —— whence then came those *Sweedes* and *Ger*
manes landed in *Scotland*? —— *For* (saith hee) *I beleeve* (and that'
a great assurance) *the maine matter* [*money*] *is wanting, and besides the*
Muster place (what, not a field neare *Hamborough*?) *and meanes for*
Transportation, about which Montrosse *is still treating with the King of*
Denmarke &c. And hee further addes, *That there is at present one at*
Noremberg *solliciting the Emperours Commissioners, and* Sweedes, *and*
German *Princes for mony and men for the same Designe.* By which he may
gather then the *Cavaliers* are not idle, nor quite out of hopes to shake
the foundation of their *new-Common-Wealth*; so that yet they'll have
no time to sing *lullabye* to their *Soules*; they are not so safe as imagined.

But I have done with the Annuall because he hath done with his Intelligence, and
(as he saith) failed in his Expectation of the certainty of Affaires in *Ireland*; but that
defect I shall timously supply: For, by Letters from *France* (for this weeke I have
seene none else that mention any thing of *Ireland*) it is assured us, that an Expresse is
come to the Queene of *England*, wherein it is signified that imediatly after the conjun-
ction of *Oneale* and *Ormond, Inckequine, Ards*, and the rest of the *Irish* Forces;
Cromwell advanced, with intention to hinder the same, or at least to distract and a-
maze them by his suddaine Approach, but finding them all united and in readinesse
beyond expectation, they engaged him to Fight, and that upon some disadvantage:
Neverthelesse the Rebells stood stiffly to it, and fought with great Resolution; the Bat
tel began about six in the Morning, and continued, more or lesse, till six at night; by
which time the Rebells were totally Routed, 4000 killed, 2000 taken prisoners, the
rest pursued to the very walls of *Dublin*, with great Execution. In this Action it is
said they have lost most of their prime Commanders, and some report *Cromwell* him-
selfe to be mortally wounded. And thus much we receive by the way of *France*, for by a
neerer it is scarce possible, considering the strictnesse used in the stopping of all per-
sons and Letters which might give us the truth of Affaires there; But I am strongly in-
duced to beleeve the truth hereof by a Letter I have seen from a well-affected brother
in *Chester*, to his friend in *London*, wherein he saith, *The News there, concerning their*
Army in Ireland, *is such, and as Related so incredible, and lamentable* (*if true*) *as hee*
dare not mention it; but referres to his next, wherein he hopes to give him more Com-
fort, &c. In the afore-mentioned Letters from *France*, we are also informed That
there was a Designe of surprizing the King in *Jersey*, by the meanes of a man of War,
with the assistance of some of his good Servants about him; to which end the Ship had
cast Anchor there, under the notion of a Revolter, but the Plot being discovered, she
was seized on in good earnest, and honest men put in her, and there remaines for the
service of him she came to betray. Since which his Majesty is removed, some thinke
for *Scotland* (but that is groundlesse) others for *Ireland* (and that is more probable)
But whither, as yet we are unceitaine.

The last weeke I told you that *Thursday* (the 18. instant) was appointed for Mr.
Lilburne to bee brought to his Tryall; and so it was; but the *Juncto* have very pru-
dently deferred it for ten daies longer, and perhaps when they are expired, will a-
gaine for as many more: — Indeede la! they have a Woolfe by the eares.

The Resolves of the *Regicides* touching the subscribing to an Engagement, where-
in they Declare and promise to bee true and faithfull to the Common-Wealth of
England as the same is now Established, without a King or House of Lords, being
already in Print, I thinke needelesse to mention; And I hope the snares therein are
so apparent, the weakest eye may discerne (and if they have grace avoid) them.

The Snares *and* Treason-Traps *they lay in* wait
For us, *may catch* them, *in their owne* deceipt.

FINIS.

For instance, the following week, the 15-22 October edition of the same newsbook Wharton reports the following fictitious incident:

> Immediately after the conjunction of O'Neale and Ormond, Inchequine, Ards, and the rest of the Irish forces, Crumwell advanced, with intention to hinder the same, or at least to distract and amaze them by his suddaine approach, but finding them all united and in readiness beyond expectation, they engaged him to fight, and that upon some disadvantage. Nevertheless the rebels (Cromwell's army) stood stiffly to it and fought with great resolution, the battel began about six in the morning, and continued more or less till six at night, by which time the rebels were totally routed, 4,000 killed, 2,000 taken prisoners, the rest parsued to the very walls of Dublin, with great execution. In this action it is said they have lost most of their prime commanders, and some report Crumwell himself to be mortally wounded.

This is a fabricated battle and is just one example of the desire of early propagandists to invent stories that would reflect negatively on their enemies and stir up public opinion against them. It is essential to realise that the propaganda war was also vicious and yet McElligott wonders about the grounds on which I might dismiss this 'primary source'. As Professor Micheál O'Siochrú says, 'Royalist reports on Ireland became increasingly far-fetched, seizing on any slight piece of good news as evidence of a major setback for the Parliamentarians. Fictitious Royalist armies marched on Dublin, while Cromwell suffered defeats wherever he went...'

George Wharton (1617-1681) was an astrologer and royalist who published annual polemical almanacs during the mid-seventeenth century that drew him into fierce battles in print with his parliamentarian rivals. In 1645 he was commissioned captain of a regiment of horse and he fought for the King for a couple of years after which he returned to writing. In his *Bellum Hybernicale* (December 1646) he antagonised Parliament further when he justified the rebellion of 1641 in Ireland on the grounds of Ireland's long history of repression, and suggested that the English and Scots were equally to blame for the massacres. He was horrified when the king was executed and in his almanac of 1650 he described Parliament as 'the most prodigious Monsters that ever the earth groaned under' and he threatened them with execution and hell-fire themselves, an act for which he was subsequently arrested.

If McElligott, an expert in the period, offers Wharton's hyperbole as evidence, are we really now saying that we are relying on disreputable partisan authors with axes to grind who wrote newsbooks and pamphlets with outrageous abandon, as proof of Cromwell's guilt? We need only to point to the gross inaccuracies of the stories in the newsbooks and pamphlets that emerged in 1641 describing the 'massacres' of that year to see what the burgeoning newspaper business was effectively responsible for just eight years earlier. The general consensus of contemporary opinion suggests that in 1641 the press was responsible for circulating erroneous stories that as many as 154,000 Protestants were mercilessly massacred by Catholics in the rebellion of that year, stories that Oliver Cromwell himself is said to have believed as he approached Ringsend in August 1649.

Also in his *Bullán* article McElligott analyses how the period was taught in Irish schools and notes a 'decline of the cult of violence in Irish schoolbooks'. Writing in 2001 – and when one considers the textbooks already quoted above – his conclusions, while pertinent at the time, seem now to be dated:

> In the past few years the texts that were introduced in the 1980s have, in their turn, been replaced by a new generation of texts and a new primary school history curriculum that strives

> to present history in a balanced and unemotional manner. It is to their credit that the authors of these books have rejected the simplistic notions and ridiculous excesses of some revisionists in favour of a rounded, sophisticated, and non-sectarian approach to Irish history. We have come a long way in the last thirty years.

When one considers that the textbooks already quoted above (*Timeline* and *Earthlink*) have been published since McElligott wrote these words, it seems that we simply took one step forward only to take two more backwards.

Failing to convince the reader that the surviving evidence supports the civilian massacre theory, McElligott only offers two additional sources, neither of which makes any difference to this debate. So rather than dismantling my thesis in a scholarly and academic fashion with rational argument, which one would expect if he had the evidence at hand, McElligott descends into invective. He writes:

> On every single point that he uses to rehabilitate Cromwell – the letter to the House of Commons, the numerous seven-teenth century accounts of the fall of Drogheda, and the rules of war – Reilly has manipulated the facts in order to arrive at his preordained conclusion. Indeed *Cromwell, An Honourable Enemy* is such a painfully bad book that were it not for the rave reviews it has received in some quarters, such a lengthy deconstruction of the text might seem like taking a hammer to crack a nut.

It's such a pity that McElligott chose not to perform a 'lengthy deconstruction of the text'. It might have been much more useful and could have added significantly to our appreciation of the events had he done so.

Another of the high-profile detractors was Professor Micheál

O'Siochrú, who also vociferously nailed his colours to the mast immediately after the book was first published. In an article entitled '*Propaganda, rumour and myth: Oliver Cromwell and the massacre at Drogheda*' (in *Age of Atrocity* 2007), O'Siochrú deals with the civilian massacre theory comprehensively and defends the notion of a massacre of 'many' of the local, defenceless population. In defence of his case, in the first instance, he points to Irish poetry and folklore citing the eloquent words of contemporary poet Dáibhí Cúndún, who wrote 'in the 1650s'. According to O'Siochrú, Cúndún; 'refers directly to Cromwell's complicity in the massacre at Drogheda, in which he claims that civilians, as well as soldiers, were killed.' Folklore and poetry are often quoted in connection with Cromwell and there is no question that folk memory has its place in history in general and in the seventeenth century in particular. But as an argument in this particular controversial debate with the absence of corroborative proof from firsthand accounts, the 'evidence' of poets adds nothing to the discussion.

O'Siochrú then proceeds to outline arguments to support the traditional version of events. In so doing he analyses the popular sources, such as letters involving Inchiquin and Ormond, James Buck, and the sensationalist Restoration account of Thomas Wood as they have generally been interpreted by Irish nationalist interests. He takes the same view – and uses the exact same arguments – as McElligott concerning the 'and many inhabitants' dilemma and concludes, 'Oftentimes the most straightforward answer is the correct one. In his report, Cromwell, who witnessed the attack on Drogheda at close quarters, simply acknowledged that the casualties included a number of civilians.'

O'Siochrú then presents the details of Wharton's *Mercurius Elencticus* declaring, 'In early October the *Mercurius Elencticus*, until then the most moderate of the Royalist newssheets (at least in its Irish coverage) made a number of specific and lurid allegations. The dead at Drogheda included women and children...' It is quite surprising that both McElligott and O'Siochrú attach such significance to this document despite the harebrained opinions/stories that Wharton offers his readers week after week and the context of the publication in the propaganda war.

But interestingly he also raises another primary source that was also absent from *Honourable Enemy* when he writes, '*The Man in the Moon* picked up on the allegations of civilian deaths the following week, claiming that of the 3,000 dead, 2,000 were women and children.' To his credit O'Siochrú attaches a caveat to this statement when he says, 'Whether based on firsthand accounts from Ireland, gleaned from rumours circulating around London, or simply invented, these stories added to Cromwell's growing reputation for cruelty in Ireland.' And yet O'Siochrú chose not to complete the entire quotation, whereas, had he done so, it would have proved that the information here was notoriously unreliable.

(211) (Numb. 26.)

The Man in the Moon.

Discovering a World of

KNAVERY

Under the

SUNNE;

Both in the *Parliament*, the *Councel* of *State*, the *Army*, the *City* and the COUNTRY.

With *Intelligence* from all Parts of *England*, *Scotland*, and *IRELAND*.

Die Lunæ, From *Octob.* 17. to *Wednesday October* 24. 1649.

Noll cannot *thrive* on *Irish*-Coast,
get *Victory* nor *Riches*;
For *Usquebah* his *Nose* they toast,
and make him wrong his *Breeches*.

Return he must, he cannot *live*,
that *Aire* is too pure;
No *nourishment* it can him give,
that *Serpents* can't endure.

Yet he bares up, though Rowted quite,
'tis *Honor* for his Grace;
But now he need not fear their might,
his *Copper* shields his *Face*.

His *heart* is double, trebble *Gilt*,
his *Nose* 'gainst *Foes* gives *Fire*;
For all the *Blood* that he hath *spilt*,
he now Receives his *Hire*.

CROMWEL would needs go for *Ireland*, though he went without *Doublet* or *Breeches*; and now he is like to come home without *Head* or *Armes*: *Ha, ha, ha*; I could cry

Cc now,

now, but that I cannot: Is it poſſible that that invincible Conqueror *Cromwel* ſhould be overcome? who the Devil can beleeve it? nay then I ſee there is no truſt in *Horſe-fleſh*, ſince the Iriſh Papiſts are turn'd *Jews*, and begin to Sacrifice *Bulls* again: would I were but the Prieſts Boy to ſtrike in with my *Fleſh-book* (ſince *Noll* is gon to the Pot) to fetch up a Joynt of the *Bull* of *Ely* to preſent to the *Juncto*, or their Devils *Councel* of *State* for a Breakfaſt, it may be they would forgive me the *Ten pounds* I am indebted to them (by their late Act) for Writing this *Pamphlet* againſt their pretended *Authority*: or Remit me of my *Forty dayes impriſonment for non-payment of the ſame.* Is not *Lilly* now a *Witch* or a *Cunning-man*, that forewarned his Excellence of his *Fate*, and receiving a *Wound*? how good had it been, if he had tane his Counſel and ſtaid at home? but queſtionleſs he was Ripe for the Devil, and could not prevent his *Fate*, as appears by the proverb,

> He needs muſt go, when *Devils* do him drive,
> When *Rebels* fall, then *Loyalty* doth thrive.

The News from *Ireland* is now forbidden ſo much as to be peep'd into by the *Juncto*: the *Poſt* that brought *Letters* ſworn into Secrecy, and the Letters buried in the Grave of Oblivion: Order likewiſe gon to Sea-ports to ſwear all that come over Secrecy; yet all will not do: faith they may e'ne hang up their Harps and themſelves too, for they have loſt their other Inſtruments: That wonderful Miracle, *Ene almoſt as great as the Reſurrection from the dead*, is now beſhitt; their intended *Feaſting-Day*, turn'd into a *Day of Howling, Wo, and Lamentation*: and that God (who hates all unrighteous dealing) hath juſtly delivered them up as a Prey, to thoſe they thought they had deſtroyed: this 'tis to reckon their Chickins before they be hatch'd: ſuddenly (when they thought themſelves Cock-ſure, and like the Devil Cry'd, *All's mine*:) their Deſtruction ariſeth, after they had wrought home all their Miſchiefs, and were Ripe for Hell: then unexpectedly (in *Cromwels* furious Carrier, when all fled before them) *Vengeance* over-takes him, and deſtroyes their Army, kills 6000 on the place, and has the execution upon them twenty miles together.

The manner of it this: After theſe bloudy Monſters had Sa-

(213)

Sacrificed in *Tredagh*, Men, Women, and Children to their curſed Rage, yet could not take the White Tower, nor the Windmill-Mount, whereupon (my Letter ſaith) That their Commanders (a thing odious ſo much as to be mentioned) got four of the Commanders Wives, and their ſucking Infants, and placed them before them where they thought their Cannon ſhould play moſt, and finding they would not refrain ſhooting, Raviſhed them in the ſight of their Husbands, and ſlew their tender Infants; a Fact odious to God and man? But what wickedneſs is it that ſuch graceleſs Monſters will not Commit? they account Murder and Adultery, nay the breach of all the *Commandements* no more ſin (as I have heard ſome of them ſay) then after they had learned their *Leſſon* of their School-maſter, to leave going to School. Their barbarous Cruelty in that abhorrid Act not to be paralled by any of the former Maſſacrees of the Iriſh, ſparing neither Women nor Children, but putting them all to the Sword 15000 indeed they killed, but 2000 were Women and Children, and divers aged Perſons that were not able to ſupport themſelves, much-leſs unable to Reſiſt them: the Town thus gained with the loſe of 5000 of their own, they were gallantly Reſiſted by the Windmill-Fort, and White-Tower, both by the great skill of that gallant Engineer Sir *Arthur Aſhton* made inpregnable, and held out four dayes after they had the Town, *Cromwel* thinking to ſtarve them out: in the mean time they ſent *Venable* with 500 to take in *Trim* and *Dundalk*, which were both delivered unto them, and ſome Offers of the Governor of *Killkenny* of 20000.l. to ſpare that place from Plunder: the enemy going confidently on; the Marqueſs of *Ormond* in the Night had put into that Garriſon 2000 Foot, and 500 Horſe; *Venable* Summons the Town, they Deny to yeeld, whereupon he falls to Storm; *Montroſs* comes in the Rear of them with 3000 Foot, and 1000 Horſe; the Town Sallyed out, and Charged them very deſperately, and a hot Diſpute was for four Hours, many falling on both ſides, till at laſt *Cromwel* finding himſelf over-powred, flies out in two Wings, but before he could get his men in Order, one Wing was Rowted, 500 killed, the reſt run; the other Wing ſtood to it about an hour

Cc 2

Referring to the parliamentarian army *The Man in the Moon* (Oct 17-24 1649) states:

> Their barbarous cruelty in that abhorrid act, not to be paralled by any of the former massacres of the Irish, sparing neither

> women nor children, but putting them all to the sword. 3,000 indeed they killed, but 2,000 were women and children and divers aged persons that were not able to support themselves, much less unable to resist them, the towne thus gained with the loss of 5,000 of their own.

Eager to paint the rebel parliamentarian army in as bad a light as possible, John Crouch, the writer of *The Man in the Moon* claims that the Parliamentarian army lost 5,000 men at Drogheda. This is a big miss. The losses on Parliament's side at Drogheda are known to have been miniscule in comparison to the Royalist casualties, 64 at the lowest estimate and 150 at the highest. While on one hand O'Siochrú acknowledges the facile nature of the Royalist pamphlets, like McElligott, his use of Crouch's inflammatory allegation to support his argument seems incongruous. McElligott himself even gives us more reason to doubt the veracity of *The Man in the Moon*. The following is an extract of a biography of John Crouch written by McElligott:

> Crouch, John (b, c.1615, d in or after 1680), writer and bookseller, was born the son of a yeoman named Thomas Crouch in Standon, Hertfordshire. He had at least one brother, Gilbert Crouch, who acted as a land agent for the earl of Shrewsbury. John Crouch began an apprenticeship with the bookseller Nicholas Salisbury on 6 November 1632 and served his time until 2 December 1639. He evidently worked as a bookseller during the 1640s and there is no evidence that he wrote any books or pamphlets during the 1640s. Between 1652 and 1657 he and a printer named Thomas Wilson owned and ran a print shop at the sign of the Three Foxes in Long Lane in Smithfield.
>
> In February 1648 Crouch wrote the first part of a two-part satirical, anti-puritan pamphlet entitled Craftie Cromwell.

> Between April and November 1648 he wrote five further anti-puritan pamphlets, the Kentish Fayre, and four plays based on the character of Mrs Parliament. He also wrote three numbers of a royalist newsbook entitled *Mercurius Critticus* and a counterfeit edition of John Hackluyt's royalist newsbook *Mercurius Melancholicus*. In April 1649 he wrote the first of fifty-seven issues of *The Man in the Moon*. The eight-page weekly was printed by John's kinsman Edward Crouch. It recounted little news and relied instead on obscene stories and rhymes to fill its pages. Its principal targets were parliament, the army, the council of state and the official newsbooks. In general it had three main lines of attack: the humble social origins of England's new rulers, their alleged sexual immorality, and their contempt for, and oppression of, the poor.

Perhaps it is not surprising that O'Siochrú does not reveal the true character of his source. It would certainly detract from the integrity of his citation and expose the evidence of *The Man in the Moon* as highly questionable at the very least.

But it doesn't stop there. The evidence of Thomas Wood, whose historian brother Anthony added the á between the first name and the family name to make himself sound more distinguished, is perhaps one of the accounts of the assault of the town of Drogheda that is the most shocking, not to mention the most controversial, and as such needs closer examination. In *Honourable Enemy*, repeating the arguments of S.R. Gardiner and Robert H. Murray, I focussed on the implausibility of Wood's story to expose the holes therein. Conversely, McElligott and O'Siochrú both seem to use it as important primary source evidence and see no problem in doing so. In fact O'Siochrú unambiguously treats the Wood brothers' tract as hugely significant, so much so that his words are worth repeating here:

> In some instances, parliamentary soldiers returning home from service in Ireland provided eyewitness testimony. Thomas Wood, for example, fought at Drogheda, and regaled his family in England the following year with colourful and lurid stories about the killing of civilians, which his brother later published.

This is the Wood tract:

> Thom. Wood, eldest brother to A[thony] W[ood], died of the flux at Drogheda commonly called Tredagh, in the month of Decemb. He was borne at Tetsworth, neare to Thame in Oxfordshire, where his father then had a farme, educated mostly in the free school at Thame under his kinsman Mr. W. Burt, was made student of Ch. Church in 1638, as I have before told you, and afterwards was the first, or one of the first yong scholars in Oxon. That threw off his gowne and ran to Edgehill battle. See more under the year 1642. At his returne thence, he was actually created bach. Of arts among soldiers that had done service at the said battle: and then his father, seeing that he could not persuade him from being a soldier, he bought a horse, armes, cloaths, &c., set him up for a troper, and got him a place to ride in the troop of captaine Tho. Gardiner of Cudeson neare Oxon. Afterwards he became a stout and desperate soldier, was in several battles, and besieged in divers garrisons, particularly, if I am not mistaken at basing in Hampshire, and was made a lievtenant of horse. When the warr was terminated, and the King's cause utterlie vanquished, he returned to his college, was actually created Mr. of arts, an. 1647, but in the next yeare [1648], he, to avoid being taken and hanged for it, fled to Ireland, where finding out his quondam school-fellow at Thame, called col. Hen. Ingoldesbie, he became a lievtenant in his regiment, afterwards a captaine, and, as I have heard, had a commission, a

little before his death, to be a major. About a yeare before that time viz in 1650, he returned for a time to Oxon, to take up his arrears at Ch. Church, and to settle his other affaires at which time being often with his mother and brethren, he would tell them of the most terrible assaulting and storming of Tredagh [Drogheda], wherein he himself had been engaged. He told them that 3,000 at least, besides some women and children were, after the assailants had taken part, and afterwards all the town put to the sword on the 11 and 12 Sept. 1649; at which time Sir Arthur Aston, the governor had his brains beat out, and his body hack'd and chop'd to pieces.

He told them, that when they were to make their way up to the lofts and galleries in the church and up to the tower where the enemy had fled, each of the assailants would take up a child and use it as a buckler of defence, when they ascended the steps, to keep themselves from being shot or brain'd. After they had killed all in the church, they went into the vaults underneath where all the flower and choicest of the women had hid themselves.

One of these a most handsome virgin and arrayed in costly and gorgeous apparel, kneeled down to Thomas Wood with tears and prayers to save her life; and being strucken with a profound pity, took her under his arm, went with her out of the church, with intention to put her over the works and to let her shift for herself; but then a soldier perceiving his intentions, ran his sword through her belly or fundament; whereupon Mr Wood seeing her gasping, took away her money, jewels &c., and flung her down over the works.

In the latter end of 1680 when the Parliament sate at Oxon. A. Wood was walking with Sir Hen. St. Georg Clarentius, king of armes, in the school-quadrangle. Sir Hen. Then meeting with

> col. Hen. Ingoldesbie before mentioned and telling him who A.W. was. A.W. thereupon did discourse with him concerning his brother Thomas, and among several things that the colonel told him, was that Thomas was a good soldier, stout and ventrous, and having an art of merriment called buffooning, his company was desired and loved by the officers of his regiment. He told him then, he buried [him] in a church at Tredagh, answerable to his qualitie, but could not tell him when he died. This Thos. Wood was a tall, proper and robust man, like his father, but black and swarthy, unlike in that to any of his brethren, or father...

O'Siochrú's notes reveal the document source – 'Anthony Wood, *The life of Anthony á Wood from the year 1632 to 1672 written by himself* (Oxford, 1772), pp. 68-69.' McElligott uses a different source reference for the Wood story – Llewlyn Powys, ed., *The Life and Times of Anthony A. Wood* (London: Oxford University Press, 1961), pp. 41-42. As it happens, there are several other editions of Anthony á Wood's life and times, some of which are appended to his tour de force *Athenea Oxionienses*, a publication in which he lists the monuments, muniments, and the bishops that had attended Oxford University up to that time, and all of which had an editor. When he published the second volume in 1692 he incurred the wrath of Edward Hyde, the Earl of Clarendon whom he was found guilty of libelling. Interestingly, O'Siochrú chooses to ignore the fact that Wood's book is edited whereas had he followed the academic source reference style (like McElligott) the title of the book should read, 'Hearne Thomas, ed, *The life of Anthony á Wood from the year 1632 to 1672 written by himself and published by Mr Thomas Hearne* (Oxford, 1772). Indeed, the preface of the book, written by the editor Hearne, is quite illuminating:

> It was originally proposed to publish a life of Mr Anthony A

> Wood from those materials which were collected by the late Dr Richard Rawlison and printed by him, in duodecimo, (tho' never made public) in the year 1711.

So up to 1772 Wood's life was 'never made public'. Anthony Wood, a staunch royalist, who was always suspected of being a Catholic had his life's historical works published after his death in various publications, and all with various editors (including the Rev Sir J Peshall 1773, John Gutch 1786, Phillip Bliss 1813, Andrew Clark 1889), some of which included the story of his life, which in turn contains the account of his brother Thomas at Drogheda. Wood's biography was not in fact published by himself in the literal sense, but was transcribed by Hearne from pocket diaries, documents and manuscripts that Wood left to a Dr Thomas Tanner, among others, on his deathbed. The title page from the 1772 publication, partially referenced by O'Siochrú, proves this:

> *The Life of Mr Anthony A Wood (From the time of his birth Dec 17th 1632 to July 6th 1672), written by himself and now first printed, from a copy transcribed by the publisher, from the original in the hands of the Reverend Dr Thomas Tanner.*

Most significantly, rather than being a primary source in the strictest sense of the expression, McElligott and O'Siochrú fail to reveal that Thomas Wood's fireside stories first came to public attention in the year 1772. That's 123 years after the events. When the provenance of Anthony Wood's account is combined with the melodramatic exploits of his action hero and mercenary soldier brother Thomas Wood (who fought for both parliament and the king) and the story itself, it becomes obvious why it should not be treated with any real significance. The fact that Wood's commanding officer thought that Wood was the company clown and was proficient in the 'art of merriment and buffooning' throws further suspicion on his brother's words, if they even were his brother's words.

Unfortunately, O'Siochrú and McElligott both fail even to introduce balance by admitting that the evidence for a large-scale killing of the local population in all of its forms is inconclusive. This is sad especially given the impact that this topic has made on Anglo-Irish relations over the centuries.

But the book *Age of Atrocity* also included another challenge to *Cromwell, An Honourable Enemy,* this time by one of the foremost Oliver Cromwell experts, Prof. John Morrill of Cambridge University, an Englishman. In *The Drogheda Massacre in Cromwellian Context,* Morrill tackles my arguments and is far from complimentary in his conclusions. In his opening remarks, referring to McElligott's article above, Morrill declares:

> Jason McElligott has given us an outstanding summary of the nationalist and revisionist cases and a totally convincing and necessary explanation of why Tom Reilly's claim that there was no civilian massacre at Drogheda is not to be trusted. In essence Reilly fails the test of source criticism at every turn. He argues a case and unreasonably privileges second-and third-hand evidence that supports his presupposition and unreasonably dismisses contrary evidence. When it comes to first hand evidence, he reasserts an already discredited attempt to deny that Cromwell confessed to the deaths of civilians.

Morrill then 'rehearses' McElligott's interpretation of the three words 'and many inhabitants' that are at the end of the list appended to Cromwell's letter in the official parliamentary pamphlet and he writes:

> There is no getting around these words...Reilly tries to do so by drawing attention to Carlyle's false claim in the first

> edition of L&S (*Letters and Speeches of Oliver Cromwell,* by Thomas Carlyle) that the appendix is an eighteenth century addition...this claim was simply incorrect. This in itself is fatal to Reilly's thesis and it is disgraceful that so many reviewers have not checked this.

First McElligott then O'Siochrú and now Morrill all hone in on the three words 'and many inhabitants' and all three dismiss Firth's suggestion that the printer John Field inserted the words spuriously. They easily prove that Carlyle got it wrong when he claimed the three words were not in the original document. While I had initially embraced Carlyle and Firth's assertions fourteen years ago, these three academics have forced me to look at this piece of evidence differently. But not as they might think. The fact is we absolutely and categorically do NOT know that these are the words of Oliver Cromwell himself. That's how we can get around these words.

Morrill then proceeds to nail his colours to the mast with regard to the civilian massacre theory. He clearly lays out his thought process as follows:

> Hugh Peter, close to Cromwell and on his council of war, suggested that the total number killed was 3,552 and he gives the number of military survivors as 400. Cromwell thinks that there was 2,782 killed apart from the 'many inhabitants' (although his 2,500 infantrymen and support service men is clearly a rounded number). The implication of both Cromwell and Peter is that about 700-800 civilians died and I see no reason to doubt that figure.

I could give some reasons to doubt that figure. Hugh Peters was not even in Drogheda when the battle took place and the precise nature of his estimate (3,552 - not a man more, not a man less) is uniquely precise and as such unlikely to be accurate. Indeed in his article Micheál O'Siochrú reminds us that casualty lists were notoriously inaccurate in the early modern period and he also suggests that 'Peters almost certainly based his estimate on the defenders' muster rolls.' In his book *God's Executioner* O'Siochrú elaborates; 'If, as the evidence suggests, some of the garrison fled over the north wall of the town, and the parliamentarians spared other defenders, then the casualty figures presented by Cromwell and others, based on the captured muster rolls, are clearly inaccurate.'

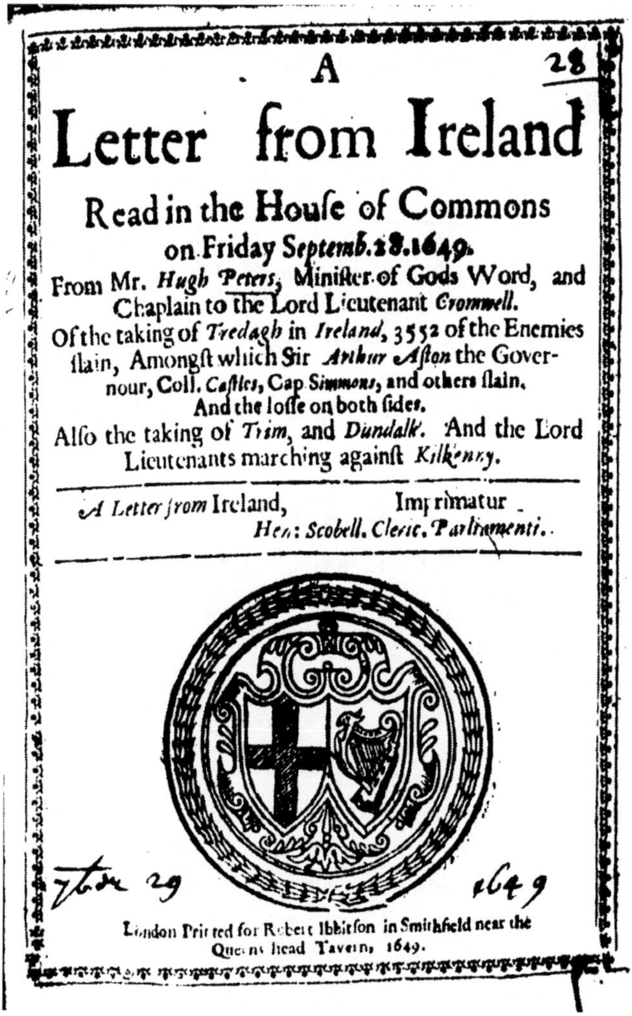

A

28

Letter from Ireland

Read in the House of Commons on Friday Septemb. 28. 1649.

From Mr. Hugh Peters, Minister of Gods Word, and Chaplain to the Lord Lieutenant Cromwell.

Of the taking of Tredagh in Ireland, 3552 of the Enemies slain, Amongst which Sir Arthur Aston the Governour, Coll. Castles, Cap. Simmons, and others slain. And the losse on both sides.

Also the taking of Trim, and Dundalk. And the Lord Lieutenants marching against Kilkenny.

A Letter from Ireland, Imprimatur

Hen: Scobell. Cleric. Parliamenti.

7ber 29 1649

London Printed for Robert Ibbitson in Smithfield near the Queens head Tavern, 1649.

(4)

A

Letter from IRELAND,

Read in the Houſe of Commons on *Friday* Septemb. 28. 1649.

From Mr. *Hugh Peters*, Miniſter of Gods Word, and Chaplaine to the Lord Lieutenant CROMWELL.

Of the taking of *Tredagh* in *Ireland*.

Alſo the taking of *Trimme* and *Dundalke*.

SIR,

THE Truth is Tredagh is taken, Three thouſand five hundred fifty and two of the Enemies ſlaine, and ſixty foure of ours.

Col-

(5)

Collonell Caſtles, and Captaine Simmons of note.

Aſhton the Governour killed, none ſpared.

Wee have alſo Trimme and Dundalk and are marching to Kilkenny.

I came now from giving thanks in the great Church, we have all our Army well Landed.

Dublin Septemb, 15. 1649.

I am

Yours

Hugh Peters.

A Letter from *Ireland*,

Imprimatur

Septemb. 28. 1649.

Hen: Scobell
Cleric Parliamenti.

FINIS.

Hugh Peters was Cromwell's chaplain in Ireland and was writing his letter from Dublin at the time. His actual words are:

Sir, The truth is Tredagh is taken, three thousand five

> hundred and fifty two of the enemies slaine, and sixty foure of ours. Collonell Castles and Captaine Simmons of note. Ashton the governor killed, none spared. We have also Trimme and Dundalk and are marching to Kilkenny. I came now from giving thanks in the great church. We have all our army well landed.

It is difficult to see how Morrill interprets Peters' short letter to be proof of civilian casualties when Peters himself refers to the 3,552 as 'the enemies' and says nothing of inhabitants or civilians. The enemy were the enemy. They were not the local common people, women and children. And in any case, why would this precise estimate of Peters' carry any more weight than other writer's account, some of whom were eye witnesses? In actual fact, if we consider the word 'many', which has been attributed to Cromwell regarding inhabitants, we know for a fact that according to Inchiquin, 'many officers and soldiers escaped out of Drogheda'.

Another contemporary document issued by newsbook author Henry Walker via the printer Robert Ibbotson says 'But many they found in houses, in a quiet and orderly posture, they gave quarter to.' So if Peters was using the muster rolls, as O'Siochrú suggests, then his estimate is already shot to pieces. For Morrill to suggest that Peters was allowing for the numbers that escaped and others that were spared, and that he implied that the numerical difference was simply made up of civilian deaths – when such a thing was explicitly forbidden by Cromwell – this is completely at odds with the surviving evidence. Furthermore, Morrill is using a source that we know is already incorrect. Peters says that there were 'none spared.' Eye witness testimony from many others flatly contradicts this.

Elsewhere, of Cromwell Morrill says:

> He is deeply prejudiced but there is a large gap between

> prejudice and a will to exterminate...He is even more emphatic on his plans for a civil settlement. *I shall not willingly take or suffer to be taken away the life of any man not in arms but by trial to which the people of this nation are subject by law for offences against the same.*

Here Morrill is quoting from Cromwell's declaration to the Catholic clergy in the winter of 1649 where he repeats, often, that unarmed civilians were to be unmolested. This does not seem like the mindset of a man who simply lost his self-control at Drogheda and allowed his army to do the same, killing hundreds of innocent people. Morrill seems to think that he did but as we have seen, Cromwell repeated his policy concerning civilians often, and this is what's called 'evidence'.

On first reading Morrill's piece, the wholesale dismissal of my thesis by such a heavyweight in the business early in the narrative suggested that the perceptiveness of the writer and his ability to see the events clearly and intuitively meant that a stiff challenge was about to appear in the second part. In places the work is ground-breaking and insightful but concerning the civilian massacre theory, inconsistency prevails. For instance he says:

> He (Cromwell) killed most of the garrisons at Drogheda and Wexford, many in cold blood after they had surrendered, and in each case a significant number of civilians were killed, either caught in the crossfire, or at least in the heat of the action, albeit vindictively.

Here Morrill is at least willing to consider the real possibility that civilians were killed being 'caught in the crossfire'. Unfortunately he does not make enough of this point. This is precisely the nub of the argument. This is the controversy that has raged for centuries and that is the subject of this book. Was there a policy to slaughter the innocent – or were the innocent simply caught up in the crossfire? Either Cromwell did it or he didn't do it. But Morrill fails to address the point fully and believes 700-800 civilians were killed at Drogheda, neglecting to say whether he believed they were armed or unarmed. After all, an armed civilian is no longer a civilian.

After calling my thesis untrustworthy Morrill announces that he is reluctant to enter into the controversy. However, making a clear distinction between 'civilians' and 'combatants' he says; 'What is not clear is how many civilians, as against how many combatants, died in cold blood. The sources that discuss this are amongst the least reliable and nothing is to be gained by re-visiting that debate.' Then he proceeds to enter the debate.

Morrill also sees the events at St. Peter's Church quite differently to most others where all of the contemporary evidence points in the totally opposite direction. Discussing the events at St. Peter's Church he says, 'It is not clear if those in the church included civilians. It seems perfectly possible.' In *Honourable Enemy* I had established that the first reference to civilians occupying the church building or the church steeple appears in 1820 in Johnstone's *History of Drogheda*. Exclusively, all of the primary source documents describe the occupants of the church in military terms.

Otherwise, Morrill is more discerning about Cromwell and brings some fresh insights that are at odds with the general Irish perception of the man and his attitude to Catholics that deserve to be repeated here. He writes:

> Cromwell was not amongst the most anti-Catholic and probably not amongst the most anti-Irish of Englishmen in the 1640s and 1650s. He was anti-Catholic and anti-Irish but he was no less so than many of those he served alongside in the army and the Long Parliament...Cromwell's letters and speeches are surprisingly short of strong anti-Catholic

> rhetoric. He does not make the same intimate connection between Laudian bishops and Popery that one finds in Pym or Prynne, for example...No Catholic priest in England was tried and executed while he was Lord Protector...His speeches as Lord Protector were equally silent on the special culpability of the Catholics...All laws penalising Catholics for absenting themselves from Protestant worship were repealed, and penalties for attending Catholic worship largely unenforced...He was friends with all those "with the root of the matter in them" all who were seekers after God's truth, for he did not believe that any one church had a monopoly of truth, though we cannot find any sign that he found the root of the matter in any Catholic. But persecution was not a route to conversion. Cromwell himself would give liberty to evangelise to all those who sought truth through the sovereign authority of Scripture, and he would give a *de facto* liberty to practice any other form in private.

Gardiner has suggested, and Morrill agrees, that Cromwell was strongly opposed to the Act of Settlement of 1652 (the act that somewhat ironically was to morph into the Cromwellian Plantation), which was a far cry from the penalties he outlined in his declaration to the bishops in December 1649 where a much more lenient Cromwell elucidates his ideas, which Morrill paraphrases as follows,

> Banishment would only be used to commute the sentences of those guilty of capital offences. Estates would be confiscated only from those who had taken part in the massacres or taken up arms in the defence of the rebellion, and those laying down their arms would be given merciful consideration.

Morrill highlights a side to Cromwell that few scholars have reported when he says; 'Even at an individual level, he

(Cromwell) could exercise acts of compassion for Catholics. When he discovered that Bishop David Rothe was dying, he rescinded the order banishing from Ireland clergy whom he had taken prisoner at Kilkenny, so that the old man could die amongst his own people.'

Also on the positive side, and even more significantly, Morrill submits a seldom-quoted interpretation of one of Cromwell's most controversial comments following the assault on Drogheda that – if it were true – would change many aspects surrounding the events at Drogheda. It is worth including here verbatim:

> But what of the chilling phrase 'this is a righteous judgement of God upon those barbarous wretches, who have imbrued their hands with so much innocent blood?' It has generally been assumed by all who have written about it that it referred to the 1641 massacres, and that it has often enough been said that he knew he was lying – that he knew perfectly well that the garrison consisted of English and Ormondist troops, none of whom could have taken part in the 1641-2 massacres. Drogheda had *never* been a confederate town. So why do we assume that he was referring to the 1641 rebellion? In the course of his post-Drogheda letters Cromwell only mentions by name English officers and members of Irish noble families. In that list of those killed, he privileges the names of English officers along with those from Irish noble families – the Earl of Westmeath and Sir James Dillon, brother of the Earl of Roscommon. Is it not possible that Cromwell's reference is to the blood guilt of those who refused to accept the judgement of God in the first Civil War, those who committed sacrilege by renewing the war and carried a culpability far higher than that of those who fought to establish God's judgement in that first war, the culpability for shedding innocent blood that brought Charles I to the scaffold. It was a reference to that same rage which overtook him throughout 1648 and led to the

> summary trials and death sentences on the leaders after the sieges and battles of Pembroke, Preston and Pontefract. It was a rage that had allowed him to refer to those English rebels who obstructed the Lord's work as acting 'barbarously' so this was not a term he held back to use on the Irish. Is this why the heads of the English officers like Sir Edmund Verney were sent to be put on spikes in Dublin? Is this why he singled out English officers to be denied mercy at Gowran? And was the concern to highlight the English officers intended to send a clear message to royalists amongst the English readership of the letter not to cross to Ireland to continue the struggle?

If Morrill is right (as well as some nineteenth century commentators, Prof Ronald Hutton has also offered this as a possibility) then this goes a long way to restoring Cromwell's integrity, not to mention his credibility. It has been generally assumed that the 'barbarous wretches' were the Irish. It is unthinkable to believe that Cromwell didn't know that he was not dealing with those likely to have been involved in the massacres of 1641 at Drogheda since he was acutely aware of the composition of the garrison. His accusers contend that he simply ignored this fact and massacred the garrison using 1641 as justification, all the time knowing that they could not have been involved. Take away the lie and the entire affair takes on a different dimension. If Cromwell was referring to those English royalists at Drogheda who returned the country (England) to war in 1648 then the treachery disappears from his comments. Furthermore, it gives us more reason to believe him especially when he talks of excluding civilians from the violence, which McElligott, O'Siochrú and Morrill are disinclined to do.

With Morrill's distinctive insights into Cromwell the man it is difficult to reconcile how the assiduous academic can balance his 'compassionate' Cromwell with a Cromwell who he believes, butchered 700-800 civilians at Drogheda. Morrill neglects to distinguish between women and children in his article despite the fact that Morrill himself even concedes that the sources that discuss civilian deaths 'are amongst the least reliable'.

As a consequence the thesis in *Honourable Enemy* remains in one piece, despite its flawed methodology. If Morrill believes that number juggling with the death tolls of Hugh Peters and Oliver Cromwell proves that Cromwell deliberately killed local innocent civilians at Drogheda then he will have to do a lot better than this. Because we need to be clear about that word civilians. Are we talking about unarmed common people such as blacksmiths, merchants, teachers, gentlemen, yeomen, carpenters, tailors, cobblers, washerwomen, housewives, spinsters, domestic servants, school children, toddlers, babies? Or are we talking about armed inhabitants? The former is a war crime. The latter is an accepted consequence of war.

Not long after *Age of Atrocity* appeared in print I heard the news that RTE had commissioned a major documentary on Cromwell in Ireland. I immediately contacted the production company with a view to highlight the revised version of events to them but they were disinclined to engage with me. I then discovered that they would be using footage of unarmed civilians and I despaired. It soon transpired that Professor Micheál O'Siochrú was to present the series and that there would be an accompanying book. Perhaps this would now be the ultimate rebuttal of my work. Perhaps O'Siochrú had properly constructed the evidence to confirm the massacre of innocents instead of relying on vague interpretations of inconclusive evidence. Here now was the ultimate opportunity to finally put this controversy to bed with both a book and a documentary. Never before had Cromwell been so much to the foreground in Irish popular culture in modern day Ireland.

The first episode of the two-part documentary programme was aired on Tuesday 9 September 2008 at 10.15pm on RTE I, with the second episode going out the following Tuesday. When discussing the storming of Drogheda in the commentary O'Siochrú declared, 'In total at least 3,000 people died in Drogheda, including the garrison and an indeterminate number of civilians.' Contributing to the programme, Professor John Morrill said that among the numbers killed are 'clearly civilians, as well as soldiers.' The emphasis on the word 'people' and the careless use of the word civilians meant that this was an appalling retrograde step in our understanding of the period. Were they armed, or were they not? Did this include women and children or did it not?

The experts had expounded their view. Unfortunately they didn't qualify the use of the words 'civilians' and 'people'. However, the inference in the commentary and from the contributors was clear and the damage was done. These civilians were unarmed. So say the experts. How can anyone question the experts?

But it was to the book *God's Executioner, Oliver Cromwell and the Conquest of Ireland* by Professor Micheál O'Siochrú that I next turned. This was a much more suitable medium for a detailed discussion on the subject. O'Siochrú promises much in his opening remarks about the controversy:

> The storming of Drogheda on 11 September shocked contemporary opinion and established Cromwell's reputation for cruelty and savagery, which has persisted in Ireland until the present day. And yet, despite all the subsequent condemnation and outrage, as well as some crude attempts at justification, doubts persist over exactly what happened on that day. Not surprisingly, few eye-witness accounts survive from the royalist side, although hundreds of the garrison did manage to slip away over the north wall in the confusion of the battle...Unfortunately, apart from the reflections of the Anglican clergyman, Dean Nicholas Bernard, the town's inhabitants left no diaries or letters describing the tragic

> events...As a result, we must rely heavily on parliamentary statements, with all the attendant problems of bias (deliberate or otherwise) and a lack of corroborating evidence. The following construction is based almost entirely on the reports of those actually present at Drogheda in an attempt to separate fact from fiction, and reality from propaganda, be it parliamentarian or royalist.

While O'Siochrú neglects to mention this writer's work by name or title in either his article above or the book now under discussion, it is certainly implied when he mentions that 'some crude attempts at justification' had been made. However, in an article in *History Ireland* that same year (Sept/Oct 2008 issue), he makes specific reference to my work:

> One book relating specifically to the topic of Cromwell and Ireland, Tom Reilly's *Cromwell: An Honourable Enemy,* has proved particularly controversial. As the title suggests, Reilly approached the topic from the premise that Cromwell's brutal reputation in Ireland was entirely unjustified, the result, he argues, of a deliberate distortion of the facts by nationalist historians. It is an interesting if hardly original idea, but in his eagerness to prove this thesis Reilly simply dismissed or ignored contrary evidence. As C. H. Firth said of Thomas Carlyle's approach to Cromwell, 'like too many other historians he found in the past just what he went to the past to find.'

One of the main difficulties that some historians had with *Honourable Enemy* was my assertion that NO civilians were *deliberately* targeted and killed by Cromwell or his men at Drogheda or Wexford. Fundamentally, this is still my belief, but it behoves me to qualify this interpretation since it caused so much debate. Obviously, civilians could easily have been killed by accident in both battles and it is futile to say that no civilians whatsoever died at Drogheda and Wexford. They clearly did. It's the deliberate slaughter of large numbers of non-combatants, women and children included, that is in question. There was a significant difference between the storming of Drogheda and the storming of Wexford in the make-up of the defenders, and the political inclinations of the two populations. Both events need to be treated quite differently. Drogheda was no Wexford, and vice versa.

Unlike Wexford, Drogheda had never declared for the Confederacy. Only eight years earlier the town had been besieged by Irish rebels under the command of Sir Phelim O'Neill. A five month long siege ensued and the inhabitants of the town were reduced to eating rats and horsemeat according to some reports. Before Cromwell opened fire it was the defenders' plan to maintain the siege for as long as possible to reduce the attacking army using the Irish weather and whatever illnesses might befall them. So with another long siege on the horizon, it seems likely that many of the town's inhabitants would have departed the town and left it to the opposing armies to fight over. We know that Dean Nicholas Bernard had sent his wife and children out of the town, and it seems possible that others would have done the same. In his book O'Siochrú states:

> The real controversy, however, revolves around the issue of civilian deaths. It seems highly unlikely that while storming a town in the face of stiff resistance, 10,000 parliamentary troops would at all times have distinguished, or been able to distinguish, between enemy soldiers and non-combatants.

Other writers have also proffered this latter point as a possible scenario. I would contend that this is a moot point. We do not know how many civilians stayed in the town for the siege. These parliamentary troops were one of the most professional armies in

Europe at the time and their orders were very clear – they were not to engage with any 'persons not in arms'. This is what the evidence clearly states. Is O'Siochrú seriously suggesting that the attackers were unable to distinguish between common men and the defending soldiery and they simply killed everything that moved when their orders emphatically forbade this? The parliamentarian publication, John Dillingham's *The Moderate Intelligencer* of 27th Sept – 4th October 1649, publishes an eye witness account that clearly implies 'common men' were exempt from the battle; 'Where their horse were, we don't know, probably they went as common men.' Besides, both armies wore basic uniforms to distinguish themselves from each other and it's hard to believe that the highly skilful parliamentarian infantry – who had been wearing red coats since 1645 - engaged in combat would not be able to tell the difference between a fully armed Royalist soldier - who generally wore blue in the Civil War - and a lay member of the local community. (The cavalry wore buff coats). The fact that any innocent laypeople still left in the town had no weapons surely would have been the giveaway.

My contention in *Honourable Enemy* that Cromwell stayed within the rules of war during the storming of both towns has also come under scrutiny. Jason McElligott has discussed this issue exhaustively and for me does an excellent job of proving that Cromwell did indeed step outside the military conventions that were prevalent at the time that simply stunned his contemporaries.

But even here the lines are ambiguous. In *God's Executioner,* O'Siochrú appears to have two separate schools of thought on the matter. In the first instance he says, 'Moreover, although this savage act sent shock waves throughout Ireland and abroad, in refusing quarter to enemy troops Cromwell had acted entirely within the accepted conventions of warfare at the time.'

And in the second, while discussing the events at Millmount in Drogheda, where the governor Aston and several others were disarmed after quarter was apparently given and they were subsequently slaughtered, O'Siochrú takes a different tack when he writes: 'Such a calculated act of cold-blooded murder, not taken in the heat of the action, was not only highly dishonourable but also a clear breach of the contemporary military code.'

The firsthand evidence may be problematic but one of the primary source documents that has come down to us is the evidence of one of Drogheda's inhabitants, whose accounts of the events are about as trustworthy as we have. Protestant minister, Dean Nicholas Bernard, is seen as an excellent witness and his accounts of both sieges (1641 and 1649) are very detailed. He was the resident cleric at St Peter's Church during the 1640s and his writings reveal him to be very much on the Royalist side. O'Siochrú uses Bernard's evidence to support the civilian massacre theory and as a consequence his thought process is worth close assessment here. This is mainly because O'Siochrú uses a single incident at Bernard's house to then generalise arbitrarily about the siege in the rest of the town, quite a sizeable leap, especially when the incident is seen in context. Paraphrasing Bernard's words, O'Siochrú writes:

> He [Bernard] describes how, "in the heat of prosecution" immediately following the assault, parliamentary troops shot through the windows of his house, where over thirty Protestants had gathered seeking sanctuary, killing one person, and seriously wounding another. The soldiers broke into the building, discharging their weapons, before the timely intervention of an officer known to the dean restored order. This account raises a number of key issues. According to Bernard, the soldiers fired on civilians sheltering indoors, which belies claims that the parliamentarians only targeted those in arms. Moreover, the group was only saved from further harm when an officer recognised Bernard and

> identified his companions as Protestants. The implication of this sequence of events for the town's Catholics do not require any further explanation...Therefore, according to the one surviving civilian account of the storming of Drogheda, troops of the New Model Army deliberately attacked non-combatants in their homes.

O'Siochrú fails to reveal the real reason why the parliamentarians targeted the dean's house. But Bernard clearly tells us himself. In his tract (where he is called Doctor and is referred to in the third person) the document reads, 'Then came five or six who were sent from a principal office – the doctor's former acquaintance – under pretence of a guard for his house, but had a command for him, as soon as they were entered to kill him, which an ear-witness had assured him of.'

So Bernard's house was targeted deliberately and this is a key aspect of the dean's evidence. Furthermore, he was taken prisoner to Dublin following the siege, had several charges levied against him, was interviewed by Cromwell himself and kept in custody for six months. His tract implies that it was Cromwell who saved his life (much to the chagrin of Hugh Peters who seems to have wanted him killed) and that after his imprisonment he was 'sent up to the army at Clonmel, and permitted to come then with Cromwell into England'.

But it was an incident at the house involving the parliamentarian army that O'Siochrú uses to shore up his large-scale civilian massacre allegation. Again, it is the parts of the evidence that he omits that change the connotation of the evidence completely. The story that O'Siochrú paraphrases is repeated here verbatim in Bernard's words:

> Then a cornet of a troop of horse came to his relief and pretending that he had an order from the General to take care of that house, the soldiers withdrew, and so at the back door

> he brought in his quartermaster, whom he left to secure it. About a quarter of an hour after, another troop of horse came to the window, and demanded the opening of the door. The quartermaster, and himself [Bernard], with an old servant (for he had sent his wife and children out of the town) stood close together, and told them that it was the minister's house and that all inside were Protestants. As soon as they heard the Doctor named, and his voice, one of them discharged his pistol at him wherein being a brace of bullets, with the one the quartermaster was shot quite through the body, and dyed in the place, and the other shot his servant through the throat, but recovered; the Doctor only was untouched.

Bernard seems to have been incredibly lucky. Not only did he miss being hit by the brace of bullets, but it later transpired that the officer who he knew (Colonel Ewers) was admonished for saving his life by others, and he was told in no uncertain terms by his captors that he should expect to die yet. The Protestant minister was a supporter of Ormond's and had publicly proclaimed both his support for the Stuarts and his hostility for parliament vociferously and often, transgressions that easily explain why he would be targeted by the attackers. But O'Siochrú, implies instead that the attackers simply happened upon the preacher's house and the incident ensued.

To use the death of the quartermaster (obviously a soldier) and the wounding of his servant (presumably a civilian 'in office with the enemy') as evidence that a large scale massacre of civilians took place, as O'Siochrú appears to do, seems precarious to say the least, especially since Bernard himself says nothing of the deaths of any of the local population. This is not the smoking gun that O'Siochrú wants it to be.

He is on much safer ground when he points to the death of a local alderman named Henry Mortimer. This is another important piece of evidence that was absent from *Honourable*

Enemy. Mortimer's name is mentioned in *The Court of Claims*, where petitions were drafted to resolve land disputes following the Restoration. This is a significant source because here for the first time, we actually have names of local inhabitants who were killed during the assault. Quoting from *The Court of Claims* and after identifying a couple of soldiers O'Siochrú writes, 'Alongside these military personnel, however, others, such as James Fleming, are described as "murdered", while Henry Mortimer, an alderman of the town, was killed "being then about seventy years of age".'

Here in a nutshell is the sum total of names of local inhabitants that we know were killed during Cromwell's attack on the town from a contemporary source, albeit one thirteen years after the events. Without question Fleming and Mortimer are local contemporary names. However, there are several things that we should be sure of before we begin to use these two examples to stretch the story to a large-scale massacre of civilians. Firstly, we don't know whether or not they were armed. Secondly, we don't know if they were two of the unlucky inhabitants that Morrill alludes to who were simply caught in the crossfire. When it comes to the deaths of these two inhabitants doubts persist. We know they died, but we don't know how or why. O'Siochrú, however, concludes: 'The issue remains contentious to the present day but the surviving evidence clearly shows that a significant number of non-combatants were killed during the storming of the town.'

Interestingly, Mortimer's family name appears in the local municipal records on several occasions during the 1650s and always in connection with a transfer of land or property. He himself is mentioned six times, all obviously posthumously. The fact that his name appears in *The Court of Claims* by definition means that it was in connection with a land dispute. And while the following is purely speculation, the one thing we do know about those who took up arms against parliament in Ireland is that they lost their property to varying degrees, so it's actually possible that Messrs Fleming and Mortimer had taken up arms to defend their town.

Curiously, O'Siochrú seems to give the same credence (as McElligott) to the oft-published John Evelyn's diary, (first published in 1818) since he also uses a quotation from the entry of 15th October 1649, but he leaves out the part that McElligott emphasises. Of the assault on the town O'Siochrú says, 'The Venetian ambassador in Paris received a letter from England (dated late September 1649) which told of "a sanguinary encounter" at Drogheda, which according to the exiled royalist John Evelyn 'makes us very sad, forerunning the loss of all Ireland.' O'Siochrú's source reference to this quotation is from a version of Evelyn's work that was published in 1959!

Having freshly analysed the evidence it is now my contention that both *Mercurius Elencticus* and *The Man in the Moon* have almost been singlehandedly responsible for spreading the civilian death massacre stories that were to make such an impact on Irish historiography to the present day. They were the first (and only) newsbooks to make the allegations at the time. Cromwell was framed. George Wharton and John Crouch were the framers.

Chapter Three

The very day before Oliver Cromwell swung his legs out of bed (11 July 1649) to travel to Ireland he could have easily strolled into Drogheda through any of the main gates and he would have been welcomed with open arms by the military occupants. That day, and for two long years beforehand (since 19 June 1647), Parliament were in control of Drogheda. In his letter to Parliament after the battle, Cromwell clearly knew this when he said 'The design was to endeavour the *regaining* of Drogheda...' This little-known fact has tremendous significance. Drogheda was not on his agenda the day he left for Ireland, because as far as he was concerned, it was in the control of his party and he would not have known that the situation had altered the previous day. This proves that the inhabitants of the town had no truck with parliamentary troops, and vice versa, since there is no recorded instance of discord between both the military and the civilian occupants of the town during the preceding two years. It was Parliamentarian soldiers who would be accused of atrocities at Drogheda, and it was Parliamentarian soldiers who lived side by side with the local population in the town for two long years, an aspect of the story that Irish nationalist historians tend to casually ignore.

It was only on 11 July that the town surrendered to the Royalists when the garrison of 700 foot and 255 horse soldiers delivered up the town to Lord Inchiquin, who had been despatched there by Ormond for that very reason. Of the total number of the garrisoned soldiers defending the town that day (mostly made up of the Colonel Michael Jones' regiment), 600 foot and 220 horse soldiers then declared for the Royalists, and may have remained in situ. This left a balance of 135 soldiers who stayed in Jones' regiment and, one assumes, made their way back to Jones at Dublin. This is an interesting point because to speculate even further, we know that Cromwell's attacking army at Drogheda included the regiment of Col Michael Jones. So it is entirely possible that these 135 men returned to Drogheda, were involved in the successful assault, and if we were to accept the traditional viewpoint, that they proceeded to engage in the massacre of those very inhabitants with whom they had fraternised for the previous two years.

An analysis by Meave Garrett in her unpublished thesis *Municipal and Central Government in Ireland under Charles II* in 1972 of the residents of the town in 1641 came to the conclusion that there were about 3,000 people living within the town walls in 1641, where Catholics outnumbered Protestants by five to one. In a poll-tax census carried out in 1659 the number can be calculated to be approximately 3,500 where the majority are now Protestant. While the numbers are not definitive, if the civilian inhabitants had been practically wiped out, it is very unlikely that within a ten year period the town's population would have replenished itself. The minute book of the Drogheda Corporation from 1649 still exists. Within its pages is ample evidence that the town did not lose thousands or even hundreds of its citizens. Several local politicians are documented as attending the Corporation meeting in April, and the one in October. This proves that they were alive before and after the siege. Hundreds of local peoples' names are mentioned in the records throughout the 1650s and beyond.

This was a period when the Cromwellian settlement was in full swing. Landed gentry of high ranking military positions who had pledged their allegiance to the King during the Irish wars were being transplanted from their lands and moved to Connaught. In May 1660 the Catholic inhabitants of Drogheda successfully petitioned Charles II to have their possessions, privileges and tenant rights restored to them. Here Cromwell makes no mention of preferential holdings available for plantation within the borough of the town to his superiors.

The difference in the social, economic and political dynamics between Drogheda and Wexford can never be over-emphasised when it comes to the storming of both towns – one was chalk, the other cheese. Drogheda had managed to keep the insurgent native Irish Catholics at bay outside the town walls just eight years previously, and as well as being well aware of this, Cromwell would have approved of the town's actions. Conversely, the town of Wexford was on the side of the 1641 besiegers of Drogheda.

No Drogheda Corporation records exist prior to 1649. The traditional viewpoint is that the previous Corporation records were burned in the storm. While no eye witness gives us details of fires being set *throughout* the town, there is substantial indirect evidence that at least some of the town was plundered and burned. Proof exists that the Corporators did not have a meeting in their own chambers between 6 April 1649 and 29 July 1656. Since the town had been in Royalist hands, some of the principal buildings may have been destroyed by either them or the Parliamentarians. An entry in the records six years after the battle confirms the fact that the Corporation headquarters at the Tholsel had been left in some disarray by the marauding soldiers. During an assembly 'Heald at Tredath, the 8th day of May 1655 ...At which time and place it was then, by the whole consent of the towne agreed upon, that the Tholsell of the said towne bee, with all competent speede built, and repaired ...' From the records that do survive, it is clear that a red book and a white book, both of which contained ancient laws and customs, were not destroyed. However, they have been lost in the intervening period. By October 1649, the short Royalist occupancy of the town had abruptly ended and Parliamentary administration in the shape of the local Corporation would now govern regional affairs. The Corporators of Drogheda settled down to a period of little unrest, while the conquered Royalist hierarchy, both Protestant and Catholic aristocrats throughout the country, lost their lands to the new English Adventurers and Commonwealth soldiers.

Prior to the storm, the allegiance of some of the Protestant municipal authorities appear to have been in favour of the King. During a sermon to his flock, Dean Bernard expressed the view that their lives may well have been in danger as well as their goods. He may have felt that as supporters of the King they could have been exposed to the wrath of the Parliamentary troops. He confirms that his congregation survived the siege safely. To suggest that as Protestants they could expect no hostility from Cromwell is naive. *The dividing line in this war was between Royalist and Parliamentarian, not Protestant and Catholic.* Those Protestants in league with Irish Catholics had little in common except their opposition to the rebel English government and their absolute contempt for each other. It can also be said that religion often created the boundary for many of the participants. Cromwell sometimes thought less of fellow Protestants who were allied to Catholics than the Catholics themselves. The Royalist ranks were a theological mix of both religions.

Cromwell's admission of guilt concerning the deaths of civilians, on the face of it, appears confirmed in those last three words at the foot of the published version of his despatch to the Speaker, Lenthall, on 27 September. In his defence, at best, the point could be made that he means *armed* inhabitants. At worst it could be argued that he refers to a large scale massacre of Drogheda's unarmed innocents. As it happens, no primary document whatsoever exists that provides details of the deaths of persons not in arms.

These three small words need to be examined carefully. On the face of it, Cromwell freely admits that 'many inhabitants' were slain. If the assumption were to be made that they were unarmed and that this was his way of telling the world of his treacherous deeds, then this seems like an enormous turnabout from the Commander-in-Chief of the Commonwealth forces. This same man, a month earlier, had issued explicit orders to the entire Parliamentarian forces 'not to do any wrong or violence towards Country People or persons whatsoever unless they be actually in arms.' These instructions were decidedly conclusive and did not differentiate on theological grounds. All persons whatsoever, not in arms, either Catholics or Protestants, were not to be harmed. Immediately prior to the sacking of the town he had hanged two of his soldiers who had disobeyed this order. Is it likely that he could now casually justify the deaths of hundreds, if not thousands of innocent civilians, even as the unfortunate but necessary result of collateral damage, or as the intentional consequence of enraged behaviour and an attacking army out of control? This massacre he would have had to have carried out by discriminating in the tumult of a storm between which of the inhabitants had Royalist sympathies and which had Parliamentarian leanings – this would seem like a most preposterous notion.

Yet these three words are exceptionally incriminating, and a case could possibly be made for a commander in a fit of rage and an army out of control to have slain many defenceless inhabitants, irrespective of political persuasions, as Cromwell himself seems to have alleged. But did he? Do these words actually come from the pen of the future Protector? The actual letter that Cromwell wrote to the Speaker with quill and ink on vellum paper has not survived. The manner in which the text of the despatch has come down to us is through the official government printers, and other licensed contemporary pamphlets that transcribed it.

The list is outlined in the pamphlet *Letters from Ireland relating the Several great successes it hath pleased God to give unto the Parliament's forces there, in the taking of Drogheda, Trym, Dundalk, Carlingford and the Nury. Together with a list of the chief commanders, and the number of the officers and soldiers slain in Drogheda* which is the official Parliament pamphlet published on 2 October 1649 that historians go to for Cromwell's letters about Drogheda. The list reads as follows:

A List of the Officers and Soldiers slain at the storming of Drogheda

Sir Arthur Ashton, Governor

Sir Edmund Verney Lieutenant Col to Ormond's Regiment

Col Fleming of Horse

Lieutenant Col Finglasse of Horse

Major Fitzgerald of Horse

Eight Captains Lieutenants Cornets of Horse

Cols Warren, Walls, Byrne of Foot, with their Lieutenants, Majors, &c.

The Lord Taaff's brother, an Augustine Fryer

Forty-four Captains, and all their Lieutenants, Ensigns &c.

Two hundred and twenty Reformadoes and Troopers

Two thousand Five hundred Foot Soldiers, besides Staff Officers, Chyrurgeons, &c and many inhabitants.

The best way to evaluate the primary source documents is to take them in date order – from 11 September 1649 onwards. Since this assessment is being carried out specifically to address the civilian massacre theory, the objective here is to first identify the source then to ascertain precisely what that person tells us about the events. Aside from private letters, the newsbooks of the day, the early newspapers, provide us with much of our information. The burgeoning newspaper industry was in its infancy at the time. The first newsbook – a precursor to the first newspaper - in England appeared on the streets on 29th November 1641. It was published by John Thomas and it was entitled *Heads of Severall Proceedings*. As soon as the Civil War got under way, so too did the war on paper. The periodical press therefore by 1649 was in full swing and each newsbook came out once a week and was in either an eight, or sixteen-page format. Born out of political conflict, they were a collaborative affair with an author, a printer and a publisher all having a part to play in the production. As well as the regular weekly edition, if a writer received news between issues, they would sometimes publish this news in isolation in a separate pamphlet instead of waiting for his day to come around. In 1649, the first year of the Commonwealth, as well as the official government newsbooks, the opposition press, Royalist newsbooks, were published every week despite Parliament's attempts to prevent them. It was easy enough for a politically-inclined author to find a printing press, a willing printer and publisher to promulgate their opinions. Unfortunately, these publications, both Royalist and Parliamentarian, are known to have sometimes had intentions to deceive rather than inform, the former much more so than the latter. Both parties had factional interests often driven by an intense bias. Many of the royalist 'mercuries' were copied by interlopers where competitors simply stole their opposition's credentials, their titles and their typography and published their counterfeit publications with impunity.

It is also important to realise that there were licensed newsbooks and there were unlicensed newsbooks. Around the time that news was breaking in London about the fall of Drogheda, the House of Commons passed a new licensing act, The Licensing Act of 1649 had been planned from at least May of that year, the previous Licensing Act of 1647 lapsed and this new act replaced it. On 12 May 1649 the Council of State commissioned the president of that body, John Bradshaw (who had been a lawyer) to prepare and bring in an act prohibiting the printing of invective and scandalous pamphlets against the Commonwealth. The great seventeenth century poet John Milton is believed to have assisted Bradshaw in the setting up of the act. One of the new government's earliest priorities was to control the press, as they realised how potent this new genre could be and the impact it was having/could have on an impressionable public. The general public were gradually becoming well-informed and discerning, and as a result a market was created with a demand for cheaply printed newsbooks and was growing exponentially. The 'Act against unlicensed and scandalous Books and Pamphlets; and for better regulation of printing' was agreed by the House of Commons on 14 September, three days after the fall of Drogheda. Law-breakers could be fined or imprisoned; £10 for authors, £5 for printers, and £2 for booksellers. Any member of the public found in possession of an unlicensed newsbook was subject to a £1 fine. Printers could also lose their printing equipment and had to enter into a bond of £300 as well as now having to print the name of the licenser on all of their publications. Existing licensers had their powers revoked and were replaced by three licensers; the clerk to parliament, the secretary to the army, and anyone whom the Council of State would directly appoint.

As a result of the act, when Drogheda fell most unlicensed newsbooks, with the exception of some notable rogue printers, closed down. So all the existing newsbooks were without a license and anyone intending to continue to publish must now seek a new one. As news of Drogheda was winding its way to London, three newsbooks emerged to fill the vacuum, *A Brief Relation of Some Affaires and Transactions Civall and military Both Forraigne and Domestique,* (licensed by Gualtar [Walter] Frost, secretary to the Council of State), *Perfect Diurnall of Some Passages and Proceedings of, and in Relation to the Armies* (mostly licensed by John Rushworth) and *Severall Proceedings in Parliament* (licensed by Henry Scobell). These three newsbooks replaced the eight or ten previously licensed newsbooks, and of course, there were those who flouted the law, took their chances and published their tracts anyway like the royalist *The Man in the Moon* and *Mercurius Elencticus,* for instance, to influence public opinion and undermine the fledgling government.

At that point Richard Hatter entered some publications into the Stationers' Register over at Stationers' Hall even though he did not have the credentials to do so under the three pre-requisites. He was part of the army secretariat, but was clearly not the secretary to the army and so the Council of State moved quickly to prevent him from licensing further publications, and John Rushworth, the *bona fide* army secretary, took up his position as the Commonwealth's official licenser on 30th October.

Around the turn of the nineteenth century JG Muddiman, writing under the pseudonym JB Williams, one of the earliest seventeenth century news industry experts, saw the new Licensing Act as a ban on news from Ireland and an attempt by the new regime to cover up news of a massacre of the garrison and the bulk of the civilian population at Drogheda. Using Richard Hatter's publications, Muddiman constructs an account of his version of events. This does not stand up to scrutiny. Muddiman was no fan of Cromwell's and was determined to prove that a large-scale massacre of innocent civilians took place at both Drogheda and Wexford on top of the slaughter of soldiers. He interpreted Hatter's dismissal as proof that Parliament wanted to suppress the news that 'many inhabitants' were killed at Drogheda, since Hatter's publications allude to the slaughter of the entire garrison as well as inhabitants but other publications also do, as we shall see.

With Cromwell abroad in Ireland and with Parliament in such a precarious position of power (with just 25 per cent of the 'popular vote') there were those back in London who craved news of the Irish expedition. Many English people had looked on in horror as Parliament had cut the king's head off and the majority was hostile to the party in power. Meanwhile Europe was watching the next development with interest as the stability of the three kingdoms on its western edge was now in question. In short, Parliament's continuance in power depended of the success of the Irish mission.

Publishers all over the capital were champing at the bit for morsels of information about Drogheda, both Royalist and

Parliamentarian. But due to bad roads and adverse weather conditions none was forthcoming in the days immediately after the siege. Cromwell himself was back in Dublin by 17 September, the day he wrote his first letter to Lenthall. Meanwhile, back in London almost a week had passed since the breach was stormed and news was trickling in, perhaps from sailors who had heard stories through the grapevine. *The Kingdom's Weekly Intelligencer* reported on 17 September that St Mary's Church had been beaten down by Parliament's large siege pieces. The next day, *The Impartiall Intelligencer* said that yes, the assault on the town had begun but they did not have enough information to say which way the battle had gone. On the 20 September *The Moderate Messenger* reported that Colonel Hewson's regiment had made an unsuccessful assault on the breach, information the author said was in a letter from Liverpool dated the 14th and received on the 17th. *Perfect Occurrences* went one step further in their edition of 21 September reporting that the breach had been gained and that part of the town was captured.

(2)

TWO

FIGHTS

IN

IRELAND

ON

Sunday, Munday, Tuesday, and *Wednesday* last, between the Forces commanded by the Marq. of *Ormond*, and the Lord Lieutenant *Cromwell*.

SIR,

UPon the Lord Governour *Cromwels* neer approach with his Army, to the frontier and impregnable Garrison of *Tredah*, his Lordship sent a Summons to the Governour Colonell *Ashton*, for the

(2)

the surrender thereof to the power and obedience of the Parliament of *England*, but the Governour returned a very resolute and peremptory Answer, intimating, *That he abhord with his soul the brand of perfidiousnesse, that he was resolved to display the banner of loyalty, and to stand in the defence and preservation of the trust reposed in him to the last man, &c.* Whereupon, the Lord Governour immediatly called a Councel of Officers, for the well-ordering of the Army, to the end the work might appear more facile and easie, and indeed so excellent were the debates and consultations thereof, that their Design was lookt upon with great admiration.

And upon Saturday morning being the 8. of this instant *Septemb.* twelve thousand Horse, Foot, and Dragoons, marched up in *battell-array*, with Trumpets sounding, and Drums beating against the Town, where they soon encamped themselves, cutting off divers passes, & using the rarest stratagems of war, for streightning the enemies quarters.

About 7 at night, the Army advanced somewhat neerer, and divers strong Guards both of Horse and Foot were placed within twice musket shot of the walls, where the Foot intrenched themselves. And about 5 in the morning, the besieged discovered us, who drawing neerer to each other, said, *they would give us a dinner to welcome us into* Ireland; and indeed they were very circumspect in keeping of their word, for between 11 and 12 they gave us a visit, sallying forth with a considerable party of Horse, and lining the obscure places with many hundreds of foot, but failed in their promise; for upon their first charg against one of our horse-guards, they were so gallantly received, that they soon

(3)

ſoon quitted the place, our horſe purſued them within musket ſhot of their works, receiving a great volley from their Ambuſcado, in which we loſt 4 men, and 7 horſe; of the enemy kild and taken 13. The next morning being *Munday* they attempted another ſally, but not daring to put it in execution, retreated in again without action, remaining all day very ſilent, till the Curtain of the moſt high Canopy began to expell and darken the ſplendor of *Sols* beauty, who even at the cloſe of the day, upon the relieving our guards, gave us a volley both with great and round ſhot, which grazed and did no execution.

On *Tueſday* being the 11. inſtant, about break of the day, we received a new allarum from theſe troubled ſpirits, who (upon an unexpected ſalley) ſuddenly fell upon Col. *Hewſons* foot guard, but were repulſed, and the loſſe equally ballanced.

On *Wedneſday* being the 12. inſtant, Lieu. col. *Aſhton* (a great Papiſt, and Nephew to the Governour) about two of the clock in the morning made a very deſperate ſalley upon two of our foot-guards, with 500. Iriſh, which by reaſon of the ſudden ſurprizall of our Perdews, and Centinels, cauſed great difficulties to intervene, yet notwithſtanding, the Wings of providence ſeeming as a great Bulwark to preſerve and defend us, our men received their furious onſet, but being overpowred, the Vau-guard retreated to the next, and bodying, advanced to the other ingaged, fell upon the *Iriſh* killed 40, took 20 priſoners, and forced the reſt to a diſhonorable retreat, with the loſs of ten; beſides thoſe in the former engagements, priſoners exchangd were equall, about 50. above 100 killed and wounded, whereof on our part 30.

From the Siege at Tredah Sept. 13. 1649.

The above is an anonymous account of sally activity from an eye witness at Drogheda published in London before news of the successful attack broke.

But it was on Saturday 22 September that the author of *Perfect*

Occurrences, that well-known pamphleteer Henry Walker got hold of two letters with the news that everybody was waiting for. One was from Liverpool and is dated 14 September giving a second-hand account from the captain of a ship recently arrived from Dublin that Drogheda had indeed fallen. Walker had mixed feelings about the letters. On one hand he knew that he was the first with the news but on the other, it was a Saturday and *Perfect Occurrences* came out every Friday, and he had just missed the previous day's edition. But even worse, the previous day, Parliament had enacted the new act. But Walker wasn't going to be stopped breaking the news so, along with his regular printer Robert Ibbittson, (In Ibbitson's will, he calls Walker his 'loving friend') he went to press.

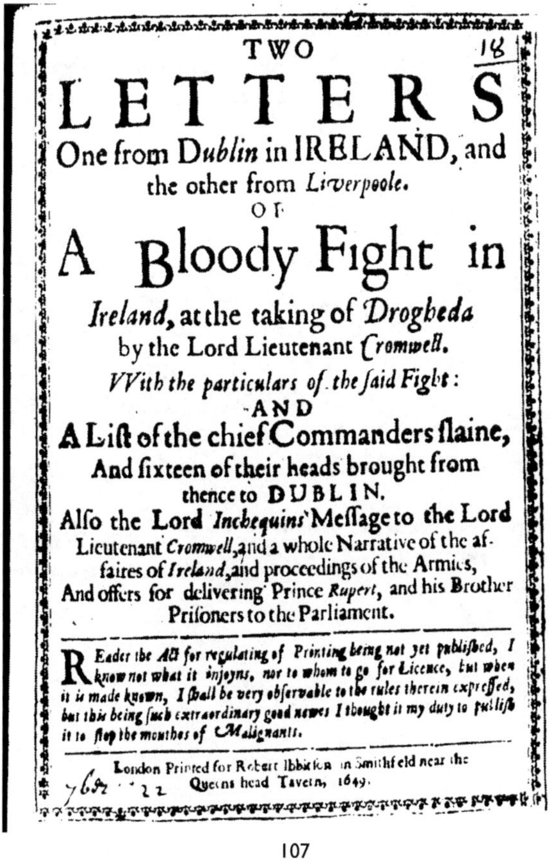
TWO

LETTERS

One from *Dublin* in IRELAND, and the other from *Liverpoole.*

OF

A Bloody Fight in *Ireland,* at the taking of *Drogheda* by the Lord Lieutenant *Cromwell.*

VVith the particulars of the said Fight:

AND

A List of the chief Commanders slaine, And sixteen of their heads brought from thence to DUBLIN.

Also the Lord *Inchequins'* Message to the Lord Lieutenant *Cromwell,* and a whole Narrative of the affaires of *Ireland,* and proceedings of the Armies, And offers for delivering Prince *Rupert,* and his Brother Prisoners to the Parliament.

Reader the Act for regulating of Printing being not yet published, I know not what it injoyns, nor to whom to go for Licence, but when it is made known, I shall be very observable to the rules therein expressed, but this being such extraordinary good newes I thought it my duty to publish it to stop the mouthes of Malignants.

London Printed for Robert Ibbitson in Smithfeld near the Queens head Tavern, 1649.

(2)

On *Wednesday* 12. *Septemb.* 1649. The Lord Lieut. ſtormed the Garison of *Drogheda*, where he found much oppoſition, yet through the glorious power of God (which was wonderfully ſeen there) they made entry into the Town, neer the Mount by the Church, where they found reſiſtance, offered *Quarter*, but it would not be accepted of, ſo that they were forced to fight their way into the Town, which they did with great reſolution, and courage, and killed of the Enemy neer 3000. Amongſt which Sir *Arthur Aſton* (their Governour) and divers other conſiderable men, putting all to the ſword that were in the ſtreets, and in the poſtures of Souldiers, But many whom they found in houſes, and in a quiet and orderly poſture they gave quarter to.

There are 16 of the chief of their heads cut off, and ſent to *Dublin*, to be hanged up on poles as Traytors. It is ſaid that amongſt the reſt there is *Aſtons* the Governours, and the Lord *Grandeſey*, young *Villers*, and *Armeſtrong* (that Apoſtate) and young *Varney*, and *Goodwin* and others.

We have alſo news that there are 2 or 3000 come in from *Ormond* and *Inchequin*, to the Lord Lieutenant *Cromwell*, and that the Lord *Inchequin* is mediating for his Peace; that he may be received to mercy, and that he will with his Officers and Souldiers goe out againſt P. *Rupert*, to bring him, and his brother P. *Maurice* in Priſoners, and ſurrender them to the Lord Lieutenant, if he and his Officers may be received to mercy.

It is ſaid that we have loſt ſome, and ſome Officers wounded. Amongſt which Col. *Jones*, but the more exact

(3)

exact narrative hereof I ſhall ſend you by the next. In the mean time I have ſent you theſe incloſed particulars from a very good hand from *Dublin*.

Liverpoole 14 *Septem.* 1649.

A Letter from Dublin.

SIR,

OUr News from *Ireland* (God be thanked) is very good: On the 17th. and 18th. of *Auguſt*, there was little action, but waiting to heare of the reſt of our Fleet, 19. being the Lords day, were ſpent in holy exerciſes; about ſix a clocke at night, they received the happy newes of the Arrivall of the reſt of our Fleet; and Major Generall *Ireton* who had beene nine dayes at Sea, and the news of *Derry* being relieved by *Owen Roe*,

The 20th. was ſpent in landing the Forces that came with the ſecond Fleet (the 21, and 22.) were ſpent in refreſhing and drenching of our poor horſe almoſt ſtarved at Sea. The 23. was a publick day of Thankſgiving kept for the ſafe landing of our Forces, with a Proclamation, commanding the Magiſtrates of the Town and Officers of the Army, to ſuppreſſe to the utmoſt of their power, ſwearing and drunkenneſſe. The 24. was ſpent in Councell and Court-Marſhalls where divers perſons were ſentenced for miſdemeanors; on the 25. was a generall Muſter of the whole Army in two Greens near *Dublin*, the Horſe and Dragoons

A 3 goons

Walker transcribed the letters in a standalone pamphlet and published them for general circulation with a caveat to appease the authorities:

> Reader, the act for regulating of printing being not yet published, I know not what it injoyns, nor to whom to go for license, but when it is made known, I shall be very observable to the rules therein expressed, but this being such extraordinary good newes, I thought it my duty to publish it to stop the mouths of malignants.

Walker prints the following words on the front cover: *Two Letters, One from Dublin in Ireland and the other from Liverpoole of A Bloody Fight in Ireland, at the taking of Drogheda by the Lord Lieutenant Cromwell. With the particulars of the said fight and, a List of the chief commanders slaine, and sixteen of their heads brought from thence to Dublin.*' (The 'list of the commanders slaine' referred to is not to be confused with the other list in *Letters from Ireland* as the anonymous writer simply mentions the names of six individuals in the text and does not actually print them in list format, rather he cites them as narrative.) Both letters are reasonably short, and while neither writer is an eye witness to the actual events, neither mention the involvement of civilians or inhabitants. In fact, after stating that 3,000 of the garrison had been slain, the first letter corroborates other eye witness testimony that 'many' royalist soldiers were actually spared:

> They made entry into the town, neer the mount by the church, wherein they found resistance, offered quarter, but it would not be accepted of, so that they were forced to fight their way into the town, which they did with great resolution, and courage, and killed of the enemy neer 3,000. Amongst which Sir Arthur Aston (their governour) and divers other considerable men, putting all to the sword that were in the streets and in the

> postures of soldiers. But many whom they found in houses, and in a quiet and orderly posture they gave quarter to.

The other letter in the pamphlet is written on 12 September without knowledge of the battle and merely says, 'On Sept 12, being this present day, is newes come hither that their guns have been heard to play hard, and it is said that we are entered Tredah, we are hourely expecting the particulars.'

But Walker was upstaged by other newsbooks that also published news of the taking of Drogheda that same day. *A Modest Narrative of Intelligence* reported that Drogheda had been captured and added that ships were unable to leave Dublin due to the lack of wind on the Irish Sea. *The Moderate Messenger* was more circumspect with the news that was now abroad and cautioned that, *'Reports are commonly accompanied with such incredible stories, that it diminisheth that credit which otherwise would be given thereto.'*

Cromwell's chaplain Hugh Peters arrived in Dublin to join the expedition late on the day of the actual storming of Drogheda, 11 September. Four days later, Peters heard directly from messengers from Drogheda about what had happened there. Peters then wrote his telegram style letter directly to Henry Walker, who obviously had friends in high places. The sender and receiver considered the other to be his 'affectionate friend'. Walker didn't receive the letter until the 28th but when he did he knew that he had his scoop and he appears to have immediately taken the letter to the House of Commons, where it was read out. That same day he went to print (licensed by Scobell) in a second separate pamphlet. He entitled the publication, *A Letter from Ireland, Read in the House of Commons on Friday Septemb 28. 1649 From Mr Hugh Peters, Minister of God's Word, and Chaplain to the Lord Lieutenant Cromwell. Of the taking of Tredagh in Ireland, 3552 of the Enemies slain, Amongst which Sir Arthur Aston, the Governour, Coll Castles, Cap. Simmons and others slain. And the losse on both sides.*)

Perfect Occurrences of every daie journal in Parliament (Henry Walker)

(1273) Numb. 144.

Perfect Occurrences.
OF
Every Daie iournall
OF THE
PARLIAMENTS
Armies Proceedings:
AND OTHER
MODERATE INTELLIGENCE.
From Friday Septemb. 28. to Friday Octob. 4. 1649.
Collected by Henry Walker Cleric.

Printed at London by J. C. for John Clowes, & Robert Ibbitson, and are to be sold near Cripplegate, and in Smithfield,

Beginning Fryday Septemb. 28

(Or more at large) Terror and Dread is the Cavaliers portion. They are undone in all their wretched designes; But the busines of Ireland, quite breaks their hearts.

Newes came this day that the Lord Lieut. had taken Tredagh: And there slain Sir Arthur Aston (the Governour.) Sir Edmond Varney, Lieutenant Col. to Ormonds own Regiment of Horse. And also, Col. Fleming, Lieut. Col. Finglasse, Major Fitzgarret, And Capt. Sir Robert Harpoole, all of Horse. And 6. Captains, 8. Lieutenants, and 8. Cornets of Horse more. And of Foote, Col. Warren, Col. Wall, Col. Byrine. And the Lord Taffes 2. Brothers, one of them being an Augustine Fryer, And 41. Captains, 44. Lieutenants, and all the Ensignes and other Officers of 44. Companies, some very few only excepted: 220 Reformadoes and Troopers. And 2500. Foot-Souldiers, besides staffe-Officers, and Chirurgions, with many Inhabitants.

Mr. Peters Letter was also read as followeth.

N nnnnnn SIR,

Meanwhile, Walker was still working on his newsbook edition for that week (one of the five newsbooks to be licensed by Hatter), and he held the front pages for this news, where he subsequently prints the list. The list is therefore in general circulation on 28

September, five days before Parliament prints Cromwell's letters. (This is not even the earliest date, as we shall see.) Walker does not identify its author. *Perfect Occurrences* dated 28 September – 4 October starts with the words:

> Beginning Fryday September 28. Terror and Dread is the Cavaliers portion. They are undone in all of their wretched designs. But the business of Ireland quite breaks their hearts. News came this day that the Lord Lieutenant had taken Tredagh and there slain Sir Arthur Aston the governour, Sir Edmund Varney, Lieutenant Col to Ormonds own Regiment of Horse. And also, Col Fleming, Lieut Col Finglasse, Major Fitzgarret, And Capt. Sir Robert Harpoole, all of Horse. And six Captains, 8 lieutenants, and 8 Cornets of Horse more. And of Foote, Col Warren, Col Wall, Col Byrine. And the Lord Taffe's Brothers, one of them being an Augustine Fryer. And 41 Captains, 44 Lieutenants, and all the Ensignes and other Officers of 44 Companies, some very few only excepted. 220 Reformadoes and Troopers. And 2500 Foot Soldiers, besides Staff-Officers, and Chiurgions, with many inhabitants.

'News came this day' very clearly proves that the list was in circulation (general, not print) as early as 28 September, at least. Walker then re-prints the list later on in the document in list format at the end of his transcription of Cromwell's letter to Lenthall of the 17th. Interestingly, the list changes slightly from the one he prints on the cover in that Sir Robert Harpoole is now missing, so instead of ten named persons there are now nine, the same nine that appear in *Letters from Ireland...*

There is no doubt that this is the same list that appears in *Letters from Ireland,* the document that incriminates Cromwell. They are one and the same. This same list is reproduced in seven newsbooks in total that week with some slight differences, with the exception of *Perfect Diurnall* where the names of 26 persons are named as opposed to nine or ten, in spelling, general typography, words used and layout, but this one in *Perfect Occurrences* is uncannily similar to the one in *Letters from Ireland* even to the point where numbers are spelled out in words rather than typed in figures, and most capital letters match each other with the exception of just one (The word Brother v brother). Here Walker gives a total of nine named individuals, the exact same named individuals as the list in *Letters from Ireland*.

But Walker gives us two reasons to believe that they are not the words of Cromwell. Firstly, Cromwell's letters may not have been opened until 2 October as it is recorded that they were read to the Council of State that day and since Walker reveals that he received a version of this list on 28 September, there is significant doubt (as we shall see further) that the list was Cromwell's own. Furthermore - and even though Walker repeats the list later on in the same edition of *Perfect Occurrences* (with slight differences) – nowhere does he suggest for a moment that this list was written by Cromwell himself. In fact he gives no source for the list.

Gathering the snippets of information from the dates and times of the publications and the activities of both the Council of State and the House of Commons, it is possible to stitch the sequence of events together.

Cromwell employed one of his officers, a Captain Samuel Porter, as a messenger to travel to London with his official despatch announcing the fall of Drogheda. In the sealed package was his letter to John Bradshaw, the President of the Council of State, that was dated 16 September as well as his letter to William Lenthall, Speaker of the House of Commons that was dated the 17th.

Since Hugh Peters had written his letter on the 15th Porter was also the bearer of this (private) letter that was addressed to Walker. Arriving in London on Friday 28 September with both letters, Porter passed them on to the addressees. Cromwell's short letter to Bradshaw seems to have been opened that day as is evident in the *Kingdom's Weekly Intelligencer* and *The Perfect Weekly Account*, both of whose authors say they are in receipt of the letter of the 16th on the Friday and they both published it in full. It would not appear on the streets until later that week as the news for the week was still coming in. Peters' letter to Walker was subsequently printed on its own and was the first with the news. The House of Commons sat again on Tuesday 2 October when Cromwell's lengthy letter to Lenthall was read to the House. But in the meantime, over the weekend, Cromwell's second letter dated 27th had also arrived and was also read on 2 October. Both were then ordered to be printed and it was at that stage that the incriminating list seems to have been added to his two despatches in *Letters from Ireland*.

But that week the list then began to appear all over London, in several publications and in isolation, mostly without Cromwell's letter preceding it. In the context of this investigation it is important to analyse each of these documents. As well as two official Parliament publications, five other newsbooks published the list – just the list, and not the preceding letter. This already indicates that the list is separate from the letter. Furthermore, it will also be shown that none of the publications attribute the list to Cromwell.

Meanwhile, on 29 September Walter Frost, Secretary to the Council of State, published a general notification to the clergy to let Londoners know that Drogheda had fallen to parliament.

177

Die Saturni, 29 *Septembr.* 1649.

At the Council of State at *Whitehal.*

WHereas it hath pleaſed God to bleſs the endeavors of the Forces of this Commonwealth, againſt the Iriſh Rebels and their Adherents, in the Town of *Drogheda*, which was taken in by ſtorm, there being in it a ſtrong Gariſon of the choice of *Ormonds* Army put into it; there were about Three thouſand of the Enemy ſlain, and of our men, onely Sixty four private Souldiers, and two Officers.

IT is thereupon this day Ordered, That all the Miniſters in *London*, and within the Lines of Communication, do publiſh the ſame to the people to morrow, being the Lords day, the thirtieth of this inſtant *September*, in their ſeveral Churches and Chappels; and ſtir up the people to give thanks to God for his goodneſs, in ſtill owning and bleſſing the endeavors of this Commonwealth, for the ſetling of Peace againſt the Enemies thereof.

9.

ORdered alſo, That this be printed, and ſent to the Lord Major of London, *to cauſe the ſame to be ſent to all the Miniſters within his Iuriſdiction, for the purpoſe aforeſaid.*

By Command of the Council,

Gualter Froſt, Secr'

London, Printed by *Iohn Field* for *Edward Husband*, Printer to the Parliament of *England*, 1649.

One of the first publications that printed it was *The Perfect Weekly Account*. The list appeared in the edition of Wednesday 26 September – Wednesday 3 October 1649. It is possible that Daniel Border was the author in this case (Bernard Alsop was the printer) although Border has also been accused of producing a counterfeit version of the true journal of the same name.

The Perfect Weekly Account (Daniel Border)

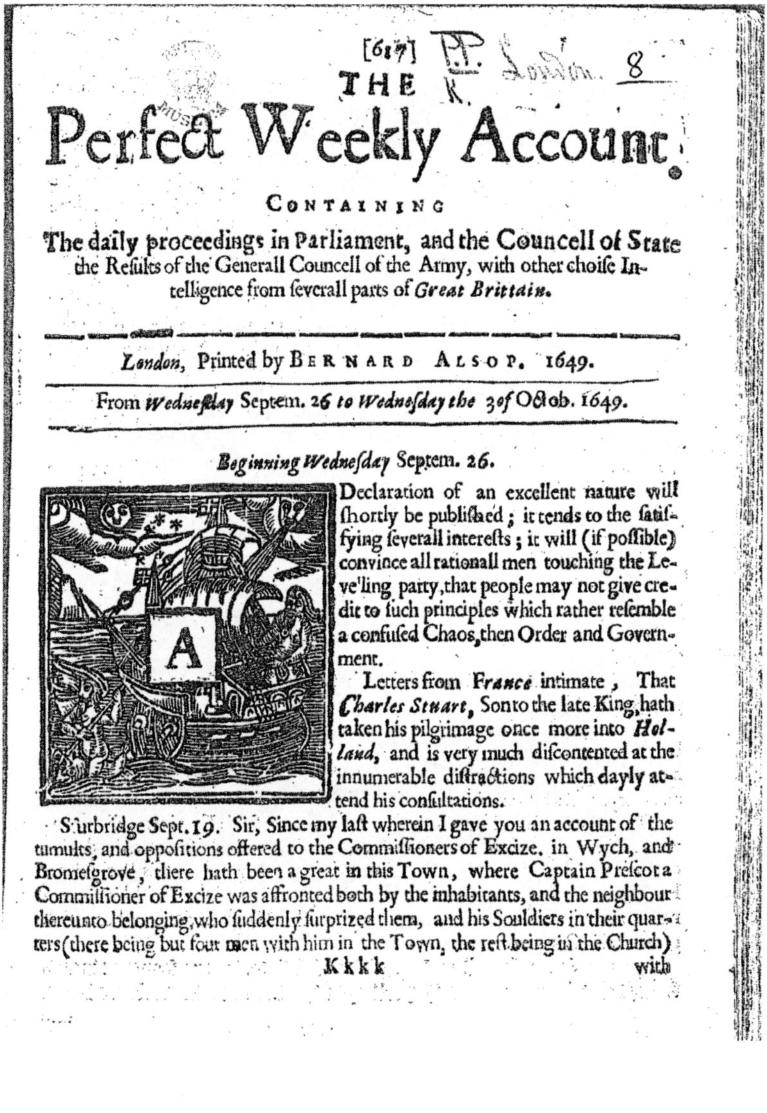

[617]

THE

Perfect Weekly Account.

CONTAINING

The daily proceedings in Parliament, and the Councell of State the Results of the Generall Councell of the Army, with other choise Intelligence from severall parts of *Great Brittain*.

London, Printed by BERNARD ALSOP. 1649.

From *Wednesday* Septem. 26 *to Wednesday the* 3 *of* Octob. 1649.

Beginning Wednesday Septem. 26.

A Declaration of an excellent nature will shortly be published; it tends to the satisfying severall interests; it will (if possible) convince all rationall men touching the Levelling party, that people may not give credit to such principles which rather resemble a confused Chaos, then Order and Government.

Letters from *France* intimate, That *Charles Stuart*, Son to the late King, hath taken his pilgrimage once more into *Holland*, and is very much discontented at the innumerable distractions which dayly attend his consultations.

Sturbridge Sept. 19. Sir, Since my last wherein I gave you an account of the tumults, and oppositions offered to the Commissioners of Excize, in Wych, and Bromesgrove, there hath been a great in this Town, where Captain Prescot a Commissioner of Excize was affronted both by the inhabitants, and the neighbour thereunto belonging, who suddenly surprized them, and his Souldiers in their quarters (there being but four men with him in the Town, the rest being in the Church)

Kkkk with

[618]

with more then 300 men armed with Muskets, Guns, Swords, Bills, Pitchforks, and divers other sorts of weapons; which affront was offered before the Commissioners demanded any mony of them, but tde rude multitude told them in plain terms, that if they had any they would take it from them; which accordingly they did, and took away the Commissioners and Souldiers mony, Horses, Arms, Cloaks, Cloaths, wounded some of them very dangerously, shot the Commissioners in three three places, disarmed all the Souldiers in the Church and dispersed them, that there was not six of them left together. This Kyot was begun by one Nicholas Den a Leveller, condemned by a Councell of Warre, to be shot at Burford, and from his sentence of death delivered. The rest of the company being generally of that faction: yet this man still continues in his affronting, ridiculous, and factious ways without any submission at all, sends into the Country, beats Drums to raise what further force and power he can can to suppresse all Parliamentary proceedings. The last night they had 40 Musketiers upon the guard, sent to the Commanders and souldiers, that unlesse they would depart Kinver Church (where now they are for their defence) they would beat them out.

But the Commanders and Souldiers are resolved to stand it out untill they have assistance from the L. Gen. who hath written to the Governor of Stafford to apprehend Den, and suppresse the tumult.

Thursday.

THe Officers of the Army kept a day of humiliation, and amongst other things the increase and growth of Atheism and prophaneness of the Times; there preached before them Mr. *Sedgwicke*, Mr. *Marshall*, and Mr. *Strong*.

Divers Turkie Marchants ships were certified to be safely arrived in the River of *Thames*.

A Letter from *Dover* advertiz'd, that about 800 l. in Gold was taken in a ship going beyond Sea.

Aix in *Province* Sept. 14. The Plague continues in *Marseilles*, and thereabouts, with such violence, as that almost all the Fryers and Religious men, which hazarded themselves to stay there for the assistance of such as fell sick, are dead, and carryed away to another World thereby.

The Souldiers likewise continue their retiring out of this Province, whose Governour the Count of *Alets* is now at *Toulon*, where he hath bin entertained with extraordinary cherishments; and Commis. sent unto him from this Parl. with a Protestation to keep, from henceforth, a most perfect intelligence with him; and not to make hereafter more then one body for the Kings service, and common good of this Country.

Edenburgh, Sept. 23. Our Committee of Estate, was no sooner returned from Saint Johnstones, but they fell upon the Letter to our declared King, and

(619)

and who ſhould be diſpatcht with it, and agreed upon Mr. George Windram of Lilerton, for his incouragement (he refuſing other wayes) there was a farther mitigation, and the demands made lower, that Condiſcention on our part may appear to the full, and you will hear the matter of the Covenant, will be inſiſted rather then the form of words.

It was intended he ſhould have gone this day, but that the laſt night Major Boſwell that delivered the Letter to the King at Homby, and hath ſtill adventured upon deſperate ſervices, it's not known whether a brought Letters or a verball Meſſage: he ſaith he comes to the Eſtates, but it's thought but will only make addreſſes to the Marq. of Argyle, and the Chancellor, which if then it's for more ſecrecy: beſides here is no Committee to receive what he brings: the Expreſſe that was ſent to the Queen and Chancellour of Sweden, brings nothing that is pleaſing, at leaſt it's ſo divulged: there is here an expectation of a ſudden alteration, but in regard things have been ſo off and on, we know not what to ſay, this ſeemes more and more apparent, that ſomewhat will be brought into this Kingdom, both of men, moneys, ſhips, and ammunition: whether againſt the Presbyters or for them, a little time will ſhew, a ſmall matter will unite us, and our Royall Maſter, yet come he not ſingle, we are afraid touch will not be kept: it's very credibly certified hither, that Owen Mac-Art, is agreed, and joyned with Ormond: ſomewhat is talked of the ſiege of Tredah, but that we credit not: the baniſhed out of Ulſter are commiſſerated, and put in hope of a livelihood: here are apprehenſions that if things ſhould draw neer to a concluſion between our intended King, and the people, that ſome of Eminency will obſtruct it by throwing in objections, becauſe they think they cannot be ſecure upon any terms.

Friday.

This day came Letters in confirmation of the great ſucceſſe in Ireland; and the particulars more fully related under the Lord Governour Cromwells ow hand, as followeth.

Sir, It hath pleaſed God to bleſſe our endeavours at Droghedah, after Battery we ſtormed it the enemy were about 3000. ſtrong in the Town; they made a ſtout reſiſtance, and neer 1000. men of ours being entred the enemy forc'd them out again; but God giving a new courage to our men they attempted again, and entred beating the Enemy from their defences, the enemy made three Retrenchments both to the right and left, where we entred; all which they were forced to quit. Being thus entred we refuſed them quarter, having the day before ſummoned the Town. I believe we put to the ſword the whole number of the Defendants, and I do not think 30 of the whole number eſcaped with their lives;

Kkkk 2 thoſe

(620)

those that did are in safe custody for the Barbadoes. Since that time the Enemy have quitted to us Trim and Dundalk. In Trim they were in such hast that they left their Guns behind them. This hath been a marvellous great mercy; the enemy not willing to put an issue upon a field Battel had put into this Garrison almost all their prime Souldiers, being about 3000, horse and foot, under command of their best officer Sir Arthur Ashton being made Govenour, they were some seven or eight Regiments, Ormonds being one under the command of Sir Edward Verney. I do not believe, neither do I hear that any Officer escaped with his life save onely one Lievtenant, who I hear going to the Enemy, said, That he was the only man that escaped of all the Garrison.

The enemy were filled upon this with much terrour; and truly I believe this bitternesse will save much effusion of blood through the good hand of God; I wish that all honest hearts may give the glory of this to God alone, to whom indeed the praise of this mercy only belongs: For instruments they were very inconsiderable the work throughout.

We are marching the Arwy to Dublin, which we hope will be here to morrow night, where we desire to recruit with victuall, and then we shall (God willing) advance towards the Southern Design (you know what) onely we thinke Wexford will bee our first undertaking, in order to the other. I desire you to let us have the continuance of your assistance; I thought fit to ride you notice thereof to prevent inconveniency; and to the end the ships may ride it out in Kingsale, as farre as God give them leave, and they are possibly able to do. I hope we shall begin our march on Thursday or Friday morning next at the farthest.

Capt. Brandley did with 40 or 50. of his men, very gallantly storm a Tenalia; for which he deserves the thanks of the State.

Sept. 16. 1649.

O. CROMWELL.

From St. Germans they write that the declared King of Scots after his going thence, stayed certain dayes at Caen in Normandy, in his way to Jersey: And by other Letters the fourteenth of September he was lodged at the house of one Blatchford; and on the fifteenth he with his train rod away thence toward the Sea to ship as given out for Jersey. If he went then onward he went fit for Col. Popham to receive and entertain him: he went from St. Germans and six Coaches of six horses each, besides many went on foot not only under Officers and Servants, but many Gentlemen two of good quallity who were loath to stay behind, and yet had not means to mount themselves: others that were in the same condition but could not go so far on foot, are gone to Paris with intention to follow if Jermyn can furnish

nish them with money, whom they sollicite earnestly for it, but as yet without fruit for ought we can hear, the said proclaimed King hauing distributed his mony to his Ambassadours, whom he hath sent to severall Plaoes Cottington and Hide for Spain, who had 12000 Livers, and Culpepper as much, who is gone to Russia, and the rest their proportion, he had but 300 Pistols left him when he left St. *Germayn*, he hath received nothing of the French since he came thither, nor at his going away, nor was there any order taken to defray him in his Journey from this place to *Jersey*.

And even at a stately house of the Duke of *Vendosme* called *Annet*, where he lay the first night after his departure hence, he had nothing allowed him but bare lodging.

He made many Knights before his going hence, and gave the Order of the Garter to the Palatine *Edward*, and the Duke of *Buckingham*.

He also issued many Commissions both to English, Dutch, and French, to take prizes from the English Marchants.

The E. of *Seaford* the Scotch-man came down hither on Sunday last, the day before the said proclaimed King went hence, he went back the next day having refused (the second time) to go along with him.

The Queen went to *Paris* on *Tu:sday*, and the next day *Jermin* gave a great Feast to the Ambassadors, they are all at *Paris* still, except *Culpepper*, who went thence on *Thursday*, the rest go not till next week, and perhaps some of them not then, specially *Hatton* who is designed for *Sweden*, but he is not yet resolved whether he shall go himself, or make a Deputy, that power being given to him. The Queen (*Charles Stuarts* Mother) was about the streets in *Paris* with three murning Coaches, but her servants have no money, and her self is in very little better case.

The Duke of *York* swore to a Gentleman upon his going hence, that since the time his Brother came from *Holland*, he had not had two pistols in his possession, that he had not at that time one penny, that he went that journey as forced, and out of meer obedience to the Command of his Brother, who would have it performed.

Upon the first notice of *Charles Stuart* his motion toward *Jersey* (though some relations made him already to be arrived there) order was given to Colonell *Popham*, one of the Parl. Generals at Sea, then in the Downs, to sayl over with such ships as he should think fit to *Gernsey*, and *Gersey*, and to wait for him, he came thither time enougo, and if the weather will suffer him to continue, t'will be hard for *Charles Stuart* to come to *Gersey*, unless in some fog he should slip, which will not be without danger.

Saturday

(621)

Saturday.

B*Erwick* 18 Septemb. Sir, The Bigot Presbyterians are in a great pang of zeal to be in action for their King, if he will but gratifie the Kirk in what they desire they will easily unite with all the rest of his party there yet, that make those that are indeed conscientious among them to dislike, and by that dislike they are in more danger every day to make defection to the Sectaries, which are daily increasing among them, of which they sadly complain.

This day (according to custom) the Aldermen and Common-councell-men of the City of *London* had a Sermon in *Lawrence* Church; after that they repaired to Guild-hall for the choise of a Lord Major for the year ensuing, where that which is most observeable, was this: The City having good experience of the wisdom, fidelity, and other rich endowments, which God hath bestowed upon the present Lord Major, whereby he is thought every way fit for the Gubernation of this famous City, a great number of the Citizens gave their voyces to have him continued Lord Major for the next year; but the election fell upon Alderman F*ooke*, who is likewise a Gentleman full of worth, and parts fit for a Magistrate.

Hamburgh 14 Sep. The business of P*oland* is strangely and beyond expectation composed; the King comming with fresh supplies to relieve his Army, being much streightned by the *Cossacks*, he granted them their full desires, and so they that had him at a great advantage (had they pursued it effectually) submitted to him.

The chief Articles granted them are, as followeth:

1 That the Greekish Religion shall be freely exercised throughout all P*oland*.

2 That the Jesuits and Jews shall not be prejudiciall to them.

3 That the King shall entertain constantly a standing Army of 40000 *Cassackes*.

4 And to be commanded by their present Generall, who shall follow the Kings directions.

'Tis believed by many men there, that the whole business was a plot of the King to render himself Soveraign, and that it causeth jealousie in the great Ones and Gentry of that Kingdom.

Last night came to this town a speciall Couzier, to give notice, that the Emperour refused to subscribe to the Agreement at *Nuremberg*.

The S*wedes* thereupon forbear to disband, and to be ready at an hours warning to march, and some who were marched toward the East Sea, to be transported for S*weden* were countermanded.

This caused a great disturbance amongst the States of the Empire assembled at *Nuremberg*, and among the people there, which people were so inraged against the

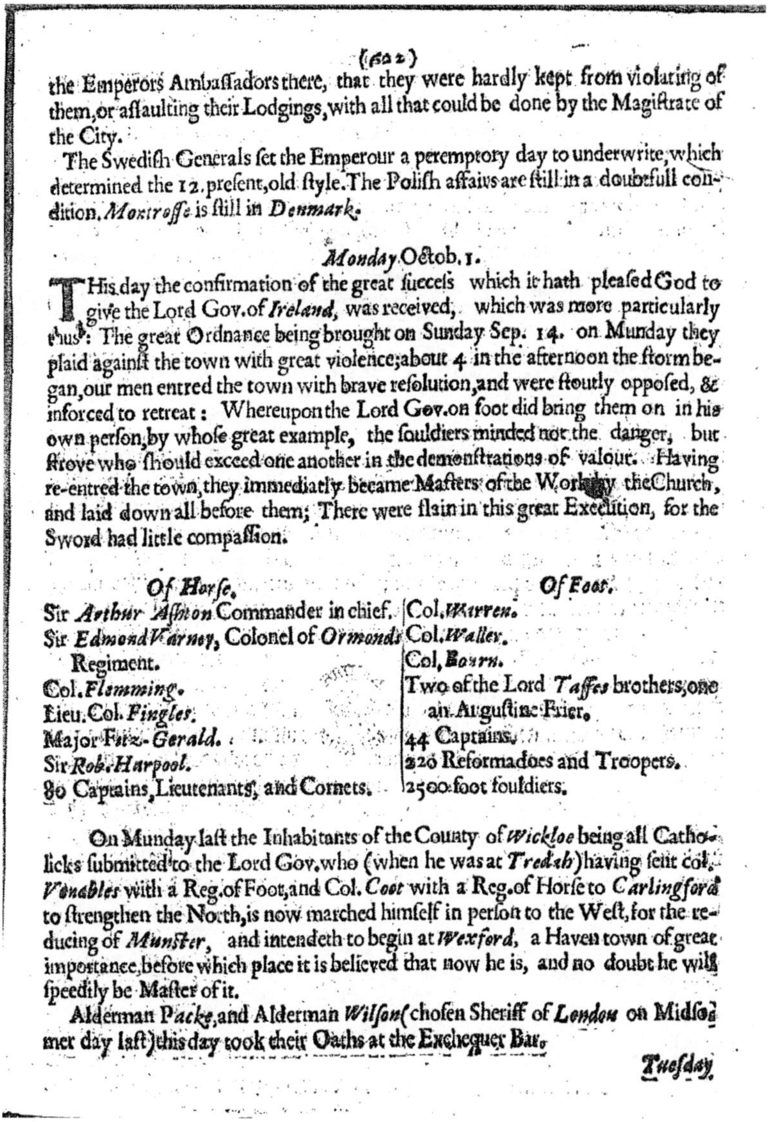

(602)

the Emperors Ambaſſadors there, that they were hardly kept from violating of them, or aſſaulting their Lodgings, with all that could be done by the Magiſtrate of the City.

The Swediſh Generals ſet the Emperour a peremptory day to underwrite, which determined the 12. preſent, old ſtyle. The Poliſh affairs are ſtill in a doubtfull condition. *Montroſſe* is ſtill in *Denmark*.

Monday Octob. 1.

THis day the confirmation of the great ſucceſs which it hath pleaſed God to give the Lord Gov. of *Ireland*, was received, which was more particularly thus: The great Ordnance being brought on Sunday Sep. 14. on Munday they plaid againſt the town with great violence; about 4 in the afternoon the ſtorm began, our men entred the town with brave reſolution, and were ſtoutly oppoſed, & inforced to retreat: Whereupon the Lord Gov. on foot did bring them on in his own perſon, by whoſe great example, the ſouldiers minded not the danger, but ſtrove who ſhould exceed one another in the demonſtrations of valour. Having re-entred the town, they immediatly became Maſters of the Works by the Church, and laid down all before them; There were ſlain in this great Execution, for the Sword had little compaſſion.

Of Horſe.	*Of Foot.*
Sir *Arthur Aſhton* Commander in chief.	Col. *Warren.*
Sir *Edmond Varney*, Colonel of *Ormonds* Regiment.	Col. *Waller.*
Col. *Flemming.*	Col. *Bourn.*
Lieu. Col. *Fingles.*	Two of the Lord *Taffes* brothers, one an Auguſtine Frier.
Major *Fitz-Gerald.*	44 Captains.
Sir *Rob. Harpool.*	220 Reformadoes and Troopers.
80 Captains, Lieutenants, and Cornets.	2500 foot ſouldiers.

On Munday laſt the Inhabitants of the County of *Wickloe* being all Catholicks ſubmitted to the Lord Gov. who (when he was at *Tredah*) having ſent Col. *Venables* with a Reg. of Foot, and Col. *Coot* with a Reg. of Horſe to *Carlingford* to ſtrengthen the North, is now marched himſelf in perſon to the Weſt, for the reducing of *Munſter*, and intendeth to begin at *Wexford*, a Haven town of great importance, before which place it is believed that now he is, and no doubt he will ſpeedily be Maſter of it.

Alderman *Packe*, and Alderman *Wilſon* (choſen Sheriff of *London* on Midſomer day laſt) this day took their Oaths at the Exchequer Bar.

Tueſday

Irrespective of authorship, this version of *The Perfect Weekly Account* reports on the events on Monday 1 October, the day *before* Cromwell's letter was opened and the full details in *Letters from Ireland* were published by Parliament, as follows:

Monday Octob. 1
This day the confirmation that the great success which it hath pleased God to give the Lord Gov. of Ireland, was received, which was more particularly being thus: the great Ordnance being brought on Sunday September 14· On Munday they plaid against the town with great violence; about 4 in the afternoon the storm began, our men entered the town with brave resolution, and were stoutly opposed, & inforced to retreat: Whereupon the Lord Gov on foot did bring them on in his own person, by whose great example, the soldiers minded not the danger but strove who should succeed one another in demonstrations of valour. Having re-entered the town they immediately became masters of the works by the church and laid down all before them. There was slain in this great execution, for the sword had little compassion:

Of Horse	Of Foot
Sir Arthur Ashton Commander in chief	Col. Warren
Sir Edmund Varney, Colonel of Ormond's Regiment	Col. Waller
Col Flemming	Col. Bourn
Lieu. Col Finglas	Two of the Lord Taffe's brothers, one an Augustine Frier
Major Fitz-gerald	44 Captains
Sir Robert Harpool	220 Reformadoes and Troopers
80 Captains, Lieutenants and Cornets	2,500 foot souldiers

Border includes Harpool (or Harpoole) and names ten persons in total but he does not print the words 'and many inhabitants' with this list. Furthermore, nowhere does Border, in his introduction to the list, suggest that these are the words of the Lord Gov. Cromwell. He merely prints the list without identifying its author. In contrast elsewhere, Border reveals that he had received Cromwell's letter to Bradshaw on the previous Friday and was at pains to point out that they were Cromwell's own words:

> Friday (28th September) This day came letters in confirmation of the great success in Ireland and the particulars more fully related under the Lord Governour Cromwell's own hand, as followeth:

Border then prints Cromwell's letter to Bradshaw, but without the list of the defenders of Drogheda that appears in *Letters from Ireland* indicating perhaps that even this list is separate from the letter and not the work of Cromwell himself.

The Kingdom's Faithfull and Impartial Scout (Daniel Border)

[257] Numb.36

The Kingdomes Faithfull 26

AND IMPARTIAL

SCOUT; P.P. London. R. Will...

COMMUNICATING

The daily proceedings of the Parliaments Armies in *England* and *Ireland*, the great Success and Achievements against the Marquess of *Ormond*; and other moderate Intelligence, from *Scotland*, *France*, *Denmarke*, and *Holland*.

From Friday the 28. of Septem. to Saturday the 5. of ~~Septem.~~ Octob. 1649.

LONDON, Printed for R. WOOD, and G. HORTON, and are to be sold neer Creple gate, and at the Royall Exchange in Cornhill, 1649.

Beginning Friday Septemb. 28.

Necessity is not ruled by Law, the force is so great; through many dangers she finds out the way, but it sufficeth not to the strength of armes, to have flesh, bloud, and bones, unless they have also sinews to stretch out, or pull in, for defence of the body: So an Army consisting of many men, and furnished with warlike habillements, is but lame, and unserviceable, if God give not a blessing upon their undertakings.

Ἐμοῦ θανόντος γαῖα μιχθήτω πυρί

Me moriente, terra misceatur igni.

The many thousands raised by *Ormond* and *Inchiquin* (so much boasted of by the malignant party) are in a dying condition, the loss of *Tredah* being like to prove fatall to them; for hereby (to their sorrow is it spoken) a free passage is open to the North of Ireland, good quarters obtained, and the main Body of our Army marching towards the most fertile parts of that Country, the Roman Catholicks of the Province of *Wicklow* brought to subjection, hath caus'd all things to be very plentifull in *Dublin*, and more gold and silver seen, then in the raign of severall late Kings. And least any one that shall read the Preface to this Book, shall take up a prejudicate opinion, and think that we exceed the bounds of truth, I shall refer them to these ensuing Letters, impartially communicating as followeth:

SIR, We sate down before Tredah, the last of Aug. with about 9000 Foot, & 5000 horse; the 5 of Sep. the enemy made a salley forth upon the West side of the Town,

Mmm but

[258]

but were beaten in again with some loss ; the 6. a barrel of the Enemies powder was blown up, and the 9 *Ormond* sent 500 foot, and 500 horse which attempted to get into the town; but being gallantly received by our men, many of the foot were lost, and the horse returned back to their Garrison at Trim; the 10. the Canons began to play on the South side of the town, and about 12 of the clock they had batter'd down a Church: after this we made our Battery against the walls, and plaid upon them all that night, and about 2 of the clock the next morning a breach was made so wide, that 20 men a breast might march into the Church-yard; but the Enemy had made so many double Breast-works, that a farther entrance was thought almost impossible to be made; yet the 11 day about 12 of the clock, our horse and foot drew very neer the town on every side therof, and about 2 in the afternoon the Lord Gov. gave command to fall on: then col. *Castles* men fell on the breach, and after a very hot dispute was forced to retreat a little, untill col. *Hewson* brought up his Reg. who fell on very resolutely, and although the Rebels were as gallant in their own defence as possible men could be, yet in a short time our men began to get ground, and being seconded by more foot, the enemy were forst to run, and were so gallantly pursued, that they had not time to rally; they kept a Mount (the strongest that hath bin seen) in which they had 300 foot, 6 great Guns, & 50 barrels of powder, with match & bullet proportionable; as also victuals to have lasted 9 months, in it (amongst others of eminency) was Sir *Arthur Ashton*, & Sir *Rob. Thorell*, which Fort was suddenly entred by our men, which put the Enemy into such an amazement, that some fled to the Towers of the wall, and others to the Church, where they were all killed and taken: the Commanders were rich in money and apparell, there was in all about 3000 slain, & what was found became free booty.

Dublin 17 Sept. 1649.

As for the further perticulars touching the aforesaid renowned atchievement, I shall endeavour (according to the best informations from the hands of great worth and eminency) to give you a more fuller relation touching the occurrences of this nature, which (for ample and generall satisfaction) take as followeth.

The 4th. instant we sate down before Droghedah strongly fortified, and wel manned with an expert Governour Sir Arthur Ashton, his men, as before, most Irish, and select, our Artillery, comming by Sea with our necessaries, and winds being uncertain, it was, the 10th. before our Batteries were finished, that day we made a small breach on the 11. a large, yet so, as no horse could enter or foot without much difficulty, we being necessitated to use Ladders in some places: About four in the afternoon the assault began, and but one South side of the Town, the North being not attempted, we not thinking it discretion to divide our Army to both sides the River, least the Enemy should (which we had intelligence he intended) fall upon one part or other, from within and from without; the first attempt was upon a Tenalia newly made, and without the Wall. which flanked the breach, which was taken without any considerable losss, by a party commanded by valiant Captain Branley, whom the Lord Lievt. recommends to Parliament, after which the breach was stormed, which held a hot dispute for a quarter of an hour, each fighting, as if the gaining or losing thereof, had been the loosing or gaining of Ireland, and to say the truth, it was little lesse as by the sequel you will find; the violence of our enemy made our men give back, so fierce was the opposition, which the Lord. Liev. seeing, run on foot to the Souldiers, & and encouraged them, which occasioned

the

[259]

the ſetuing of the Charge and it was done with that reſolution, that they immediately, carried the town, putting to the ſword as faſt as they could, in which ſlaughter there fell. Sir Arthur Aſhton a Papiſt, as were moſt of the Garriſon, the reaſon given of his death is ſaid to be the rage of Colonel Caſtles ſouldiers, for the death of their Colonell, alſo for that Aſhton gave not a civill anſwer when ſummoned.

Thus is that ſtrong place overcome to the terrour of the Enemy in all parts: As for the ſeaſonableneſs of it, and the neceſſity of the taking the way we did, it appears, firſt, becauſe proviſions would have fail'd had we made a long work, beſides, in Sir Arthur Aſhtons Pocket was found a Letter wherein Ormond, Caſtlehaven, and others write, that they would, if they held out but to the thirtienth, relieve them, by raiſing the ſiege, and ſay the ſame Letters, with 4000. horſe, and Owen Roes foot, which they preſumed upon: and as we are aſſured, are ſince joyned with them, but too late, for this place, what they may do afterward; this place being taken two dayes before: and though ſome are of opinion, that the enemies rage will be the greater, by the ſlaughter at Tredagh, yet we find the terrour great that is upon them, Trim being quit before Major Coddugin could come to it, Ormond ſending a party to re-inforce it, but comming too late, and ſeeing ours flee, it's very advantageous to us for quarters, and out of that reſpect it was the next place to be attached: Dandalk did the like, only the Caſtle, which with other places, Colonell Venables being ſent with horſe, and foot, to reduce, hath frighted them out of Carlingford, and it's ſaid the Nurey alſo: the North now being at our devotion, except Belfaſt, Carickfergus, Charlemount, and Colerain: of whom, we hope to be Maſters, before we go to Winter-Quarters: we take notice, that the Sunday, and but two days before Tredagh was taken, Maſſe was ſaid in the great Churches of the Town; when ſuch ſottiſh Idollatry is erected, and on high, the fall, we hope will ſtill be the greater; and ſo long as our grand enemy imployes ſuch, we have faith enough to beleeve we ſhall overcome, theſe two Churches, the one was beat down, the other blown up; let him continue to plow with an Oxe, and an Aſſe, and believe it, he is like to come home by weeping croſſe. Mark Trevor with his ſtrong reſolutions for royalty, is (with a Veſſel kept for that end) fled to the Iſle of Man, and more, no doubt, will follow: Ormond, and Inchequin are at ods by reaſon of the conjunction with Owen Roe, who with the Marquis Clanrickard, Ards and Claneboyes, is marched to Kilkenny, where he tells the Councell, that if they will not put him in capacity to fight the enemy, he wil quit his command: Inchiqueen ſaith, he will go, and ſecure his party of Munſter, as well as he can, rather then joyn with the bloudy Rebels. The Lord Lievtenant is marched from hence, having firſt murſtered our men, refreſhed them, and taken proviſions with him: we do not go ſo many South, as we went North; for though we loſt but few, we believe not above a hundred ſlain out right, yet it could not be expected, but that ſome be wounded others ſick; and of them, the main ſufferers were of Venables, Huſons, and Ewers Regiments; whether we ſhall attach Kilkenny, or Wexford, time will ſhew, and what oppoſition we ſhall meet with by the way, there being many ſtraights, and ſuch as may be defended by a few men againſt many: Wexford it's poſſible may be firſt ſet upon, becauſe it's the great Receptacle for Pyrats, there being it's believed 80 ſuch ſmal Veſſels there, it's double w[illegible]led about, and no doubt well provided, if thoſe in it, who man their Ships, only e[illegible] they may make a notable defence: the Fleet will, do doubt be ayding unto us; in th[illegible]ming of Tredah, our word was: *The Lord aſſiſt us.*

[206]

This is observable that the Nobles and Gentry of Ireland;are as generally engaged in this forloen design;as wer the English for the late King;and in all likelyhood, if they persist,will come to as miserable an end.

Saturday.

BY Letters from Scotland we are advertized as followeth. Sir,*Here is still talk of an Army,that is to come out of Germany,Denmark,and Sweden,but how it will fadge we know not, for still Montrosse, and others, whom we fancy not,are imployed,and busie at Hamborough, and other places,making overtures : there are not words(we hear)wanting to these instruments:but for other things,little appears,what may be bySpring,time must shew.Major Boswell is gone from hence to Ireland, you see we suffer Royalists to crosse the Country:his Message signifies little that may prove satisfactory to the people:Mr.Windram is gone to the declared King,with as inviting a Message,as pen could draw,or people send: they promise him their personall protection,preservation,restauration, &c. and shall not so much as condition for subscribing of the Covenant;such is the World,Religion,and the glory of God,changed into all shapes, as will best stand with humane Greatnesse,and earthly Benefit.*

Hamburgh 14 Sep. The business of *Poland* is strangely and beyond expectation composed; the King comming with fresh supplies to relieve his Army, being much streightned by the *Cossacks*, he granted them their full desires, and so they that had him at a great advantage (had they pursued it effectually) submitted to him.The chief Articles granted them are as followeth: 1 That the Greekish Religion shall be freely exercised throughout all *Poland*. 2 That the Jesuits and Jews shall not be prejudicial to them. 3 That the King shall entertain constantly a standing Army of 40000 *Cassackes*. 4 And to be commanded by their present Generall,who shall follow the Kings directions.'Tis believed by many men there,that the whole business was a plot of the King to render himself Soveraign, and that it causeth jealousie in the great Ones and Gentry of that Kingdom. Last night came to this town a speciall Couzier, to give notice, that the Emperour refused to subscribe to the Agreement at *Nuremberg*. The *Swedes* thereupon forbear to disband, and to be ready at an hours warning to march, and some who were marched toward the East Sea, to be transported for *Sweden* were countermanded. This caused a great disturbance amongst the States of the Empire assembled at *Nuremberg* and among the people there, which people were so inraged against the Emperors Ambassadors there, that they were hardly kept from violating of them,or assaulting their Lodgings, with all that could be done by the Magistrate of the City. The Swedish Generals set the Emperour a peremptory day to underwrite, which determined the 12 present,old style.The Polish affairs are still in a doubtful condition. *Montrosse* is still in *Denmark*.

Monday Octob. 1.

THis day the confirmation of the great success which it hath pleased God to give the Lord Gov.of *Ireland*, was received,as also a List of the number killed, which was more particularly thus:

Of

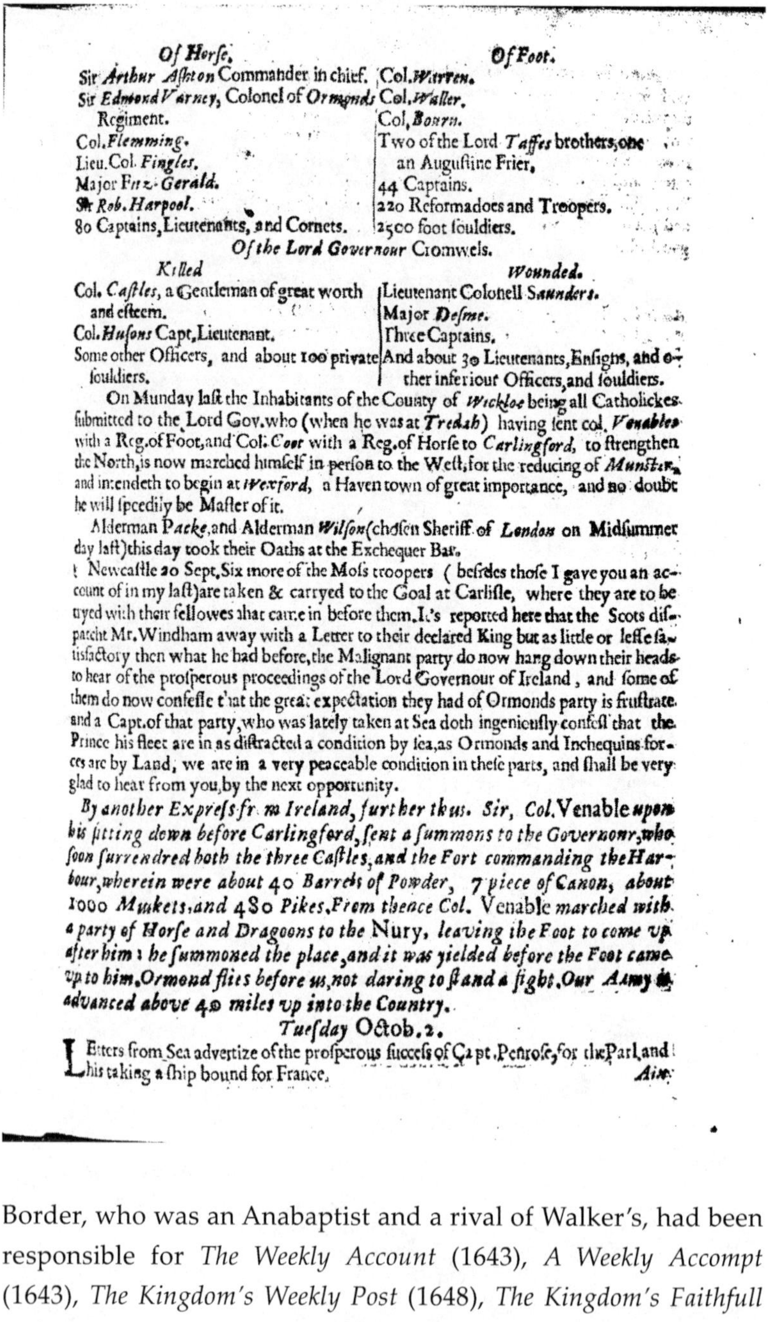

Of Horse.	*Of Foot.*
Sir *Arthur Ashton* Commander in chief.	Col. *Warren.*
Sir *Edmond Varney*, Colonel of *Ormonds* Regiment.	Col. *Waller.*
	Col. *Bourn.*
Col. *Flemming.*	Two of the Lord *Taffes* brothers, one an Augustine Frier,
Lieu. Col. *Fingles.*	
Major *Fitz-Gerald.*	44 Captains.
Sir *Rob. Harpool.*	220 Reformadoes and Troopers.
80 Captains, Lieutenants, and Cornets.	2500 foot souldiers.

Of the Lord Governour Cromwels.

Killed	*Wounded.*
Col. *Castles*, a Gentleman of great worth and esteem.	Lieutenant Colonell *Saunders.*
	Major *Desme.*
Col. *Husons* Capt. Lieutenant.	Three Captains.
Some other Officers, and about 100 private souldiers.	And about 30 Lieutenants, Ensigns, and other inferiour Officers, and souldiers.

On Munday last the Inhabitants of the County of *Wickloe* being all Catholickes submitted to the Lord Gov. who (when he was at *Tredah*) having sent col. *Venables* with a Reg. of Foot, and Col. *Coot* with a Reg. of Horse to *Carlingford*, to strengthen the North, is now marched himself in person to the West, for the reducing of *Munster*, and intendeth to begin at *Wexford*, a Haven town of great importance, and no doubt he will speedily be Master of it.

Alderman *Packe*, and Alderman *Wilson* (chosen Sheriff of *London* on Midsummer day last) this day took their Oaths at the Exchequer Bar.

Newcastle 20 Sept. Six more of the Moss troopers (besides those I gave you an account of in my last) are taken & carryed to the Goal at Carlisle, where they are to be tryed with their fellowes that came in before them. It's reported here that the Scots dispatcht Mr. Windham away with a Letter to their declared King but as little or lesse satisfactory then what he had before, the Malignant party do now hang down their heads to hear of the prosperous proceedings of the Lord Governour of Ireland, and some of them do now confesse that the great expectation they had of Ormonds party is frustrate, and a Capt. of that party, who was lately taken at Sea doth ingeniously confess that the Prince his fleet are in as distracted a condition by sea, as Ormonds and Inchequins forces are by Land, we are in a very peaceable condition in these parts, and shall be very glad to hear from you, by the next opportunity.

By another Express from Ireland, further thus. Sir, Col. Venable *upon his sitting down before Carlingford, sent a summons to the Governour, who soon surrendred both the three Castles, and the Fort commanding the Harbour, wherein were about* 40 *Barrels of Powder,* 7 *piece of Canon, about* 1000 *Muskets, and* 480 *Pikes. From thence Col.* Venable *marched with a party of Horse and Dragoons to the* Nury, *leaving the Foot to come up after him: he summoned the place, and it was yielded before the Foot came up to him. Ormond flies before us, not daring to stand a fight. Our Army is advanced above* 40 *miles up into the Country.*

Tuesday Octob. 2.

Letters from Sea advertize of the prosperous successe of Capt. Penrose, for the Parl. and his taking a ship bound for France, *Ain*

Border, who was an Anabaptist and a rival of Walker's, had been responsible for *The Weekly Account* (1643), *A Weekly Accompt* (1643), *The Kingdom's Weekly Post* (1648), *The Kingdom's Faithfull and Impartial Scout* (1649), *England's Moderate Messenger* (1649) and *The Impartial Scout* (1650). On Friday (Not Saturday, as his title page reads) 5th October, Border published *The Kingdom's Faithfull and Impartial Scout*. He opens the edition with two letters from two separate correspondents, neither of which he names, regarding the fall of Drogheda. Later in the document he tells us:

Monday 1st October – This day confirmation of the great success, which it hath pleased God to give the Lord Governor of Ireland, was received, as also a list of the numbers killed, which was more particularly thus:

Of Horse
Sir Arthur Ashton Commander in chief
Sir Edmund Varney, Colonel of Ormond's Regiment
Col Flemming

Lieu. Col Finglas
Major Fitz-gerald
Sir Robert Harpool

80 Captains, Lieutenants and Cornets

Of Foot
Col. Warren
Col. Waller
Col. Bourn
Two of the Lord Taffe's brothers, one an Augustine Frier
44 Captains
220 Reformadoes and Troopers
2,500 foot souldiers

Of the Lord Governor Cromwels

Killed
Col Castles, a gentleman of great worth and esteem
Col Huson's Capt. Lieutenant
Some other Officers, and about 100 private souldiers
And about 30 Lieutenants, Ensigns, and other inferior officers and souldiers

Wounded
Lieutenant Colonell Saunders
Major Desme)
Three Captains

Not surprisingly, Border's list of the defenders slain is exactly, to the letter, the same as the list in *The Perfect Weekly Account.* One could be forgiven for concluding that the same pieces of type were left in the same printer's chase to produce the same list. Indeed, it is impossible to conclude that both publications were not from the same hand, or at least the same printing machine, given the similarities. The text throughout both publications is identical in several places, including the list and some of the surrounding text. Interestingly, Border is the only newsbook writer to reproduce a list of the attackers who were either killed or wounded. And significantly, Border does not include the phrase 'and many inhabitants' in either of his publications. In his analysis of this issue in *God's Executioner,* Micheál O'Siochrú misses Border's *Kingdom's Faithfull and Impartial Scout.* However disingenuous it may seem, it is important to note these omissions in the work of the academic experts of the period. Another newsbook that did not attach the words 'and many inhabitants' to the list could easily be used to bolster an argument in this discussion.

Severall Proceedings in Parliament (Henry Scobell)

Numb. 1. 14

SEVERALL
PROCEEDINGS
IN
Parliament

Hen: Scobell Cleric. Parliamenti.

From *Tueſday* 25 *Septemb.* to *Tueſday* the 9th. of *October*, 1647.

Printed at *London* by *Robert Ibbitſon* dwelling in Smithfield.

Beginning Tueſday 25 *Septemb.*

THe humble Petition of divers maimed Souldiers who have loſt their limbs and of diſtreſſed widdows whoſe husbands have loſt their lives in the Parliaments ſervice under the Lord Gen. *Fairfax* was this day read and referred to the Commmittee of the Army to take ſome order for the releiſe of the Petitioners.

The compoſitions of the Delinquents of *North-Wales* were ordered to bee paid unto the Treaſurers of the Army to bee iſſued out by warrant from the Committee of the Army according to ſuch Orders and Inſtructions as they have or ſhall receive from the Parliament concerning military affaires, and not otherwiſe.

An Act for ſettling the Malitia's of the reſpective Counties in England & Wales was this day read the firſt & ſecond time and committed to a Committee of the whole Houſe which is

A ap-

(2)

appointed to sit for that purpose on this day month, And in the mean time it was referred to the Councell of State to give power and instructions to such persons within the severall and respective Counties, in England and Wales, as they should thinke fit for the preserving the peace of the Common-wealth and prevention of all tumults, Insurrections, and Invasions,

H. Scobel.

Wednesday 26 *Septemb.* 1649.

THis day there passed an Act for the continuance and maintenance of the Schoole and Alme-houses of *Westminster* with a liberall allowance for that purpose out of the revenues belonging formerly to the Colledge of *Westminster*, wherein there is likewise provision made for maintaining an able and godly Minister to preach twice upon every Lords day in the Abby Church, together with a yearly allowance for those Ministers that are to continue that famous Lecture every morning in that Church.

The Act for draining the Fennes was ordered to bee Printed.

H. Scobell.

Thursday 27. *Sept.*

THe Committee for Compositions at Goldsmiths-hal were ordered to sit this afternoon, and so *de die, in diem*, till the Compositions be perfected.

A Letter from the Generall to the Councell of State touching the suppressing the late Insurrection at *Oxford*, and the proceeding of the Court Martiall against such of the most guilty as are Members of the Army, was this day read, and the poceedings therein were approved,

This day was read a Declaration of the Parliament of *England* in vindication of their proceedings and discovering the dangerous practices of severall Interests against the present Government and Peace of the Commonwealth, together with the resolutions of the parliament thereupon.

H. Scobell.

Friday 28 *Septemb.*

THis day the Declaration was againe read by parts and passed and ordered to be Printed and Published. And it was referred to the Councell of State to consider of such Persons

(3)

ſons now in Priſon or under reſtraint as are fit to receive favour in purſuance of the ſaid Declaration, and to give order for their diſcharge with ſome directions to the Councell of State for theirs proceedings therein.

The Houſe was adjourned to Tueſday next: *H.Scobel.*

Tueſday the 2. *of* October.

THis day were read ſeverall Letters from the Lord Lievtenant of *Ireland*, one dated the 17 of *September*, 1649. relating the great ſucceſſes it pleaſed God to vouchſafe to the Parliaments Forces there in taking the Town of *Drogheda* by aſſault, wherein were ſlaine,

Sir *Arthur Aſhton* Governour,
Sir *Edmond Verney*, Lievt. Col, to *Ormonds* Regiment;
Col. *Fleming*, Lievt. Col. *Finglaſſe*, Major *Fitz-gerald*, } of Horſe
Col. *Warren*, Col. *Wall*; Col. *Byrne*, } of Foot, with their Lievten. Majors &c.
Eight { Captaines, Lievtenants, Cornets } of Horſe.
The Lord *Taffs* Brother, an *Auguſtine* Fryer,
44 Captains, and all their Lievtenants, Enſignes, &c.
220 Reformado's and Troopers,
2500 Foot Souldiers, beſides Staffe Officers, Chirurgions, &c.

A party of Horſe and Dragoons being ſent to *Dundalk* the enemy quitted it; another Caſtle between *Trym* and *Drogheda* upon the Bogues, and upon the newes of *Drogheda*, the *Scots* Companies, with the Lord *Ardes* brought to aſſiſt *Ormond*, and were in *Trym*, ran away, leaving their great Guns behind them.

Another Letter was read from the Lord Lievtenant, dated the 27 of *Sept.* 1649. and likewiſe a Letter from Col. *Venables* to the Lord Lievtenant, declaring that after he came to *Carlingford*, upon a Summons the three Caſtles, and the Fort commanding the Harbour were ſurrendred to him, wherein were 40. Barrels of Powder, 7 peice of Cannon, about 1000 Muskets, and 500 Pikes, (the greateſt ſtore in

A 2 *Ulſter*)

Henry Scobell was a clerk for parliament. He recorded the everyday proceedings in the House of Commons and licensed many of their official publications before they were subsequently released for general circulation. One of these weekly official publications dates from Tuesday 25 September to Tuesday 9 October and was called *Severall Proceedings in Parliament*. This week was the first ever edition of the newsbook. Unfortunately, it is impossible to know for certain who is writing it for the first few issues. Both Scobell and Henry Walker have been associated with it, Walker for the most part. Arguing in favour of Scobell being responsible in the early weeks is the fact that the content is essentially just a digest of the Commons Journal, which either Scobell or a deputy clerk would have assembled. In the context of this newsbook being licensed by the clerk to Parliament, to that extent at least, it is 'legitimate'. Because of this it has often been described as an 'official government publication'. We don't know as much as we might about the practices of licensing publications at this period, and while some licensers were extremely diligent and took content out, or changed it, others may have rubber stamped it without evaluating the text in detail. Since Scobell also licensed *Letters from Ireland* it is important to establish his role in all of this. In the inaugural edition of *Severall Proceedings* then the writer (perhaps Scobell) chronologically lays out the daily accounts of what transpired in Parliament and reports the news of Drogheda thus:

Tuesday the 2 October
This day were read several letters from the Lord Lieutenant of Ireland, one dated the 17th September 1649 relating the great successes it pleased God to vouchsafe the parliament's forces there in taking the town of Drogheda by assault, wherein were slaine,

Sir Arthur Ashton Governour
Sir Edmund Verney, Lieut. Col. To Ormond's regiment

Of Horse	Of foot
Col. Fleming	Col. Warren

Lieut. Col. Finglasse	Col. Wall
Major Fitzgerald	Col Byrne
Eight Captains, Lieutenants, Cornets of horse	With their lieutenants, Majors, &c.

The Lord Taff's brother, An Augustine Fryer
44 Captains and all their lieutenants, Ensignes, &c.
220 Reformadoes and Troopers
2,500 Foot Souldiers, besides Staffe Officers, Chirurgions, &c.

Without Sir Robert Harpoole this official list names nine individuals, the exact same as the list in *Letters from Ireland*. There are two further significant pieces of information that can be gleaned from this 'legitimate' parliament publication. Firstly, the writer does not clearly say (although it is a matter of interpretation) that the list is Cromwell's own and secondly, and more importantly, this list *does not* include the words 'and many inhabitants' at the end. So if one were to interpret that this was Cromwell's personally-written list, the phrase is not included. Compared to other newsbooks that week, *Severall Proceedings* was as official a government publication as you could get. It directly recorded the proceedings in the House of Commons and transcribed them for posterity. There the matter might have ended were it not for the fact that on 2 October Parliament ordered those same letters to be printed and published with a slight, yet seismic, difference. So it is obvious as to why both Carlyle and Firth would suggest that the phrase was added later by the printer (while not painting the full picture) when they perhaps should have said by persons unknown.

The Kingdom's Weekly Intelligencer (Richard Collings or Capt Thomas Audley)

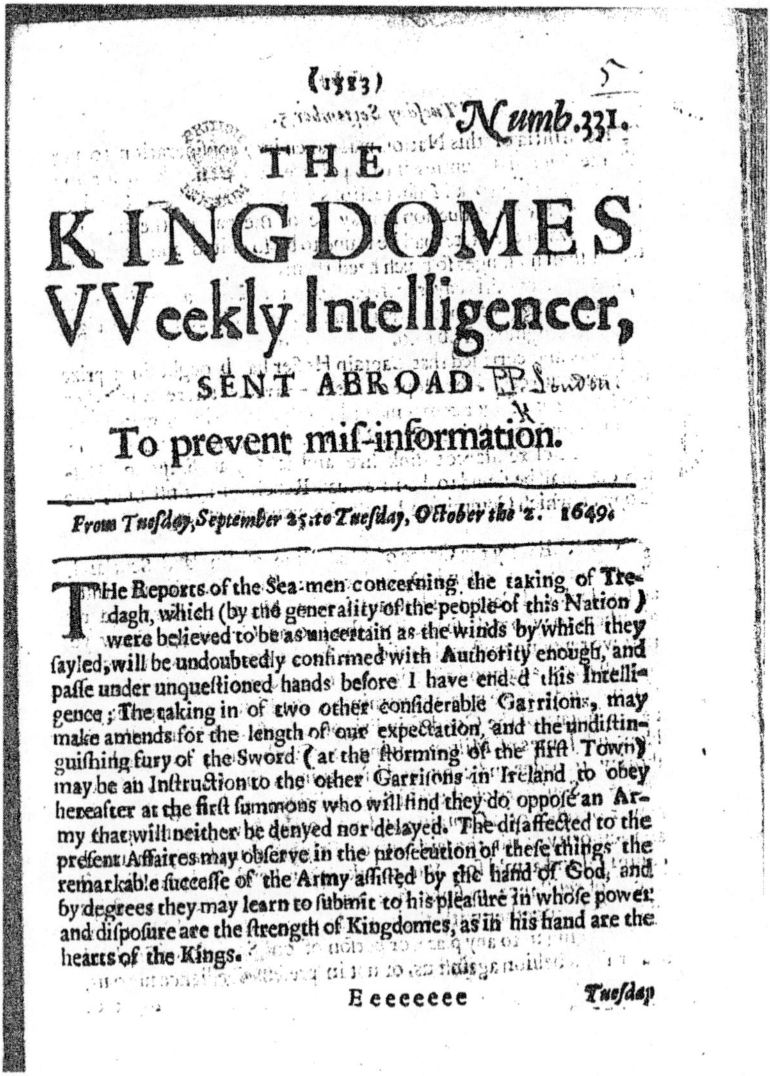

(1313)

Numb. 331.

THE
KINGDOMES
VVeekly Intelligencer,
SENT ABROAD
To prevent mis-information.

From Tuesday, September 25. to Tuesday, October the 2. 1649.

THe Reports of the Sea-men concerning the taking of Tre-
dagh, which (by the generality of the people of this Nation)
were believed to be as uncertain as the winds by which they
sayled, will be undoubtedly confirmed with Authority enough, and
passe under unquestioned hands before I have ended this Intelli-
gence; The taking in of two other considerable Garrisons, may
make amends for the length of our expectation, and the undistin-
guishing fury of the Sword (at the storming of the first Town)
may be an Instruction to the other Garrisons in Ireland to obey
hereafter at the first summons who will find they do oppose an Ar-
my that will neither be denyed nor delayed. The disaffected to the
present Affaires may observe in the prosecution of these things the
remarkable successe of the Army assisted by the hand of God, and
by degrees they may learn to submit to his pleasure in whose power
and disposure are the strength of Kingdomes, as in his hand are the
hearts of the Kings.

Eeeeeee *Tuesday*

(5)

vernour, they were some seven or eight ..., Ormonds being one under the command of Sir Edmond verney. I doe not beleeve, neither do I heare that any Officer escaped with his life, save only one Lieutenant, who I heare going to the Enemy, said, That he was the only man that escaped of all the Garrison.

The enemy were filled upon this with much terrour; and truly I believe this bitternesse will save much effusion of blood through the good hand of God; I wish that all honest hearts may give the glory of this to God alone, to whom indeed the praise of this mercy only belongs: For instruments they were very inconsiderable the work throughout.

We are marching the Army to Dublin, which we hope will be here to morrow night, where we desire to recruit with victuall, and then shall (God willing) advance towards the Southerne designe (you know what) onely we think Wexford will be our first undertaking in order to the other: I desire you to let us have the continuance of your assistance; I thought good to give you notice hereof to prevent inconveniencie; and to the end the ships may ride it out in Kingsaile, as far as God gives them leave, and they are possibly able to doe. I hope we shall begin our march on Thursday or Friday morning next at the farthest.

Captain brandley did with 40 or 50 of his men, very gallantly storme a Tenalia; for which he deserves the thankes of the State.

Septemb. 16. 1649. O. CROMWELL.

Monday October 1.

THis day the Confirmation of the great successe which it hath pleased God to give the Lord Governour of Ireland was received which was more particularly thus: The great Ordnance being brought on Sunday September the fourteenth, on Monday they played against the Town with great violence; about foure in the afternoone the Storme began: our men entred the Towne with brave Resolution, and were stoutly opposed, and inforced to retreat; Whereupon the Lord Governour on foot did bring them on in his own person encouraged, by whose great example, the Souldiers minded not the danger, but strove who should exceed one another

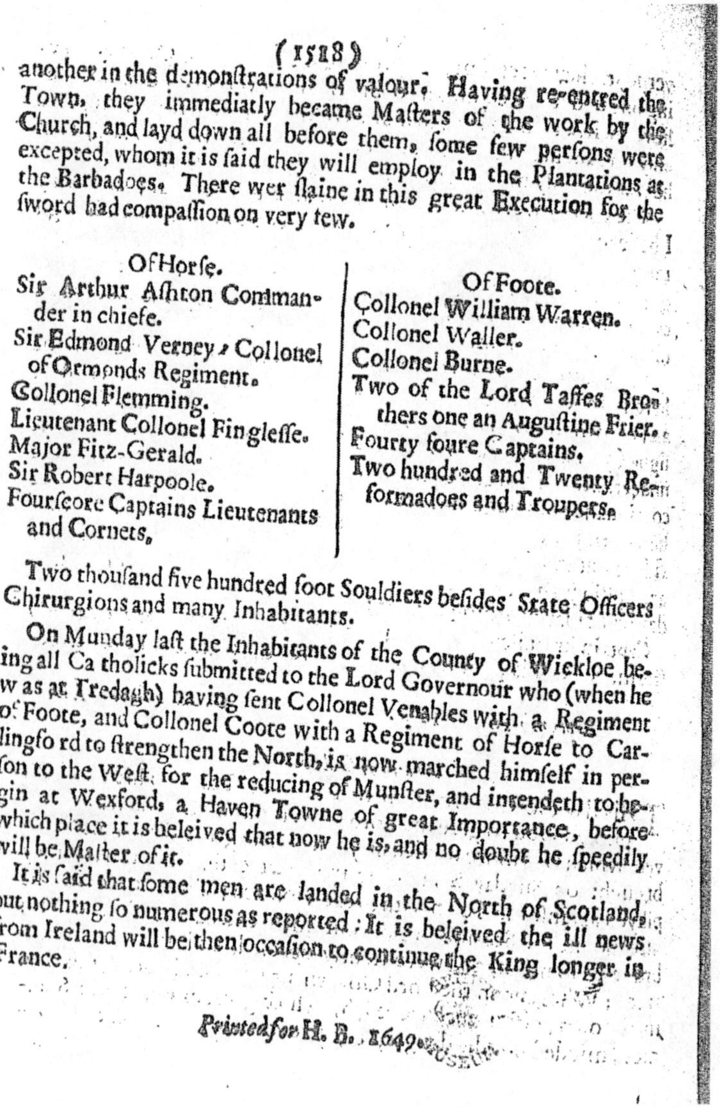

(1518)

another in the demonstrations of valour. Having re-entred the Town, they immediatly became Masters of the work by the Church, and layd down all before them, some few persons were excepted, whom it is said they will employ in the Plantations at the Barbadoes. There wer slaine in this great Execution for the sword had compassion on very few.

Of Horse.

Sir Arthur Ashton Commander in chiefe.
Sir Edmond Verney, Collonel of Ormonds Regiment.
Collonel Flemming.
Lieutenant Collonel Finglesse.
Major Fitz-Gerald.
Sir Robert Harpoole.
Fourscore Captains Lieutenants and Cornets.

Of Foote.

Collonel William Warren.
Collonel Waller.
Collonel Burne.
Two of the Lord Taffes Brothers one an Augustine Frier.
Fourty foure Captains.
Two hundred and Twenty Reformadoes and Troupers.

Two thousand five hundred foot Souldiers besides State Officers Chirurgions and many Inhabitants.

On Munday last the Inhabitants of the County of Wickloe being all Ca tholicks submitted to the Lord Governour who (when he was at Tredagh) having sent Collonel Venables with a Regiment of Foote, and Collonel Coote with a Regiment of Horse to Carlingford to strengthen the North, is now marched himself in person to the West, for the reducing of Munster, and intendeth to begin at Wexford, a Haven Towne of great Importance, before which place it is beleived that now he is, and no doubt he speedily will be Master of it.

It is said that some men are landed in the North of Scotland, but nothing so numerous as reported: It is beleived the ill news from Ireland will be then occasion to continue the King longer in France.

Printed for H. B. 1649.

The Kingdom's Weekly Intelligencer is a newsbook whose authorship is also unclear although it is generally attributed to either Richard Collings or Captain Thomas Audley, the latter being imprisoned along with publisher Robert White when it was censured. In the edition of Tuesday 25 September to Tuesday 2

October the writer attempts caution for this week and is wary of the information in the letter from Peters, which he has, but refuses to publish:

> Friday September 28. The business of this pen being as I have alwayes said and declare unto you the actions in the field, I have for the most part waved the Parliament news, and shall continue until I am better satisfied with what safety (in relation to their counciles) this pen may walk upon this paper, which I conceive was never more uncertaine than at this present. And truly for my own part, if I had their own journal lying before me, I should forebeare to give you account thereof. I shall also forebeare in this place, to give you the Letters of Master Peters concerning the taking of Tredagh. In regard he saith that at the storming of the town, there were none spared. I shall give you therefore in the roome thereof the letter from the Lord Governour himself, and affixe it for my next day's Intelligence, which indeed is able to make any dayes Intelligence most remarkable.

The next day (Saturday 29 September) the writer then transcribes Cromwell's letter to Bradshaw in full but does not publish the list of the defenders of Drogheda that follows Parliament's printing of this letter in *Letters from Ireland,* which if it were Cromwell's own, one might have expected him to do.

By Monday 1 October either Collings or Audley had gotten their hands on the list of officers and soldiers slain and the news for that exact day reads as follows:

> This day the Confirmation of the great successe which it hath pleased God to give the Lord Governour of Ireland was received, which was more particularly thus: the great ordnance being brought on Sunday September the fourteenth, on Monday they played against the town with great violence.

About foure in the afternoone the storme began, our men entered the towne with brave resolution, and were stoutly opposed, and inforced to retreat. Whereupon the Lord Governour on foot did bring them on in his own person, encouraged by whose great example, the soldiers minded not the danger, but strove who should exceed one another in the demonstrations of valour. Having re-entered the town they immediately became masters of the works by the church and layd down all before them, some few persons were excepted, whom it is said they will employ at the plantations at the Barbados. There were slain in this great execution, for the sword had compassion on very few:

Of Horse	Of Foote
Sir Arthur Ashton Commander in chiefe	Collonel William Warren
Sir Edmund verney. Collonel of Ormond's Regiment	Collonel Waller
	Collonel Burne
Collonel Flemming	Two of the Lord Taffe's brothers
Lieutenant Collonel Finglesse	one an Augustine Frier
Major Fitz-Gerald	Forty foure Captains
Sir Robert Harpoole	Two hundred and Twenty Fourscore Captains, Lieutenants Reformadoes and Troupers And Cornets.

Two thousand five hundred foot soldiers besides State Officers, Chirurgions and many inhabitants.

Harpoole makes this list giving a total of ten named persons, and the writer includes the critical three-word phrase.

A Perfect Diurnall of Some Passages in Parliament
(Samuel Pecke)

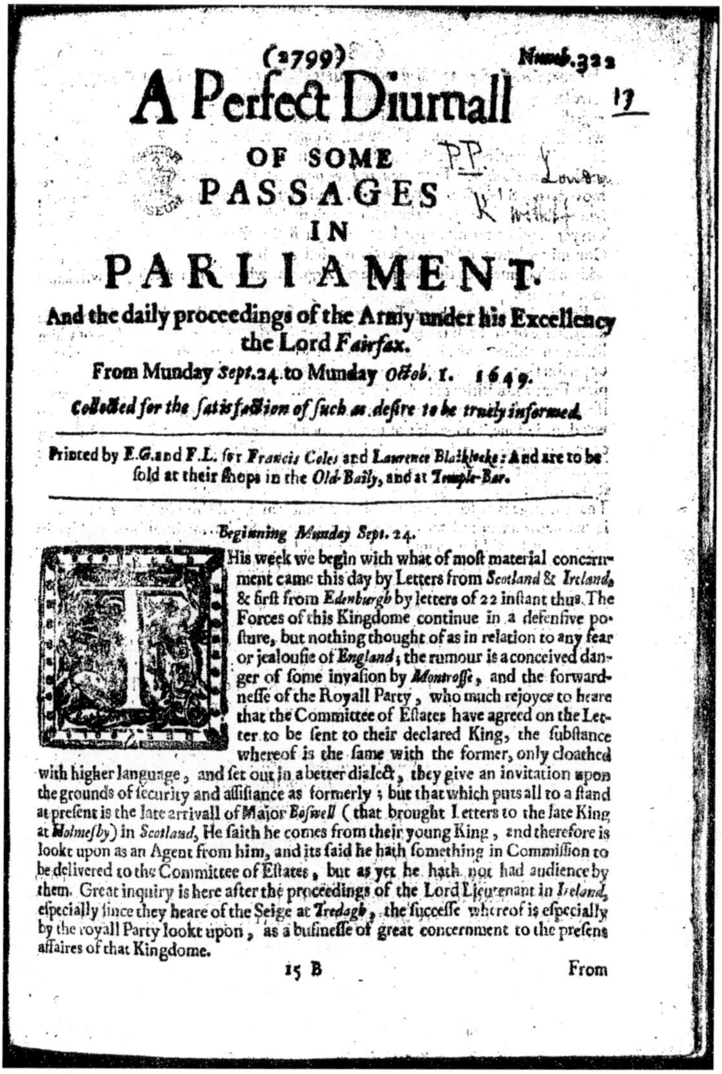

(2799) Numb. 322

A Perfect Diurnall OF SOME PASSAGES IN PARLIAMENT.

And the daily proceedings of the Army under his Excellency the Lord *Fairfax*.

From Munday *Sept.* 24. to Munday *Octob.* 1. 1649.

Collected for the satisfaction of such as desire to be truely informed.

Printed by E.G. and F.L. for *Francis Coles* and *Lawrence Blaiklocke*: And are to be sold at their shops in the *Old-Baily*, and at *Temple-Bar*.

Beginning Munday Sept. 24.

This week we begin with what of most material concernment came this day by Letters from *Scotland* & *Ireland*, & first from *Edenburgh* by letters of 22 instant thus. The Forces of this Kingdome continue in a defensive posture, but nothing thought of as in relation to any fear or jealousie of *England*; the rumour is a conceived danger of some invasion by *Montrosse*, and the forwardnesse of the Royall Party, who much rejoyce to heare that the Committee of Estates have agreed on the Letter to be sent to their declared King, the substance whereof is the same with the former, only cloathed with higher language, and set out in a better dialect, they give an invitation upon the grounds of security and assistance as formerly; but that which puts all to a stand at present is the late arrivall of Major *Boswell* (that brought Letters to the late King at *Holmesby*) in *Scotland*, He saith he comes from their young King, and therefore is lookt upon as an Agent from him, and its said he hath something in Commission to be delivered to the Committee of Estates, but as yet he hath not had audience by them. Great inquiry is here after the proceedings of the Lord Lieutenant in *Ireland*, especially since they heare of the Seige at *Tredagh*, the successe whereof is especially by the royall Party lookt upon, as a businesse of great concernment to the presens affaires of that Kingdome.

15 B From

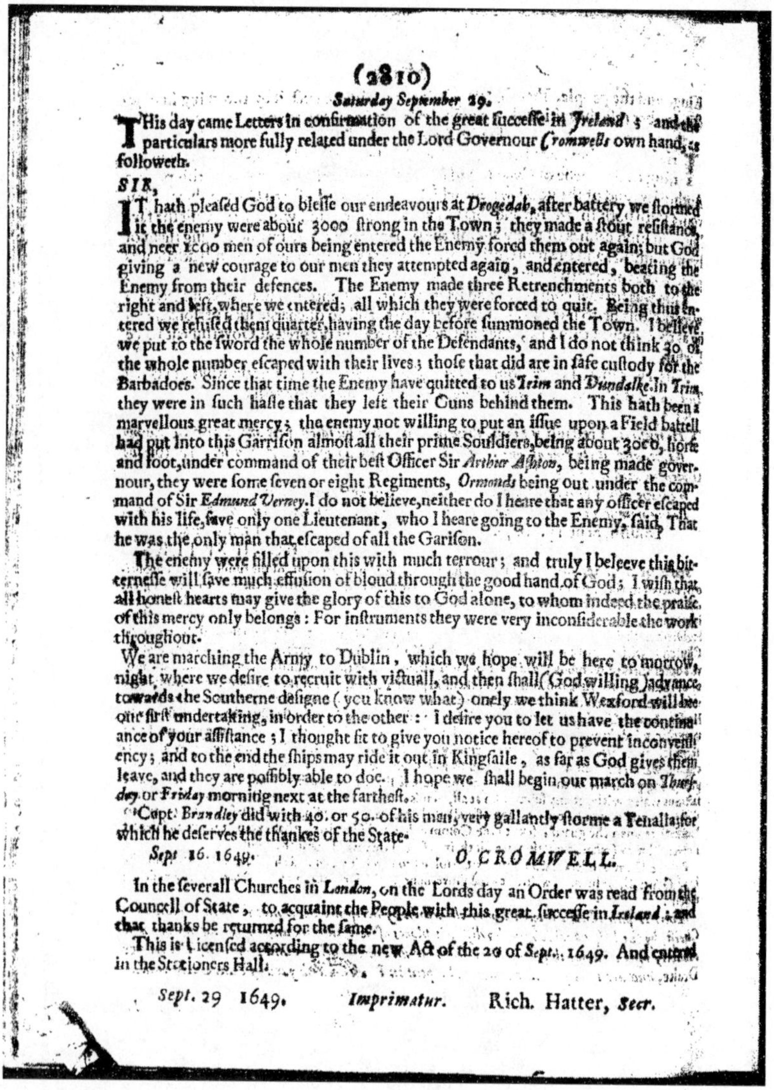

(2810)

Saturday September 29.

THis day came Letters in confirmation of the great successe in *Ireland*; and the particulars more fully related under the Lord Governour *Cromwells* own hand, as followeth.

SIR,

IT hath pleased God to blesse our endeavours at *Drogedah*, after battery we stormed it, the enemy were about 3000 strong in the Town; they made a stout resistance, and neer 1000 men of ours being entered the Enemy forced them out again; but God giving a new courage to our men they attempted again, and entered, beating the Enemy from their defences. The Enemy made three Retrenchments both to the right and left, where we entered; all which they were forced to quit. Being thus entered we refused them quarter, having the day before summoned the Town. I believe we put to the sword the whole number of the Defendants, and I do not think 30 of the whole number escaped with their lives; those that did are in safe custody for the Barbadoes. Since that time the Enemy have quitted to us *Trim* and *Dundalke*. In *Trim*, they were in such haste that they left their Guns behind them. This hath been a marvellous great mercy; the enemy not willing to put an issue upon a Field battell had put into this Garrison almost all their prime Souldiers, being about 3000, horse and foot, under command of their best Officer Sir *Arthur Ashton*, being made governour, they were some seven or eight Regiments, *Ormonds* being out under the command of Sir *Edmund Verney*. I do not believe, neither do I heare that any officer escaped with his life, save only one Lieutenant, who I heare going to the Enemy, said, That he was the only man that escaped of all the Garison.

The enemy were filled upon this with much terrour; and truly I beleeve this bitternesse will save much effusion of bloud through the good hand of God; I wish that all honest hearts may give the glory of this to God alone, to whom indeed the praise of this mercy only belongs: For instruments they were very inconsiderable the work throughout.

We are marching the Army to Dublin, which we hope will be here to morrow night, where we desire to recruit with victuall, and then shall (God willing) advance towards the Southerne designe (you know what) onely we think Wexford will bee our first undertaking, in order to the other: I desire you to let us have the continuance of your assistance; I thought fit to give you notice hereof to prevent inconveniency; and to the end the ships may ride it out in Kingsaile, as far as God gives them leave, and they are possibly able to doe. I hope we shall begin our march on *Thursday* or *Friday* morning next at the farthest.

Capt. *Brandley* did with 40. or 50. of his men, very gallantly storme a Tenalia; for which he deserves the thankes of the State.

Sept 16. 1649. *O. CROMWELL.*

In the severall Churches in *London*, on the Lords day an Order was read from the Councell of State, to acquaint the People with this great successe in *Ireland*; and that thanks be returned for the same.

This is Licensed according to the new Act of the 20 of *Sept.* 1649. And entred in the Stationers Hall.

Sept. 29 1649. *Imprimatur.* Rich. Hatter, *Secr.*

Scrivener Samuel Pecke is said to be a patriarch of English journalism and is credited with being the first English journalist to write purely in English. He was known to be a balanced writer and was imprisoned twice in his career, firstly in 1642 and then in 1646. He wrote *A Perfect Diurnall of Some Passages in Parliament*. In his edition of Mon 24 September – Monday 1 October he publishes Cromwell's letter of 16 September pointing out that these are categorically the words of Cromwell himself.

(2811) Numb. 323 17

A Perfect Diurnall OF SOME PASSAGES IN PARLIAMENT

And the daily proceedings of the Army under his Excellency the Lord *Fairfax*.

From Monday *October* 1 to Monday *October* 8 24. 1649

Collected for the satisfaction of such as desire to be truly informed

Printed by *E. G.* and *F. L.* for *Francis Coles* and *Lawrence Blaicklocke*: And are to be ſold at their ſhops in the *Old-Baily*, and at *Temple-Bar*.

Beginning Monday October 1

This day by Letters ſeverall from hands, the particulars of the late great ſucceſſe of our forces in *Ireland* was fully certified, This accompt thereof from an eminent perſon in that Army, take it as followeth.

The firſt place we marched to, when we left *Dublin*, was to *Droheda* before which wee ſate down the third of *September* being Munday, and for want of our Ordnance and other proviſions for battery, which could not get to us, becauſe of contrary winds, we continued there till the Munday morning, following before we began to batter. We plaid our Ordnance all that day, and the next day, till 5. of the clok in the after noone, in the meane time we ſent over the water to the other ſide of the Town (to hinder releif from comming to them and to prevent their running away) 2 000. horſe and foot, we made two conſiderable breaches for breadth in the wall on that ſide towards *Dublin*, but not ſo deep as we deſired, which was a great hinderance to our entring into the Town, about 5. of the clock in the afternoon that Tueſday, we began to ſtorm, the Regiments of foot drawn out for that work was Col. *Huſons*, Col. *Ewers*, and Col. *Caſtles*, we could not at firſt go on with horſe, becauſe the breach was not low enough, ſo that our foot was forſt to engage both with their horſe and foot, our men at firſt were on with much courage and reſolution, and entred the Town, but by reaſon of the numerouſneſſe and ſtoutneſſe of the Enemy, who maintained their ground as

15 C gallantly

2694

Tueſday October 2

LEtters came this day further from the Lord Governour of *Ireland* to the Parl. Councell of State; and Army, of the great ſucceſſe at *Drogheda* and other proceedings in *Ireland*, the particulars have been largly printed already, yet ſome things may be added worthy the obſervation which take in this enſuing abſtract.

Munday *September* 9 our Batteries began to play againſt *Drogheda*, Summons was ſent to Sir *Arthur Aſhton* Governour to deliver, but he returned an unſatiſfactory Anſwer, That day we proceeded to beat down the Steeple of the Church on the South ſide the Town, and a Tower neer the ſame place, The next day we prepared to make breaches aſſaultable and ſo to ſtorme, accordingly our Guns after two or threed hundre ſhot beat down the Corner Tower, and opened two reaſonalbe good breaches n the Eaſt and South wall, Tueſday about five in the evening, we begun the ſtorm, and after ſome hot diſpute, we entred about ſeven or eight hundred men, the enemy diſputing it very ſtiffely, and through the advantages of the place, our men were forced to retreat quite out of the breach, not with out ſome conſiderable loſſe, Colonell *Caſſell* being there ſhot in the head, whereof he preſently dyed, our men thus forced to recoyle, being encouraged to recover their loſſe, they made a ſecond attempt, wherein God was pleaſed to animate them that they got ground of the enemy, forced him to quit his entrenchments, and after a very hot diſpute, the enemy having both horſe and foot, and we only foot within the Wall, the enemy gave ground, and our men became Maſters though with much difficulty, the enemy retreated divers of them into the Mill-Mount, a place very ſtrong and of difficult acceſſe, being exceeding high, having a good graft and ſtrongly Palliſadoed, the Governour Sir *Arthur Aſhton*, and divers conſiderable Officers being there our men getting up to them, put them all to the Sword, having command not to ſpare any that were in Arms in the Town, that night they put to the Sword about two thouſand men, divers of the Officers and Souldiers being fled over the Bridge into the other part of the Town, where about one hundred of them poſſeſſed Saint *Peters* Church Steeple, ſome the Weſt gate, and others, a round ſtrong Tower next the gate, cal'd *St. Sundays*, theſe being ſummond to yeild to mercy, refuſed, whereupon order was given the Steeple of Saint Peters Church to be fired, the next day the other two Towers were ſummoned in one of which was about ſix or ſeven ſcore, but they refuſed to yeeld themſelves, and we knowing that hunger muſt compel them ſet only good guards to ſecure them from running away, from one of the Towers, notwithſtanding their condition, they killed and wounded ſome of our men, when they ſubmitted, their Officers were knockt on the head, and every tenth man of the Soldiers killed, and the reſt Shipped for the Barbadoes the Soldiers in the other Town were all ſpared, as to their lives only, and ſhipped likewiſe for the *Barbadoes*.

The Officers and Souldiers of this garriſon were the flower of all their Army, and their great expectation was, that our attempting this place, would put fair to ruine us, they being confident of the Reſolution of their men and the advantage of the place; if we had divided our force into two quarters, to have beſieged the North Town and the South Town, we could not have had ſuch a correſpondency be-

between the two part of our Army, but that they might have chosen to have brought their Army, and have fought with which part they pleased, and at the same time have made a salley with two thousand men upon us, and have left their walls manned, they having in the Town the numbers specified in this inclosed, but some say neer fourthousand.

It is remarkable, that these people at the first set up the Masse in some places of the town that had been Monasteries, but afterwards grew so insolent, that the last *Lords* day before the Storm the Protestants were thrust out of the great Church, called *St. Peters* and they had publique Masse there, and in this very place neare One thousand of them were put to the Sword, flying thither for safety all their Fryers were knockt, on the head promiscuously, but two, the one of which was father *Peter Taaff*, (Brother to the Lord *Taaff*) whom the Soldiers took the next day and made an end of. the other was taken in the Round Tower, under the repute of lieutenant, and when he understood that the Officers in that Tower had no quarter, he confessed he was a Fryer, but that did not save him.

A great deal of losse in this businesse, fell upon Col. *Huson*; col. *Cassel*, and colonell *Ewers* Regiments, Col. *Ewers* having two Field-Offickrs in his Regiment shot, colonel *Cassel* and a captain of his Regiment slain, col. *Hewsons* capt. Leut. slain not a 100 in the whole of ours slain but many wounded.

Thus is that strong place overcame to the terour of the enemy in all parts: As for the seasonablenesse of it, and the necessity of taking the way we did. it appears first, because provisions would have fail'd had we made a long work, besides, in Sir *Arthur Astons* pocket was found a Letter wherein *Ormond*, *Castlehaven*, & others write that they would, if they held out but to the thirteenth, releive them by raising the Seige, and say the same letters, with 4000 horse and *Owen Roes* foote, which they presumed upon: and as we are assured, are since joyned with them, but too late, for this place, what they may do afterward; this place being taken two dayes before: and though some are of opinion; that the enemies rage will be the greater, by the slaughter at Tredagh, yet we find the terror great, that is upon them *Trim* being quit before Maior *Coddugin* could come to it. *Ormond* sending a Party to re-inforce it but comming too late and seeing ours flee its very advantagious to us for quarters, and out of that respect it was the next place to be attatched. *Dundalk* did the like, only the castle which with other places, col. *Venables* being sent with horse and foot to reduce, hath frighted them out of *Carlingford* and the *Nurey* also; the North being now at our devotion, except *Belfast*, *Carickfergus* *Carlemount*, and *Colerain*, of whom we hope to be masters before we go to winter Quarters; we take notice, that the *Sunday*. and but two dayes before *Tredagh* was taken, Masse was said in the great Churchs of the town, the one was be.t bown the other blowne up *Mark Trever* with his strong resolutions for Royalty, is with a vessel kept for that end fled to the Isle of *man*, and more; no doubt will follow. *Ormond* & *Inchiquin* are at odds, by reason of the conjunction with *Owen Row*. who with the Marquis *Clanrickard*, *Ards*, and *Clauboys* is marched to *Kilkenny* where he tels the councell that if they will not put him in capacity to fight the enemy: he will quit his command,

Inchiquin saith, he will go, and secure his party of *Munster* as well as he can,

ra

(2815)

rather then joyn with the bloody Rebels. The Lord Lieutenant is marched from hence, having firſt muſtered our men, refreſhed them, and taken proviſions with him: we do not go ſo many South as we went North; for though we loſt but few, we beleive not above 100 ſlain outright; yet it could not be expected, but that ſome be wounded, and others ſick; and of them the main ſufferers were of *Venables*, *Huſons*, and *Ewers* Regiments. Whether we ſhall attach *Kilkenny* or *Wexford*, time will ſhew.

A Liſt of the principall Officers ſlain in Drogedah.

Sir *Arthur Aſhton*, Governour. Sir *Edmund Verney*, Lieu. Col. to the L. of *Ormond*.

The Horſe commanded by Major *Butler*.

Lieu. col. *Finglas*; Cap. *Plunket* the Lord *Deſmes* ſonne, and Col. *Fleming*, ſlaine.

Of Foot.

Col. *Warren*, Col. *Wall*. Cap. *Butler*, Major *Tempeſt*, Major *Fitz-Gerald*, Major *Wilkins*, Lieu. col. *Gray*, —— *Stevens*, Cap. Lieu. *Street*, *Cooly*, *Bagnall*, Captaines.

Col. *Burne*, Li. col. *Boile*, Major *Doudle*, Cap. *Croker*, *Benſt*, *Fiſher*, *Geffes*, *Bernes*, Captaines. The Lord *Taffs* brother, a Frier of the Order of S. *Auguſtin*.

In all 44 Captaines, all their Lieutenants and Enſignes, 220 Reformadoes and Troopers, 2500 Foot ſouldiers.

A Liſt of ſuch Forces as was in Drogedah, *before it was taken.*

Lord of *Ormonds* Regiment	400	Lord of *Weſtmeaths* Regiment	200
Colonel *Burnes* Regiment	400	Sir *James Dillonkey*	200
Colonel *Warrens* Regiment	900	Horſe	200
Colonel *Walls* Regiment	800	In all	3100

Ordered, that Thurſday the firſt of *November* next be appointed for a day of publique Thankſgiving, to be obſerved in all the Churches and Chappels within *England* and *Wales* to render thanks to Almighty God for his great mercy in giving ſuch wonderfull ſucceſſes to the Parliaments forces in *Ireland*.

On Munday laſt the Inhabitants of the County of *Wicklee* (being all Catholickes) ſubmitted to the Lord Governour, who (having ſent Col. *Venables* with a Regiment of Foot. and Col. *Coot* with a Regiment of Horſe to *Carlingford*, to ſtrengthen the North) is now marched himſelfe in perſon into the Weſt, for reducing of *Munſter*, and intended to begin at *Wexford*, a haven Town of great importance, and no doubt he will ſpeedily be maſter of it.

Newcaſtle, Sept. 20. Six more of the Moſſ-troopers (beſides thoſe I gave you an account of in the laſt) are taken, & carried to the Goale at *Carliſle*, where they are to be tried with their fellows that came in before them. It is reported here that the Scots diſpatch M. *Windham* away with a Letter to their declared King, but tis thought to as little purpoſe as that they ſent before. The Malignant party do now hang down their heads to heare of the proſperous proceedings of the Lord governour of *Ireland*, and ſome of them do now confeſſe that the great expectation they had of *Ormonds* party is fruſtrate: and a Captain of that party, who was lately taken at Sea, doth ingeniouſly confeſſe, that the Prince his Fleet are in as diſtracted a condition by ſea, as *Ormonds* and *Inchequins* forces are by land. We are in a very peaceable condition in theſe parts.

15 C 2 From

Pecke's edition of Monday 1 October to Monday 8 October (another of the five newsbooks licensed by Hatter at this time) carries an account of the taking of Drogheda from an un-named 'eminent person in that army'. So we know from Pecke that as well as the letter from Peters and the letters from Cromwell, that other letters had by now (Monday 1 October) reached London. This account was written by a Parliamentarian officer and is quite detailed. Pecke publishes the officer's letter on his front page indicating that he had received it on Monday 1 October. Introducing the letter Pecke writes:

> This day by letters from severall hands, the particulars of the late great success of our forces in Ireland was fully certified. This account thereof from an eminent person in that army, take it as followeth. The first place we marched to, when we left Dublin, was to Drogheda before which wee sate down the third of September being Monday, and for want of our Ordnance and other provisions for battery, which could not get to us, because of contrary winds, we continued there till the Munday morning, following before we began to batter. We plaid our Ordnance all that day, and the next day till 5 of the clok in the after no one, in the meane time we sent over the water to the other side of the Town (to hinder relief from coming to them and to prevent their running away, 2000 horse and foot. We made two considerable breaches for breadth in the wall on that side towards Dublin but not so deep as we desired, which was a great hindrance to our entering into the Town. About 5 of the clock in the afternoon that Tuesday we began to storm, the Regiments of foot drawn out for that work was Col Hewson's Col Ewer's and Col Castle's. We could not at first go on with horse, because the breach was not low enough so that our foot was forst to engage both with their horse and foot, our men at first went on with much courage and resolution, and entered the Town, but by reason of the numerousenesse and stoutnesse of the Enemy, who maintained their ground as gallantly as ever men did...there was in the Town of the Enemy at least 3,000 horse and foot,

> who were all slain, they were the choicest men in the whole army and laid there on purpose to give our army a defeat, but the Lord be praised the pit which they digged for us they fell into themselves. It is reported by all that did see it to be as hard and as desperate a service as hath been encountered with since the war began.

This is a military account written by a military man with no reference to civilians or inhabitants whatsoever. Interestingly, Pecke reports that there are now *letters* in circulation about the siege of Drogheda by several hands and this is still before Cromwell's letters are read out and published. Later on in the same edition Pecke confirms that he has letters from several hands with information that was not contained in either Cromwell's or Peters' letters when he says, 'For the affaires of Ireland, besides what is formerly mentioned we have in severall letters, that Lieu Col Saunders, Major Disney, Captain Swaston and most of the Officers of Col Ewers Regiment were wounded at the storming of Tredagh, and Captain Puckle bruised.' The following day (2 October) Pecke reveals that he has now received copies of Cromwell's letters and he announces the news thus;

> Letters came this day further from the Lord Governour of Ireland to the Parl. Council of State, and army of the great success at Drogheda and other proceedings in Ireland, the particulars of which have been largely printed already, yet some things may be added worthy of the observation which take in this ensuing extract.

Pecke then doesn't so much publish the full tract of Cromwell's letter to Lenthall but simply extracts of the letter. In fact he also includes information that is not published in the official version (*Letters from Ireland*) which was obviously not written by Cromwell, as it speaks of the Lord Lieutenant in the third person and he quite mixes it in with Cromwell's letter. The extra information could be from his correspondent whose account of the assault he reproduces on the front page. Directly after this narrative from the anonymous source Pecke then prints the two lists, the defenders and the slain. With no clear separation from the narrative to the lists it is tempting to suggest that this writer was responsible for both lists, (as Morrill, O'Siochrú, and McElligott, among others, have done with the two lists inserted into *Letters from Ireland* by attributing the separate lists to the writer of a letter therein. The methodology is the same.) But that might be one leap too far. Certainly the two lists are printed some distance away from the extracts from Cromwell's letters. Pecke's list reads as follows:

A List of the principall Officers Slain in Droghedah
Sir Arthur Ashton, Governour. Sir Edmund Verney, Lieu. Col to the L of Ormond.

The Horse commanded by Major Butler
Lieu col Finglas, Cap Plunket the Lord Desmes sonne, (Could be Dunsany) and Col. Fleming, slaine

Of Foot
Col Warren, Col Wall, Cap Butler, Major Tempest, Major Fitzgerald,
Major Wilkins, Lieu.col Gray ——-Stevens, Cap Lieu Street
Cooly, Bagnall, Captains

Col Burne, Li. Col Boile, Major Doudle, Cap. Croker, Benss, Fisher, Geffes, Barnes, Captaines. The Lord Taff's brother, a Frier of the Order of S. Augusten.

In all 44 captains, all their Lieutenants and Ensignes, 220 Reformadoes and troopers, 2,500 Foot Souldiers.

Aside from the fact that Pecke does not print the phrase 'and many inhabitants,' the second most significant thing that can be said about Pecke's transcription of the list is that it contains 26 named individuals. It is easily the most complete list of them all. But rather than provide answers it is hard to completely contextualise the story of the list here especially with Pecke's additions. Because of the fact that the same numbers (44 captains, 220 reformadoes, 2,500 foot soldiers, etc.), that the chronology of names and the words used are always the same, it is difficult to conclude that this list is from a different writer, although it is entirely possible that Pecke adds names that others don't have to the original list where nine or ten named persons appear with or without Harpoole. He certainly added text to Cromwell's letter without batting an eyelid, or explaining that there was a difference. This just highlights that the typographical niceties such as clear demarcation lines, headings and sub-headings to announce a tract of text were simply not universally adhered to and the random nature of text and passage layout oftentimes adds to the confusion in the interpretation of these publications.

The Moderate Intelligencer (John Dillingham)

(2287)

Numb. 237.

THE Moderate Intelligencer: Communicating Martiall Affairs to the KINGDOM of ENGLAND.

From *Thurſday*, *Septemb.* 27, *to Thurſday*, *Octobber* 4. 1649.

IT may not be amiſs to begin this with the arrivall of the long expected news of the victorious proceedings of the Lord Lieutenant of *Ireland*.

When right and victory goes together, it makes the favour the greater, as well as it alwayes ſhews the parties loſing, to be in diſpleaſure with the giver of Victories. It was ſaid of a great King that his Counſels had of late been worſe then formerly, for his ſucceſſe hath not been ſo good, it's certainly true of the Parliameuts enemies who ſeeme to be infatuate: the conſideration whereof, with not in the leaſt courting, were ſufficient to make the ſtrongeſt in affection ſit looſe, whereas victory muſt needs increaſe friends, and behold a Victory remarkable, firſt diſcovered by a Letter of Mr. *Peters*, the contents whereof might well be omitted, having been divulged in a whole ſheet, but in regard the numbers ſlain on both ſides are ſo ſtrong; *viz.* that more were ſlain of the beſieged then the beſiegers in the taking *Tredagh*, *viz.* 3000 of the Rebels, and but 60 of the Beſiegers, it's probable, the loſſe was equall durieg the enemies ſtanding, and that the reſt were killed not reſiſting, but of this whole action more at the latter end, when poſſible more full intelligence will be come. The fame of this ſucceſſe produced the following Letter from

Dunſtable, September 29.

The ſtrange attempts made by Thieves in theſe parts, and that are brought hither by Tra-

11 G

among which were ſome precious ſtones, the two others were full of *Agnus Dei*, which he preſented from the Pope, which were received with all the ſignes of joy and content, and did let the Cardinall Legate underſtand her high eſteem of his regale, giving him a rich Jewel. and preſents to other of his followers, he tooke leave this night of her, and the ſeventh returned towards *Bologne*, having viſited the day before the St. Cloud of our Lord, and the body of St. *Charles*, he received the complements of Cardinall *Montalto* the Governour, the Dukes of *Maceda* and *Terra nova*, and other Miniſters which he likewiſe viſited.

Behold here a Prince and Prelate in as great or greater pomp then Cardinall *wolſey*, the concomitants of ſome mens Religion conſiſts in having outward glory, pomp, and ſtate, that inriches the people, others in War, bloud, and killing, that depopulates and begers, others, in coveting wealth, and for that end multiplying places, offices; and employments, as it it were not as great an offence to God, to heap up to a mans ſelfe ſeverall employments, as to lay houſe to houſe and land to land, leaving no place for him that is as able and willing to ſerve the State as others, if reaſon go along, the concomitants of the firſt Religion is moſt lovely. *Paris*, *Sept.* 26.

We have here the particulars of the great fight in *Poland*, but not the agreement, the Venetians are beſieged in the City of *Candia* by the Turks, and other evils in that Kingdom are befallen them, the declared King of *Scotland* is up and down in *Britany* and *Normandy*, viewing the ancient poſſeſſions of *william* the Conqueror, not as *Peter* the Hermite did the Holy land, in all probability he expects ſome Ships from *Holland* to arrive for him, as alſo the getting out of Prince *Ruperts* and others from the Iriſh harbours, yet kept in by the Parliament ſhips, with whom he will paſſe ſome whether, but when is uncertain, and the longer the more hazardous. *Dublin*, *Sep.* 22.

There's no queſtion but you will ſee and receive ſeverall relations of our late expedition to *Tredagh*, and indeed from ſeverall hands truth is beſt got forth, not one but many being neceſſary to give a true account of things of this nature; according to the beſt informations gotten receive as followeth.

The 4th. inſtant we ſate down before *Dregedagh* ſtrongly fortified, and well manned, with an expert Governour Sir *Arthur Aſhton*, his men, as before, moſt Iriſh, and ſelect, our Artilery comming by Sea with other neceſſaries, and windes being uncertain, it was, the 10th. before our Batteries were finiſhed, that day we made a ſmall breach, on the 11. a large: yet ſo, as no horſe could enter, nor foot without much difficulty, we being neceſſitated to uſe Ladders in ſome places: About four in the afternoon the aſſault began, and but on the South ſide of the Town, the North being not attempted, we not thinking it diſcretion to divide our Army to both ſides the River, leaſt the enemy ſhould (which we had intelligence he intended) fall upon one part or other, from within and from without; the firſt attempt was upon a Tenalya newly made, and without the wall, which flanked the breach, which was taken without any conſiderable loſs, by a party commanded by valiant Captain *Branley*, whom the Lord Lieut. recommends to Parliament, after which the breach was ſtormed, which held a hot diſpute for a quarter of an houre, each fighting, as if the gaining or loſing thereof had been the loſing or gaining of *Ireland*, and to ſay truth, it was little leſs, as by the ſequell you will finde: the violence of our enemy made our men give back, ſo fierce was the oppoſition, which the Lord Lieu. ſeeing, run on foot to the Souldiers, & encouraged them, which occaſioned the renuing of the charg, and it was done with that reſolution, that they immediatly, carried the town, putting to the Sword as faſt as they could, in which ſlaughter there fell Sir *Arthur Aſhton* a Papiſt, as were moſt of the Garriſon, the reaſon given of his death is ſaid to be the rage of Colonel *Caſtles* Souldiers for the death of their Collonel, alſo for that *Aſhton* gave not a civill anſwer when ſummoned, Sir *Edward Varney* alſo was ſlain, who

who had the charge of the mount, alſo Col. *Fleming*, Lieuten. Col. *Finglas*, Major *Gerald*, Sir *Robert Hartpool*, Captains, Lieutenants, and Cornets of Horſe 80, where their horſe were we know not, probably they went as common men: Of foot, Collonel *William warren*, Col. *waller*, Col. *Burne*, the Lord *Taffs* brother an *Auguſtine* Frier, of Captains and inferiour Officers of foot 44, 220 Reformadoes, 2000 within the Town were put to the Sword, the reſt that had that kinde of execution leapt over the wall, who were about 500, which make in all about 2900, and being all Papiſts, no doubt, and many of them of that party call'd the Toryes, who uſed to rob and kill without-mercie, and no doubt were of that wretched party that kill'd ſo many Proteſtants at the beginning of the Rebellion, and ſo God the avenger of murther (which it is to kill contrary to his rule of direction) hath met with them, and ſooner or later will with all ſuch bloudy minded men. Thus is that ſtrong place overcome to the terrour of the enemy in all parts: As for the ſeaſonableneſs of it, and the neceſsity of taking the way we did, it appears firſt, becauſe proviſions would have fail'd had we made a long work, beſides, in Sir *Arthur Aſhtons* pocket was found a Letter wherein *Ormond*, *Caſtlehaven*, and others write that they would, if they held out but to the thirteenth, relieve them by raiſing the ſiege, and ſay the ſame Letters, with 4000 horſe and *Owen Roes* foot, which they preſumed upon: and as we are aſſured, are ſince joyned with them, but too late, for this place, what they may do afterward; this place being taken two days before: and though ſome are of opinion, that the Enemies rage will be the greater, by the ſlaughter at *Tredagh*, yet we finde the terror great, that is upon them, *Trim* being quit before Major *Coddugin* could come to it, *Ormond* ſending a Party to re-inforce it, but comming too late, and ſeeing ours flee, it's very advantageous to us for quarters, and out of that reſpect it was the next place to be attached: *Dundalke* did the like, only the Caſtle, which with other places, Collonell *Venables* being ſent with horſe, and foot, to reduce, hath frighted them out of *Carlingford*, and it's ſaid, the *Nurey* alſo: the *North* now being at our devotion, except *Belfaſt*, *Carickfergius*, *Charlemount*, and *Coleraine*: of whom, we hope to be Maſters, before we go to Winter Quarters: we take notice, that the *Sunday*, and but two days before *Tredagh* was taken, Maſſe was ſaid in the great Churches of the Town; when ſuch ſottiſh Idolatry is erected, and on high, the fall, we hope, will ſtill be the greater; and ſo long as our grand Enemy imployes ſuch, we have faith enough to believe we ſhall overcome, theſe two Churches, the one was beat down, the other blown up; let him continue to plow with an Oxe, and an Aſſe; and believe it, he is like to come home by weeping croſſe. *Mark Trevor* with his ſtrong reſolutions for Royalty, is with a Veſſell kept for that end, fled to the Iſle of *Man*, and more, no doubt, will follow: *Ormond* and *Inchequin* are at ods, by reaſon of the conjunction with *Owen Row*, who with the Marquis *Clanrickard*, *Ards*, and *Claneboyes*, is marched to *Kilkenney*, where he tells the Councell, that if they will not put him in capacity to fight the Enemy, he will quit his Command: *Inchequin* ſaith, he will go, and ſecure his Party of *Munſter*, as well as he can, rather then joyn with the bloudy Rebels. The Lord Lieutenant is marched from hence, having firſt muſtered our men, refreſhed them, and taken proviſions with him: we do not go ſo many *South*, as we went *North*; for though we loſt but few, we believe not above 100 ſlain, out-right, yet it could not be expected, but that ſome be wounded, and others ſick; and of them, the main ſufferers, were of *Venibles*, *Huſons*, and *Ewers* Regiments; whether we ſhall attach *Kilkenney*, or *wexford*, time will ſhew, and what oppoſition we ſhall meet with by the way, there being many ſtraits, and ſuch as may be defended by a few men againſt many: *wexford* it's poſſible, may be firſt ſet upon, becauſe it's the great Receptacle for Pirates, there being, it's believed, 80 ſuch ſmall Veſſels there, it's double walled

While O'Siochrú cites five newsbooks in *God's Executioner* that print the list, as well as missing *The Kingdom's Faithfull and Impartial Scout,* very significantly he fails to spot a seventh newsbook that also prints it, albeit in narrative form and not laid out in list style. But it is the same list. John Dillingham's *The Moderate Intelligencer* (27 September – 4 October) was published on Thursday 4 October and there is no question that he too publishes the same details of officers and soldiers slain. Dillingham specialised in foreign news, is well-known to have maintained contact with foreign correspondents and was also known for adopting a neutral position. Indeed, it is possible/tempting to propose the suggestion that Dillingham's correspondent is the actual author of this controversial list of officers and soldiers slain and that the other writers simply copied the names of the dead from the lengthy letter and printed them in list form that week. The chronology of names and the death toll details are virtually the same. Tellingly, Dillingham opens his piece with the date:

> Dublin Sep 22. There's no question but you will see and receive severall relations of our late expedition to Tredagh and indeed from severall hands truth is best got forth, not one, but many being necessary to give a true account of things of this nature; according to the best informations gotten, receive as followeth:
>
> The 4th instant we sate down before Drogheda, strongly fortified and well manned with an expert governour Sir Arthur Ashton, his men, as before, most Irish and select, our Artillery coming by sea with other necessaries, and winds being uncertaine, it was the 10th before our batteries were finished, that day we made a small breach, on the 11th, a large, yet so as no horse could enter, nor foot without much difficulty, we being necessitated to use ladders in some places. About four in the afternoon the assault began and but on the South side of the town, the north not being attempted, we not thinking it discretion to divide our army on bothe sides of the river least the enemy should (and we had intelligence that he

> had intended) fall upon one part or other, from within and from without. The violence of the enemy made our men give back, so fierce was the opposition, which the Lord lieutenant seeing, ran on foot to the soldiers and encouraged them, which occasioned the renewing of the charge, and it was done with such resolution that they immediately carried the town, putting to the sword as fast as they could. In which slaughter there fell Sir Arthur Ashton, a Papist, as were most of the garrison, the reason given of his death is said to be the rage of Colonel Castle's soldiers for the death of their colonel, also for that Ashton gave not a civill answer when summoned. Sir Edward Varney also was slain, who had the charge of the mount, also Colonel Fleming, Lieutenant colonel Finglass, Major Gerald, Sir Robert Hartpool, captains, lieutenants and cornets of horse 80 – where there horse where we know not, probably they went as common men. Of foot, Colonel William Waller, Colonel Warren, Colonel Burne, the Lord Taaf's brother, an Augustine Frier, of captains and inferior officers of foot, 44, 220 reformadoes, 2,000 within the town were put to the sword, the rest that had that kind of execution leapt over the wall, who are about 500, which makes in all about 2,900, being all Papists no doubt, and many of them of that party called Toryes, who used to rob and kill without mercy and no doubt were of that wretched party that kill'd so many Protestants at the beginning of the rebellion, and so God, the Avenger of Murther (which is to kill contrary to His Rule of direction) hath met with them and sooner or later, will with all such bloody minded men.

This is an extract from a longer letter from Dillingham's correspondent in Ireland, a witness to the events, and yet he repeats the exact details of the list of officers and soldiers slain, that are attributed to Cromwell almost verbatim. What's even more significant is that this letter is dated 22 September, easily the earliest date that is attributed to these words. Does that make this writer the author of the list? It could easily be interpreted that way. Scobell tells us that the list of the *defenders* of the town was enclosed with Cromwell's letters. But he doesn't say that the list of officers and soldiers slain was also enclosed. Is this the origin of the list? The surviving evidence would certainly seem to point that way. Irrespective of which way Dillingham's source is interpreted, it is certainly the case that there is no mention here of inhabitants.

So the list is getting bandied about from publication to publication that particular week and with this analysis it's impossible to conclude that Cromwell was definitely its author. Most investigators of this period generally tend to assume that the newsbooks came after Cromwell's letter and that the various newsbook authors either simply repeated or copied the list from *Letters from Ireland...* or were furnished with the letters and lists by Parliament. But the chronology of events does not support this explanation. It has been established here that the list is independent information and that the earliest known version of it was written ten days before Cromwell's letters were opened in the House of Commons.

From this analysis what now seems possible/plausible is that there is a master list compiled by the army when hostilities ceased, which keeps getting updated as news reaches them or as wounded members of the garrison then die. People copy this list at different stages and different versions end up in London. The version in *Letters from Ireland* is the least detailed. This might make sense since it was one of the earliest written versions. The list gets added to and both the original and its variants arrive in London at the same time as other officers' letters. An even later version with the fullest list of names, arrives with Samuel Pecke a few days later via another unidentified officer.

What is even more surprising about this list is that no historian has ever seemed to have evaluated it like this before.

And yet because it is so important to establish whether or not Cromwell wrote the phrase 'and many inhabitants' it is essential to assess it painstakingly. The words lose their potency if there is doubt over whether or not Cromwell wrote them. In the opinion of this writer, doubt is putting it mildly. Indeed Micheál O'Siochrú is under the impression that the list is always the same and he simply says that some of the newsbooks 'included the phrase "and many inhabitants,"'while others 'did not'. Despite the fact that we can learn so much more about this issue by looking closely at these primary documents, and seeing the list in context, neither O'Siochrú, McElligott nor Morrill seem to have bothered to do this. Had they done so they would have concluded that there is – at the very least – ambiguity over the provenance of the phrase.

Letters from Ireland... (Henry Scobell. Official Parliamentary Pamphlet)

LETTERS
FROM
IRELAND,

Relating the ſeveral great Succeſſes it hath pleaſed God to give unto the

Parliaments Forces

there, in the Taking of *Drogheda*, *Trym*, *Dundalk*, *Carling-ford*, and the *Nury*.

Together with a LIST of the Chief Commanders, and the Number of the Officers and Soldiers ſlain in *Drogheda*.

Die Martis, 2 *Octobr.* 1649.

Ordered by the Commons aſſembled in Parliament, That the ſeveral Letters from the Lord Lieutenant of Ireland, *together with ſo much of Colonel* Venables *Letter as concerns the Succeſſes in* Ireland, *be forthwith printed and publiſhed.*

Hen: Scobell, Cleric. Parliamenti.

London, Printed by *John Field* for *Edward Huſband*, Printer to the Parliament of *England*. 1649.

(5)

For the Honorable *William Lenthal* Esq; Speaker of the Parliament of *England*.

S I R,

YOur Army being safely arrived at *Dublin*, and the Enemy endeavoring to draw all his Forces together about *Trym* and *Tecroghan* (as my Intelligence gave me;) from whence endeavors were used by the Marquis of *Ormond*, to draw *Owen Roe O Neal* with his Forces to his Assistance, but with what successe I cannot yet learn. I resolved after some refreshment taken for our weather-beaten Men and Horses, and accommodations for a march, to take the Field; and accordingly upon Friday the Thirtieth of *August* last, Rendezvouzed with Eight Regiments of Foot, and Six of Horse, and some Troops of Dragoons, three miles on the Northside of *Dublin*; the Design was, To endeavor the Regaining of *Drogheda*, or tempting the Enemy, upon his hazard of the loss of that place, to fight. Your Army came before the Town upon Munday following, where having pitched, as speedy course as could be was taken to frame our Batteries, which took up the more time, because divers of the Battering Guns were on Ship-board: Upon Munday the Ninth of this instant, the Batteries began to play; whereupon I sent Sir *Arthur Ashton* the then Governor a Summons, To deliver

A 3 the

(6)

the Town to the uſe of the Parliament of *England*; to the which I received no ſatisfactory Anſwer, but proceeded that day to beat down the Steeple of the Church on the Southſide of the Town, and to beat down a Tower not far from the ſame place, which you will diſcern by the Card encloſed: Our Guns not being able to do much that day, It was reſolved to endeavor to do our utmoſt the next day to make Breaches aſſaultable, and by the help of God to Storm them: The places pitched upon, were that part of the Town wall next a Church, called *St. Maries*; which was the rather choſen, becauſe we did hope that if we did enter and poſſeſs that Church, we ſhould be the better able to keep it againſt their Horſe and Foot, until we could make way for the entrance of our Horſe, which we did not conceive that any part of the Town would afford the like advantage for that purpoſe with this. The Batteries planted were two, one was for that part of the Wall againſt the Eaſt end of the ſaid Church, the other againſt the Wall on the Southſide; being ſomewhat long in Battering, the Enemy made ſix Retrenchments, three of them from the ſaid Church to Duleek Gate, and three from the Eaſt end of the Church to the Town wall, and ſo backward. The Guns after ſome two or three hundred ſhot, beat down the Corner Tower, and opened two reaſonable good Breaches in the Eaſt and South wall. Upon Tueſday the Tenth of this inſtant, about five of the clock in the evening, we begun the Storm, and after ſome hot Diſpute, we entred about Seven or Eight hundred men, the Enemy diſputing it very ſtifly with

us;

(7)

us; and indeed through the advantages of the place, and the courage God was pleased to give the Defenders, our men were forced to retreat quite out of the Breach, not without some considerable loss; Colonel *Cassel* being there shot in the Head, whereof he presently dyed, and divers Soldiers and Officers doing their duty, killed and wounded: There was a Tenalia to flanker the South-wall of the Town, between *Duleek* Gate, and the Corner Tower before mentioned, which our men entred, wherein they found some forty or fifty of the Enemy, which they put to the sword, and this they held; but it being without the Wall, and the Sally part through the Wall into that Tenalia being choaked up, with some of the Enemy which were killed in it, it proved of no use for our entrance into the Town that way. Although our men that stormed the Breaches were forced to recoil, as before is expressed, yet being encouraged to recover their loss, they made a second attempt, wherein God was pleased to animate them, that they got ground of the Enemy, and by the goodness of God, forced him to quit his Entrenchments; and after a very hot dispute, the Enemy having both Horse and Foot, and we onely Foot within the Wall, the Enemy gave ground, and our men became masters; but of their Retrenchments and the Church, which indeed although they made our entrance the more difficult, yet they proved of excellent use to us, so that the Enemy could not annoy us with their Horse, but thereby we had advantage to make good the ground, that so we might let in our own Horse, which accordingly,

(8)

cordingly was done, though with much difficulty; the Enemy retreated divers of them into the Mill-Mount, a place very ſtrong and of difficult acceſs, being exceeding high, having a good graft and ſtrongly Palliſadoed; the Governor Sir *Arthur Aſhton*, and divers conſiderable Officers being there, our men getting up to them, were ordered by me to put them all to the Sword; and indeed being in the heat of action, I forbade them to ſpare any that were in Arms in the Town, and I think that night they put to the ſword about two thouſand men, divers of the Officers and Soldiers being fled over the Bridge into the other part of the Town, where about One hundred of them poſſeſſed St. *Peters* Church Steeple, ſome the Weſt Gate, and others, a round ſtrong Tower next the Gate, called St. *Sundays*: Theſe being ſummoned to yield to mercy, refuſed; whereupon I ordered the Steeple of St. *Peters* Church to be fired, where one of them was heard to ſay in the midſt of the flames, *God damn me, God confound me, I burn, I burn*; the next day the other two Towers were ſummoned, in one of which was about ſix or ſeven ſcore, but they refuſed to yield themſelves, and we knowing that hunger muſt compel them, ſet onely good Guards to ſecure them from running away, until their ſtomacks were come down: from one of the ſaid Towers, notwithſtanding their condition, they killed and wounded ſome of our men; when they ſubmitted, their Officers were knockt on the head, and every tenth man of the Soldiers killed, and the reſt Shipped for the *Barbadoes*; the Soldiers in the other Town were all ſpared, as to their

lives

lives onely, and Shipped likewise for the *Barbadoes*. I am perswaded that this is a righteous Judgement of God upon these Barbarous wretches, who have imbrued their hands in so much innocent blood, and that it will tend to prevent the effusion of blood for the future, which are the satisfactory grounds to such Actions, which otherwise cannot but work remorse and regret. The Officers and Soldiers of this Garison, were the flower of all their Army; and their great expectation was, That our attempting this place, would put fair to ruine us; they being confident of the Resolution of their men and the advantage of the place; if we had divided our Force into two quarters, to have Besieged the North Town and the South Town, we could not have had such a correspondency between the two parts of our Army, but that they might have chosen to have brought their Army, and have fought with which part they pleased, and at the same time have made a Salley with two thousand men upon us, and have left their walls manned, they having in the Town the numbers specified in this inclosed, but some say near Four thousand. Since this great Mercy vouchsafed to us, I sent a Party of Horse and Dragoons to *Dundalk*, which the Enemy quitted, and we are possessed of; as also another Castle they deserted between *Trym* and *Drogheda*, upon the *Boynes*. I sent a Party of horse and Dragoons to a House within five miles of *Trym*, there being then in *Trym* some Scots Companies which the Lord of *Ardes* brought to assist the Lord of *Ormond*; but upon the News of *Drogheda* they ran away, leaving their great Guns behinde

B them,

them, which we alſo have poſſeſſed. And now give me leave to ſay how it comes to paſs that this work is wrought; It was ſet upon ſome of our hearts, that a great thing ſhould be done, not by power, or might, but by the Spirit of God; and is it not ſo clear? That which cauſed your men to Storm ſo couragiouſly, it was the Spirit of God, who gave your men Courage, and took it away again, and gave the Enemy Courage, and took it away again, and gave your men Courage again, and therewith this happy Succeſs; and therefore it is good that God alone have all the Glory. It is is remarkable, that theſe people at the firſt ſet up the Maſs in ſome places of the town that had been Monaſteries; but afterwards grew ſo inſolent, that the laſt Lords day before the Storm, the Proteſtants were thruſt out of the great Church, called *St. Peters*, and they had publique Maſs there; and in this very place near One thouſand of them were put to the Sword, flying thither for ſafety: I believe all their Fryers were knockt on the head promiſcuouſly, but two, the one of which was Father *Peter Taaff* (Brother to the Lord *Taaff*) whom the Soldiers took the next day, and made an end of; the other was taken in the Round Tower, under the repute of Lieutenant, and when he underſtood that the Officers in that Tower had no quarter, he confeſſed he was a Fryer, but that did not ſave him. A great deal of loſs in this buſineſs, fell upon Col: *Hewſon*, Col: *Caſſel*, and Colonel *Ewers* Regiments; Colonel *Ewers* having two Field-Officers in his Regiment ſhot, Colonel *Caſſel* and a Captain of his Regiment ſlain, Colonel *Hewſons* Captain-Lieutenant ſlain; I do

(11)

do not think we lost One hundred men upon the place, though many be wounded. I most humbly pray, the Parliament will be pleased this Army may be maintained, and that a consideration may be had of them, and of the carrying on of the Affairs here, as may give a speedy issue to this work, to which there seems to be a marvellous fair opportunity offered by God. And although it may seem very chargeable to the State of *England* to maintain so great a Force, yet surely to stretch a little for the present, in following Gods Providence, in hope the charge will not be long, I trust it will not be thought by any (that have not irreconcileable or malicious Principles) unfit for me to move for a constant supply, which in humane probability, as to outward means, is most likely to hasten and perfect this work; and indeed, if God please to finish it here, as he hath done in *England*, the War is like to pay it self. We keep the Field much, our Tents sheltring us from the wet and cold, but yet the Country sickness overtakes many, and therefore we desire recruits, and some fresh Regiments of Foot may be sent us; for it is easily conceived by what the Garisons already drink up, what our field Army will come to, if God shall give more Garisons into our hands. Craving pardon for this great trouble, I rest,

Dublin, Sept. 17. 1649.

Your most humble Servant,

O. CROMVVEL.

B 2 *Since*

(12)

Since the writing of my Letter, a Major who brought off Forty three Horse from the Enemy, told me, that it is reported in their Camp, that Owen Roe *and they are agreed.*

A List of the Defendants in *Drogheda.*

THe Lord of *Ormonds* Regiment, Sir *Edmund Verney*, Lieut: Colonel,	400.
Col: *Bourn*,	400.
Col: *Warren*,	900.
Col: *Wall*,	800.
The Lord of *Westmeath*,	200.
Sir *Iames Dillon*,	200.
Horse,	200.

For

(13)

For the Honorable *Willaiam Lenthal* Eſq; Speaker of the Parliament of *England.*

Mr. Speaker,

I Had not received any accompt from Col: *Venables* (whom I ſent from *Drogheda*, to endeavor the reducing of *Carlingford*, and ſo to march Northward, towards a conjunction with Sir *Charls Coot*) until the laſt night. After he came to *Carlingford*, having ſummoned the place, both the three Caſtles and the Fort commanding the Harbor, were rendred to him; wherein were about Forty Barrels of Powder, ſeven piece of Canon, about One thouſand Muskets, and five hundred Pikes wanting twenty. In the entrance into the Harbor, Captain *Fern* aboard your Man of War had ſome danger, being much ſhot at from the Sea Fort, a bullet ſhooting through his main Maſt: The Captains entrance into that Harbor, was a conſiderable adventure, and a good ſervice; as alſo was Captain *Brandleys*, who with forty Seamen ſtormed a very ſtrong Tenalia at *Drogheda*, and helped to take it, for which he deſerves an owning by you. *Venables* marched from *Carlingford*, with a Party of Horſe and Dragoons to the *Nury*, leaving the Foot to come up after him: He ſummoned the place, and it was yielded before his Foot came up to him. Some other Informations I have received from him, which promiſe well towards your Northern Intereſt; which if well proſecuted, will (I truſt through God) render you a good accompt of thoſe parts. I have ſent thoſe things to be preſented to the Councel of State for their conſideration. I pray God as theſe Mercies flow in upon you, he will give you an heart to improve them to his Glory alone, becauſe he alone is the Author of them, and of all the goodneſs, patience and long-ſuffering extended towards you. Your Army is marched, and I believe this night lieth at *Arcklo*, in the County of *Wicklo*, by the Sea ſide, between thirty and forty miles from this place: I am this day by Gods bleſſing going towards it. I crave your pardon for this trouble, and reſt,

Your moſt humble Servant,

Dublin, Sep. 27. 1649.

O. Cromwel.

(6)

I desire the Supplies moved for, may be hastned: I am verily perswaded, though the burthen be great, yet it is for your Service. If the Garisons we take, swallow up your men, how shall we be able to keep the Field? who knows but the Lord may pity *Englands* sufferings, and make a short work of this? it is in his hand to do it, and therein onely your Servants rejoyce.

I humbly present the condition of Captain *George Jenkins* his widow: He dyed presently after *Tredagh* storm; his widow is in great want.

A List of the Officers and Soldiers slain at the storming of *Drogheda*.

Sir *Arthur Ashton* Governor.
Sir *Edmond Verney* Lieutenant Col: to *Ormonds* Regiment.
Col: *Fleming*, of Horse.
Lieutenant Col: *Finglass*, of Horse.
Major *Fitzgerald*, of Horse.
Eight { Captains, Lieutenants, Cornets } of Horse.
Col: { *Warren*, *Walls*, *Byrne*, } of Foot, with their Lieutenants, Majors, &c.
The Lord *Taaffs* brother, an *Augustine Fryer*.
Forty four Captains, and all their Lieutenants, Ensigns, &c.
Two hundred and twenty Reformado's and Troopers.
Two thousand Five hundred Foot Soldiers, besides Staff-Officers, Chyrurgeons, &c. and many Inhabitants.

For

(15)

For His Excellency,

The Lord Lieutenant of *Ireland.*

My Lord,

IN obſervance of your Excellencies Orders, I advanced to *Carlingford* upon Tueſday laſt, and at the ſame inſtant, Captain *Ferns* came into the Harbors mouth with his Frigot; and upon the Signal agreed upon betwixt us, came in with much gallantry and reſolution, indured many ſhots, whereof one ſplit his main Maſt, and in the Haven took a ſmall *Wexford* Veſſel; And in the three Caſtles and the Sea-Fort, we found ſeven piece of Ordinance, near forty Barrels of Powder, and as many of ſmall ſhot, above a thouſand Muskets, and four hundred and eighty Pikes (the greateſt ſtore in *Ulſter*) but little Proviſion; the next day I marched with ſome Horſe and Dragoons to the *Nury* and ſummoned the place, which alſo yielded immediately before the Foot could come. Many difficulties encounter us, yet by Gods aſſiſtance, I reſolve to break through all, to follow the leading Providence of that Divine Hand, which now ſeems to guide us forward; for except we march on, the Scots reſolve to put Iriſh into *Carrickfergus*, *Belfaſt*, and *Liſnegarvy*, becauſe their own Nation refuſes them both aſſiſtance and Proviſions; and if we prevent not the Iriſh, it will kindle a new War in thoſe Parts, more bloody then what we have yet taſted of; which to prevent, ſhall be my utmoſt and chief endeavor. *Monro* hath already put ſome Iriſh into *Colrain*: I have ſent ſeveral Meſſengers to Sir *Charls Coot*, to

know

(20)

know his pleaſure, to acquaint him with my reſolutions for this work; we are all full of (not improbable) hopes of Divine aſſiſtance in this work, which if your Excellency pleaſe but to cheriſh us in, may through Gods aſſiſtance, prove a moſt happy undertaking, which is the Prayer of, My Lord,

Nury Sept. 22. 1649.

Your Excellencies moſt humble Servant,

R. VENABLES.

We had in the Caſtle of this place, ſixty Muskets, and five Barrels of Powder.

FINIS.

Letters from Ireland... is the official Parliamentary document that Prof John Morrill says he cannot get around because of the three words 'and many inhabitants'. So that particular document needs to be closely examined here.

As already mentioned, in *Honourable Enemy* I had outlined the fact that Thomas Carlyle and Charles Firth, both biographers of Cromwell, had cast aspersions on these three words at the end of Cromwell's reproduced letter. Carlyle was incensed with the editor of the *Old Parliamentary History*, (where it was later reproduced) whom he suggested had added the words independently. Firth has alleged that the entire list given at the end of the postscript was added by the printer, perhaps in compliance with the orders of Parliament.

A close look at this document will show that Firth could well have had a point – especially when it comes to the addition of the entire list and not simply the three words at the end. It certainly looks like an addition. Furthermore, there are several anomalies in the entire document that pose more questions than they provide answers. His letter of the 27 September ends with Cromwell's signature at the foot of page 13 of the pamphlet. The next page is the highly controversial page. The letter appears to continue (after the signature) and then seems to end again where there is a heavy black line drawn across the page, indicating perhaps that the two transcripts are separated from the other – the list from the letter. Furthermore, there are differences in spelling that are most interesting and do nothing but add more intrigue to this issue. In the last line of the postscript to the letter is the English spelling 'Tredagh'. And the very next line on the page is the spelling 'Drogheda'. While spelling in the seventeenth century was not an exact science, it is strange to think that if the writer was one and the same person that the spelling of the same word changed quite dramatically from one sentence to the next.

The separation of the list from the letter and the difference in spelling could easily be used as evidence to suggest that these three words were not the words of Cromwell himself. But that's not all. We are given to believe that the two primary letters in the document are the actual words of Cromwell. There are other anomalies. Also in the document is Cromwell's letter to Lenthall dated 17 September with a list of the defendants of Drogheda. With this letter too we can see clearly that this list is appended because Cromwell signs the end of the letter on the previous page, then on the next page there is a postscript, and the list comes next. Again, there is a black line to indicate the separation of the list from the letter but in this list the writer spells the names of two officers differently to the spelling on the other list appended to the letter of the 27 September - Col Byrne becomes Col Burn and Col Walls becomes Col Wall.

With regard to this list of the defendants of Drogheda there is nothing in Cromwell's letter of the 17th that links the letter with the list. It seems that after signing off the letter Cromwell added a postscript that reads as follows, 'Since the writing of my letter, a major who brought off Forty three Horse from the Enemy, told me, that it is reported in their camp, that Owen Roe and they are agreed.' This comment had nothing to do with the separate list of defendants that follows. The list itself is separated from the postscript and while we know from Scobell that it was enclosed with Cromwell's letters (see below), we simply cannot be sure that even this list was from his own hand.

Then there is the title page of the official pamphlet itself. It could easily be argued that the title captions on the cover notify the reader of two separate forms of transcripts to come – letters AND lists, laid out in the subsequent pages in an ad hoc format, albeit in a certain context with the lists placed between the letters, which is more or less what Firth was alluding to. The text on the cover reads:

> *Letters from Ireland, Relating the Several great Successes it hath pleased God to give unto the Parliaments Forces there, in the taking of Drogheda, Trym, Dundalk, Carlingford, and the Nury.*
>
> *Together with a LIST of the Chief commanders, and the Number of the Officers and Soldiers slain at Drogheda.*

Then there is a heavy black line. Beneath the line the printer then qualifies the two title captions above as follows:

> *Die Martis, 2 Octobr 1649. Ordered by the Commons assembled in Parliament, that the several Letters from the Lord Lieutenant of Ireland, together with so much of Colonel Venables letter as concerns the Successes in Ireland, be forthwith printed and published.*
>
> *Hen: Scobell, Cleric, Parliamenti (London, Printed by John Field for Edward Husband, Printer to the Parliament of England. 1649.*

It is the full-stop at the end of the first heading that separates it from the second heading. In other words there are letters, and then there are lists. Then in Henry Scobell's explanation of the documents beneath the black line he refers only to letters from Cromwell – not lists. And as we have seen already, the list of the officers and soldiers killed is already well-travelled.

Jason McElligott, Micheál O'Siochrú and John Morrill all hone in on both Carlyle and Firth's (and my earlier) contention that the printer added either the list or the three extra words to the document. They go on to provide details of printer John Field's career and suggest that because he became the official printer to Cromwell as Protector, and that he was never punished for adding these three words, that this in some way proves that Cromwell either wrote them or approved of them being written. That may well be so. But there are three persons named on the cover of the pamphlet: Scobell, Husband and Field. In *Acts and Ordinances of the Interregnum,* (London 1911, C.H. Firth and R.S. Rait eds), the editors provide information about Husband and Field:

> The House of Lords on January 14, 1643, ordered John Browne, the clerk of the Parliament, to "provide a printer that shall print those things that are appointed by Parliament," and Browne selected for the purpose "John Wright in the Old Bailey." (Lords Journals v. 554; vi. 147). The House of

> Commons preferred a different man. Ordinances and declarations the publication of which was authorised by Henry Elsynge, the clerk of the House of Commons, usually bear the words "printed for Edward Husbands," with the addition "to be sold at his shop in the Middle Temple" or "at the sign of the Golden-Dragon near the Inner Temple."
>
> With the abolition of the House of Lords in 1649 Wright ceased to be one of the Government printers. After the House of Commons declared itself the Parliament, and called its enactments "Acts," they were printed in folio instead of in quarto form, and in much larger and better type. At first they bore the name of Edward Husband (for he had since 1645 dropped the last letter of his name), but after September 1659 the name of John Field was associated with his. By vote of January 25, 1649–50, it was ordered that "John Field, printer, nominated by Mr. Speaker, be joined with Mr. Husband, stationer" for the printing of an Act concerning the estates of Papists, "and that his name be used in printing of the same Act and all other Acts and proceedings." (Commons Journals vi. 349.) In February 1651 the name of Husband disappears, and from that date to the expulsion of the Long Parliament the Acts bear the name of "John Field, printer to the Parliament of England.

Both Husband and Field have long associations with Parliament. Oftentimes individual printers sub-contracted jobs to other printers and it might have been the case here that Field was printing for Husband in this context. The printing of newsbooks in 1649 was quite a random affair. Oftentimes when sentences did not fit the print area on the page, printers would alter to suit, depending on the type size and the ancillary font pieces and equipment available to him. It may have been the case in some instances that the resultant message was not the intended one. In this instance *it looks like the lists were simply inserted into the available space on the sheet with a black line printed above both of them to indicate this.* The circumstances surrounding the printing of this pamphlet would seem to be in haste. The letters were read out in the Commons on 2 October and the pamphlet was printed later that day. This was an information leaflet. There were letters and lists. The lists contained the names of eminent **English** royalists, whose friends and families might be hearing about their deaths for the first time upon the reading of this pamphlet. In an effort to publish the facts that they had to hand that day it could easily be the case that with little planning, Scobell, or Field simply placed both lists in the available spaces, the only available spaces after each letter, on the page for expediency. In one fell swoop this caused major headaches for later historians who would come along to evaluate their actions.

The information gleaned from the entry in the Commons' journal for 2 October is also ambiguous:

> *A Letter from the Lord Lieutenant of Ireland, from Dublin, of the Seventeenth Day of September 1649, with a list, therein inclosed, of the Defendants in Drogheda, was this day read.*
>
> *A Letter from the Lord Lieutenant of Ireland, from Dublin, of the Twenty-seventh Day of September 1649, together with a List of the Officers and Soldiers slain at the Storming of Drogheda, was this Day read.*

Questions prevail. Note Scobell does not say with 'his' list in either entry. We can say for certain that the list of the *defendants* of Drogheda was 'enclosed' with the letter of the seventeenth, and yet we can't say for certain that Cromwell wrote it. But we can't say for certain either that the list of the officers and soldiers slain was enclosed with the letter of the twenty-seventh because the entry does not tell us this. Fundamentally we know very little about the composition of these letters. For instance did the

Council of State modify or amend them in any way before publishing them. Were they written by Cromwell with the help of his officers? Cromwell's superior officer Sir Thomas Fairfax often wrote letters back to parliament that were ghost written by his secretary John Rushworth and signed by Fairfax himself.

Henry Scobell had a hand in both *Letters from Ireland* and *Severall Proceedings in Parliament,* both legitimate Parliament publications. One would imagine that the clerk to Parliament had more of a role to play in this document than the printer. And yet the three expert historians single Field out as the key man.

It is essential that this document is scrutinised in this fashion, if only to challenge John Morrill's assertion that 'there is no getting around these words 'and many inhabitants'.' We can now see that at the very least, it cannot be proven conclusively that Cromwell was responsible for writing them, or that he even approved of them being written by another hand. That's how we can get around these words. The list was separate from the letter. When all of the irregularities with this document (*Letters from Ireland*) are outlined and the circuitous journey of the separate list is taken into account it is quite interesting to reflect on the words of Jason McElligott who published very strong opinions on this subject:

> The original letter does not survive. But the official printed version confirms that 'many inhabitants' were among those killed by Cromwell's forces at Drogheda. If this pamphlet is authentic Reilly's thesis is in ruins. Reilly's belief that a loyal servant of the state like Field would, for some unexplained reason, have accused Cromwell of the slaughter of innocent civilians during one of the harshest crackdowns against the press in the seventeenth century is ludicrous. Even if Field had taken leave of his senses and inserted these words there is little doubt that he would have been severely punished. The fact that he went on to work as printer to the lord protector

> suggests that "many inhabitants" were indeed killed during the storming of Drogheda.

Morrill has also left himself exposed on this issue as we have already seen when he says:

> There is no getting around these words. Reilly tries to do so...by drawing attention to Carlyle's claim in the first edition of Letters & Speeches that the appendix is an eighteen century addition...This in itself is fatal to Reilly's thesis and it is disgraceful that so many reviewers have not checked this.

While the argument surrounding these words has been a massive issue in modern times, it should be pointed out that it is extremely unlikely that those writing in the seventeenth century would have been so sensitive to the reporting of dead inhabitants at Drogheda, simply because they might easily have been armed. This point is emphasised in the military style of the list itself. There is no question that inhabitants died at Wexford because they were involved in the defence of their town. O'Siochrú, for one, has suggested that the newsbooks that left the incriminating phrase out of their transcription of the list did so perhaps because of the uncomfortable implications that the killing of inhabitants would have had for parliament. Others have suggested that the Royalist pamphlets would have had a field day with the notion that the Parliamentarians committed atrocities and that some of the pamphleteers simply sanitised the lists to avoid this. It is only to the modern ear that the words 'inhabitants' implies unarmed local people, shopkeepers without weapons, helpless old women and weak little children. No such allegation has yet been made by any of the newsbooks that printed the list, official or otherwise. On every interpretational level so far, it is perfectly plausible to suggest that 'many inhabitants' could have been armed and involved in the fight.

Regarding the 'and many inhabitants' affair, O'Siochrú concludes, 'Oftentimes, the most straightforward answer is the correct one. In his report, Cromwell, who had witnessed the assault on Drogheda at close quarters, simply acknowledged that the casualties included many civilians.' Another writer might construct the sentence differently; Oftentimes, the most straightforward answer is the correct one, the much-travelled list of officers and soldiers slain at Drogheda was first written by John Dillingham's unnamed correspondent in Dublin on 22 September, ten days before Cromwell's letters were read out in Parliament, so we will never know if Cromwell himself acknowledged that the casualties included civilians. Did Cromwell write the words 'and many inhabitants'? We don't know. It's as simple as that.

After the newsbooks that published the list had seeped into London society and beyond, it was in the following weeks that Wharton and Crouch swung into action. On 15 October: *Mercurius Elencticus* asserts women and children were killed and on 24 October: *The Man in the Moon* says of the 3,000 killed, 2,000 were women and children.

This just might be where the civilian massacre myth began. We can conjecture that Wharton and Crouch either picked up on the words 'many inhabitants' in the newsbooks and completely ran away with themselves or simply invented the stories to rally public opinion against Parliament. Neither of their publications can be relied upon for facts, but both can be relied upon for scandal and propaganda.

Then of course there is the issue of motive. The background to Drogheda does not provide a motive for Parliament's soldiers to butcher any innocent civilians at Drogheda, like that of Dublin, the population of which was mostly English. No motive to kill. No orders to kill. No evidence that they killed.

Returning to the theme of date order and in an effort to harmonise the primary source material, on 15 September Lord

Inchiquin, who was based nearby and received many of the escapees from Drogheda, wrote a letter to Ormond to provide him with some details of the assault. Inchiquin's language is in a military context and tells Ormond that:

> Many men and some officers have made their escape out of Drogheda, amongst them Garret Dungan is one and is now at Tecroghan and Lieutenant Colonel Cavanagh. Some of every regiment are come unto me. All conclude that no quarter was given there with Cromwell's leave but many were privately saved by officers and soldiers; the governor was killed after quarter was given by the officer that first came there, that some of the towers were defended until yesterday, quarter being denied them, and that yesterday morning, the towers within, they were blown up. That Varney, Finglass, Warren and some other officers were alive in the hands of some of Cromwell's officers twenty-four hours after the business was done, but whether their lives were obtained at Cromwell's hands, or that they are yet living, they cannot tell.

If 'many' of the Royalist defenders were 'privately saved by officers and soldiers', how likely is it that the attackers would have massacred children, their mothers and fathers and that either Garret Dungan or the other escapees would either forget or neglect to mention this to Inchiquin? There are some areas regarding this whole episode where we have to speculate but here it would seem outrageous to suggest that these eyewitnesses simply left out such monumental detail. And yet, John Morrill estimates that there was a civilian body count of at least 700 -800.

On 18 September Ormond wrote to the young Charles Stuart to inform him of the loss of the town of Drogheda. Describing the shocking episode, he cuts straight to the chase when he says that the attacking army were responsible for 'the bloody execution of almost all that were in it'. Here we come to a particularly telling remark. While innumerable investigations have been made into the storming of Drogheda there is one assumption that historians have exclusively made about the event to date. And yet, with a small amount of speculation, supported by some evidence, it is possible to interpret the entire incident quite differently to accepted wisdom. So here's the thing: Why does everybody assume that the local inhabitants stayed in the town?

Granted, we do not know a lot about the movements of the inhabitants but there are some facts that are quite clear. Firstly, there was a five-month long siege of the town just eight years earlier that had dire consequences on the food and supply levels of the civilian population. Is it sensible to assume that those same inhabitants would simply stay put when they could easily flee? They had ample time to do so with the Ironsides camped outside the town for a week before hostilities began. Secondly, we know that Aston was prepared for a long siege and that they had stocked up on supplies that would last for months. (*The Kingdom's Faithfull and Impartial Scout* reported on the 5 October 1649 that there were victuals stocked up in the town to last nine months) Thirdly, it would seem to make sense that with a population of 3,000 people and a garrison of 3,000 soldiers that a reduction in the number of mouths to feed would be an obvious military decision to make. Speculation perhaps, but then does *The Moderate Intelligencer* (30 August – 6 September) provide the evidence?

> Ormond 'lies between Tredagh and Trim, intending if he can to be a spectator at the siege of the first, if not of both, which by the advantage of the river, he hopes to do rather than by the valour of his men; he hath cleared Tredagh of all superfluous and suspected persons and furnished it well with all necessities, every man in that kingdom fit to bear arms, is in posture of war.

Ormond cleared the town of all superfluous and suspected people. This is a seminal piece of evidence not usually quoted in the context of Cromwell at Drogheda. And yet it could easily be interpreted to imply that all 'superfluous' people, including men – not inclined to take up arms - and women and children were cleared from the town. Indeed it also implies that some inhabitants may well have taken up arms since every man in that kingdom fit to bear arms was in a posture of war. Unlike *The Man in the Moon* and *Mercurius Elencticus, The Moderate Intelligencer* was considered to be the one of the most reliable and respected broadsheets of its day. Dillingham, its author, who was renowned for his excellent contacts with both parliamentary officials and army leaders, seemed to portray an open mind and an impartial perspective on contemporary events to the point where his publication is often called *The Times* of its day. So if we don't ignore Dillingham's army contact's evidence then we must assume that the 'superfluous' people in Drogheda were removed from the town.

But that's not the only evidence we have for civilians being dispatched from the town. We already know that Dean Nicholas Bernard's wife and children are documented as being 'sent out of the town'. And just to copper-fasten the suggestion that this action was desirable in order to conduct a long siege, which was exactly the plan, Ormond does exactly the same thing at Wexford. In a letter to the mayor of Wexford on 9 October, 1649, two days before the Parliamentarian army managed to force their way into the town, and still hoping for a long siege there, still outside the walls of Wexford, Ormond explains why:

> Wee are come hither to countenance the maintenance and to relieve the necessities of the towne, and doe find upon examination of the conditions thereof that provision of victuals wilbe the greatest want in all probability to draw any distresse thereon, and withal finde the Country here soe

> exhausted that it wilbe difficult to supply the Towne with provision for all sortes of people there. And therefore pray and require you after examination of each Inhabitants provision that you send out the unnecessary people, as ould men, women and children with that expedition that whilst wee are here, we may send them whither they propose to go themselves most safely.

We also know that within the town of Drogheda there was a civilian conspiracy to betray the place to Cromwell. The scheme of Lady Wilmot (Sir Arthur Aston's grandmother) and her several espionage associates was exposed when her messenger, a young boy, was caught with letters in his possession that were destined for Parliamentarian hands. One of her co-conspirators was a Lady Blayney whose letter (signed A.B.) to Lieutenant-Colonel Foulkes (Colonel John Ffolk became Governor of Drogheda in 1650 according to the Corporation of Drogheda records.) opened with the line 'Sir, The hearing of your coming this way is a great joy to me, but it has driven all the lords away, and my Ladie Moore.' This is further evidence that non-military personnel had departed the scene. With the conspiracy exposed, Aston banished the undercover agents to the monastery at nearby Mellifont, where (it would make sense that) the town's civilians might have been also seeking refuge. Listening now to the voices of some of the people of Drogheda, living there, on the ground, it is difficult to see how the civilian massacre myth became so shatterproof.

So now we have evidence that would suggest that any inhabitants of Drogheda that were capable of bearing arms and inclined to take a stand against Parliament probably did so. It may well be the case that this is the 'many' referred to in some versions of the list. Furthermore, the suggestion that the majority of the civilian population departed the town seems to make sense. It also supports the words of Ormond who mentions the 'bloody execution of all that were in it' (and to a lesser extent the testimony of Hugh Peters who says that there were 'none spared') since most of the living souls within the walls were on the streets defending the town in the posture of soldiers.

Aside from his immediate family, Bernard confirms that some civilians were not in the posture of soldiers but that they were off the streets, away from the hostilities, safely ensconced behind closed doors and that they survived:

> When the town was fully taken, the Doctor's (Dean's) house was one of the first the soldiers fell upon, but by the strength of it could not enter. The mayor of the town and divers other of the principal men that were Protestants to the number of about 30 came to it for refuge.

An entry in the Drogheda Corporation records dating from 7 October 1658 (a month after Cromwell's death) suggests that the high ranking citizens of the town were keen to keep bolt holes available for shelter in times of war when they granted a lease with a caveat to Jonas Ellwood 'for sixty and one years at the rent of twenty shillings per Ann. Provided that in case of Warrs or rebellion the Corporacon if required may make use thereof for that present occasion'.

To conclude that the majority of the unarmed civilian population had departed the scene but that the Corporators remained hidden away fits perfectly well with the credible eye witness testimony and the evidence from Dillingham's contact in the *Moderate Intelligencer.*

The above quoted newsbooks and pamphlets are what we would call the popular sources. They are the documents that historians consult directly for information about the events. Other documents about the storming of Drogheda that come under the umbrella of being popular sources are the private letters written by both Inchiquin and Ormond in September 1649 and one written by a gentleman called James Buck in November of that year. As Cromwell's public enemy number one Ormond was a prolific writer and left us numerous letters and documents over which to peruse. On 18 September he wrote to Prince Rupert to tell him the news about Drogheda and the 'bloody execution of almost all that were in it.' Then on 27 September he wrote to the young Prince Charles accusing Cromwell of 'much more than anything I ever heard of in breach of faith and bloody inhumanity.' He also wrote to Lord Byron where he says that 'the cruelties expressed in Drogheda for five days after the town was taken would make as many pictures of inhumanity as are to be found in the Book of Martyrs, or in the relation of Amboyna.' The oft-quoted headlines taken from Ormond's letters do not mention civilian deaths. It is very difficult to see how Ormond could have ignored such an occurrence when it would have been such an explosive revelation with far reaching consequences. Had Cromwell engaged in civilian atrocities the groundswell of support for Parliament's tenuous grip on power would have been severely damaged. Surely Ormond would have taken the opportunity to exploit this news, if it had an ounce of truth in it. But he says nothing of large numbers of civilian deaths. As we have seen Inchiquin too is silent on the matter.

The only other surviving letter from 1649 was written by Mr James Buck from Caen, and it is addressed to Sir Edmund Verney's brother Ralph. It reads:

> Your brother and my dear friend Sir Edmund Verney – who behaved himself with the greatest gallantry that could be – he was slain at Drogheda three days after quarter was given him as he was walking with Cromwell by way of protection. One Ropier, who is brother to Lord Ropier, called him aside in a pretence to speak to him, being formerly of his acquaintance, and instead of some friendly office which Sir Edmund might expect from him, he barbarously ran him through with a tuck; but I am confident to see this act highly avenged. The next day

> after, one Lieutenant Colonel Boyle, who had quarter likewise given him, as he was at dinner with my Lady More, sister to the Earl of Sunderland, in the same town, one of Cromwell's soldiers, came in and whispered him in the ear to tell him that he must presently be put to death, who rising from the table, the lady asked him whither he was going. He answered, 'Madam to die.' Who no sooner stepped out of the room but he was shot to death. These are the cruelties of those traitors, who, no doubt will find the like mercy when they stand in need of it.

Mr Buck's letter is the only non-military letter that has survived that gives an account of the events in the town following the storming. It is impossible to know whether or not his imaginative accounts of the deaths of Verney and Boyle are accurate. It is unlikely, although not impossible, that Buck witnessed the events since he was writing from France on 8 November. Interestingly, according to the *Memoirs of the Verney Family,* Ralph was still holding out hope that Edmund was still alive as late as 4 November despite the fact that the newsbooks in London had published his name as one of the slain in September/October. Interestingly also, Buck's letter first came to public notice in 1879 when it was discovered by The Historical Manuscripts Commission in that year.

All of the popular sources dating from 1649 have now been identified and examined here. So far the evidence for a civilian massacre at Drogheda on any scale is conspicuous by its absence. Dean Nicholas Bernard's account emerges in 1651 and even here there is no evidence for a large scale massacre of Drogheda's inhabitants. There are no other documents in the public domain from 1649 to beyond the Restoration that accuse Cromwell of civilian atrocities. This is quite a salient point. There the matter should really have ended.

The following is a chronological summary, in date order, of

the popular contemporary evidence surrounding Drogheda from 1649, as we know it today:

Tuesday 11 Sept	Drogheda falls. Hugh Peters arrives in Ireland.
Wednesday 12 Sept	The defenders in the towers surrender. Resistance is ceased.
Friday 14 Sept	Anonymous letter written from Liverpool, 'Two Fights'
Saturday 15 Sept	Hugh Peters hears news from Drogheda and writes to unknown recipient in London – possibly Henry Walker Inchiquin writes to Ormond (Many men and officers have made their escape') – includes quote from Garret Dungan, 'Many were privately saved by officers and soldiers'.
Sunday 16 Sept	Oliver Cromwell writes to John Bradshaw
Monday 17 Sept	Oliver Cromwell is back in Dublin and writes first letter to William Lenthall
Tuesday 18 Sept	Ormond writes to Prince Rupert ('The bloody execution of all that were in it')
Saturday 22 Sept	Anonymous officer writes to John Dillingham for *The Moderate Intellingencer*. First time the list appears anywhere. (Where their horse were, we don't know. Probably they went as common men.) Henry Walker publishes (Ibbitson prints) 'Two Letters'.
Thursday 27 Sept	Oliver Cromwell writes second letter to William lenthall. Ormond writes to Prince Charles – 'much more than anything I ever heard of in breach of faith and bloody inhumanity'.

Friday 28 Sept	Hugh Peters' letter read by Henry Walker. Hugh Peters' letter read in House of Commons. Walker states that news arrived on this day. Also associates the list (and many inhabitants) with this day. Cromwell's letter to Bradshaw also in circulation, according to *Kingdom's Weekly Intelligencer* and *Perfect Weekly Account*.
Saturday 29 Sept	Ormond writes to Lord Byron ('The cruelties expressed there, pictures of inhumanity Fox's martyrs and tales of Amboyna.')
Monday 1 Oct	Confirmation of the fall of Drogheda arrives in London according to the *Perfect Weekly Account*. Letter from an unnamed officer arrives according to *Perfect Diurnall*.
Tuesday 2 Oct	Unspecified letters from Cromwell arrive in London according to *Perfect Diurnall*. Cromwell's letter to Lenthall of 17 Sept read in the House of Commons. Commons Journal describes it as enclosing a list of defenders – not a list of the dead. The journal also describes a list of casualties being read but does not describe it as being enclosed with Cromwell's letter. It gives no source for the list. *Kingdom's Weekly Intelligencer* declines to print Peters' letter but mentions Cromwell's letter to Bradshaw. Prints the list (with many inhabitants included). *Letters from Ireland* is also printed by Parliament and includes the list with 'many inhabitants.'
Wednesday 3 Oct	*The Perfect Weekly Account* prints the list without 'many inhabitants.'

Thursday 4 Oct	*The Moderate Intelligencer* prints a letter which contains a version of the list excluding many inhabitants. The letter and list are dated 22 September. *Perfect Occurrences* prints the list including 'many inhabitants.'
Friday 5 Oct	*The Kingdom's Faithful and Impartial Scout* prints the list. It is the same list as the one printed in *The Perfect Weekly Account* (Daniel Border being responsible for both) without the expression 'and many inhabitants.'
Monday 8 Oct	*Perfect Diurnall* prints an officer's account of the storming of Drogheda. Prints a more detailed version of the list (without 'and many inhabitants'). *Severall Proceedings* prints the list without 'many inhabitants.'
Monday 15 Oct	George Wharton prints *Mercurius Elencticus* and includes the phrase 'as well inhabitants as others, sparing neither women and children.'
Wednesday 24 Oct	John Crouch prints *The Man in the Moon* and writes '3,000 indeed they killed, but 2,000 were women and children.'
November 18	James Buck writes to Ralph Verney from France and provides testimony regarding the deaths of Sir Edmund Verney and Colonel Boyle. (Document first comes to public notice in 1879.)
Sometime in 1651	In his book *The Penitent Death of a Woeful Sinner* Dean Bernard records sermons he gave to his flock in the months following the siege 'When not only your goods, but your lives were in the like danger'.

In historical practice I would have thought that it was quite unusual for historians to look to evidence over a decade after an event to either prove or disprove facts - the expression secondary sources is often used to describe such accounts. Indeed, Messrs O'Sioichrú, McElligott and Morrill have resisted the temptation to quote from the later memoirs of Edmund Ludlow (1698), Dr George Bate (1685), Bulstrode Whitelocke (1682), Edward Hyde, the Earl of Clarendon, (who wrote a history of the Civil War which was first published in 1702-4), or the officer in the regiment of Sir John Clotworthy (1685), all of whom wrote accounts of the war and with the exception of Ludlow, all allege that Cromwell engaged in war crimes.

Professor Micheál O'Siochrú, however, does use a source from after the Restoration to bolster his argument. However, it is quite obvious that the source is wholly inaccurate and that it flies in the face of the contemporary evidence. O'Siochrú writes: 'By the 1660s, following the restoration of Charles II, Irish clerical sources confidently asserted that 4,000 civilians had died in Drogheda, the result of "an unparalleled savagery and treachery beyond that of any slaughterhouse".' This is certainly second-hand evidence. It is written by Irish ecclesiastics who were obviously prone to gross exaggeration. Four thousand dead civilians on the streets of Drogheda is clearly preposterous. This would bring the death toll to 7,000 in a town where the population was probably only 3,000. Where then did the 3,500 souls come from in the census of 1659? Who were all the people named in the municipal records in the months and years after the attack on the town? John Morrill has suggested that I dismiss secondary sources too easily. Is it any wonder? I make no apology for summarily dismissing this non-primary, post-Restoration source of Irish clerics, the motives of whom could only have been disreputable.

If we take their assertions as true, then why did that same body politic of Catholic clergymen completely neglect to mention this in their Clonmacnoise declarations during the winter of 1649, after Drogheda and Wexford, and when the topic was still current with Cromwell still in Ireland? Their motives in these declarations were to try to bind the various confederate/royalist factions together. What better motivation did they need than to publicise allegations of 4,000 indiscriminate civilian deaths at Drogheda? Because it was a different time and a different place, where these baseless allegations would have been aggressively refuted by Cromwell - then in the whole of his health - with any talk of a Restoration aeons away.

Chapter Four

After Cromwell had left Ireland on 10 August 1650, Henry Ireton, Cromwell's son-in-law, accepted the surrender of Thomas Preston, the royalist governor of Waterford, and terms were agreed. The garrison was allowed to depart with their weapons, bag and baggage. The citizens of the town could stay or go. If they chose to stay they would not be molested in their properties or their goods. Broadly speaking these were the terms that Cromwell himself had agreed with the inhabitants of other Irish towns, like Ross, Clonmel and Kilkenny, if they continued to behave in a manner acceptable to the Parliament of England. But at Waterford, Ireton added a caveat to the conditions that represented the beginning of a change in Parliament's policy of the subjugation of Ireland. Ireton added a clause dictating that, if Parliament should later decide that the Catholic inhabitants were to be removed from the city, then they would be given three months to settle their affairs before being expelled. This is in stark contrast to Cromwell's more lenient approach in the preceding twelve months where citizens of captured urban centres were allowed to remain in situ indefinitely. It also represents a shift in strategy from the guidelines as laid out by Cromwell in his declaration to the people of Ireland at Youghal.

The Puritan movement had many virulent anti-Catholic adherents several of whom were far more vociferous in their condemnation of Catholicism than Cromwell ever was. For instance, the radical Puritan John Pym had a zero tolerance approach to Catholics everywhere. In 1641 Pym was instrumental in passing a venomous anti-Catholic proclamation, and he was always to the fore in challenging Charles I's pro-Catholic sympathies. When Cromwell became Lord Protector, however, while he did not micro-manage affairs in Ireland he obviously fully approved of the eventual colonisation policy over which he presided. He effectively oversaw the widespread transplantation of thousands of innocent Catholics who were removed from their properties under the broad terms of the Act of Subscription and the subsequent Act of Explanation.

During the 1640s the port town of Wexford proved to be of significant benefit to the Catholic/Royalist coalition. Ormond may not have had been in charge of an official navy but the alliance was certainly in possession of many sea vessels, and it was from Wexford that they maintained vital communication and trade links with Europe during the wars. Furthermore, some of the local Catholic inhabitants were said to have perpetrated atrocities on the local Protestant population at this time. The well-known local Catholic cleric Bishop Nicholas French was also implicated in some of these incidents, as Cromwell himself reported to Parliament.

In the seventeenth century, the population of Wexford, including the Old English, was primarily comprised of the Roman faith. Following Sir Phelim O Neill's proclamation of 23 October, Wexford eagerly joined the native Irish insurgents on 21 December, only two months after the official date of the rising. In the county 1,500 men were mustered and in the town the number was 800. Officers were quickly appointed under the authority of the Supreme Council of the Confederate Catholics, whose seat was at Kilkenny. Colonel Nicholas Stafford was installed as governor. According to the Protestant Nicholas Rochford by his deposition of 29 July 1642:

> The Gentlemen of the county [names given] had declared themselves to be in rebellion. The townsmen of Wexford joined themselves likewise into the said rebellion, and made captains among themselves to command the several inhabitants within the parishes of the said town ... the men under the command of the Captains numbered 800.

In January 1642 an order was issued by Viscount Mountgarret and Pierce Butler of Clough that all Protestants were to vacate the town. In an attempt to depart by sea, eighty Protestants had crammed into a frigate which got into difficulties in the estuary, either by accident or design, and only one survived. The deposition of Nicholas Rochford continues to indict a certain local ecclesiastic and some officials of overt religious intolerance, when he advises us that they ' ...took an oath before Sir Nicholas French, Priest, and Sir William Devereux, Vicar General, that they shall suffer noe English or Protestants to live in this Kingdom, or beare any office here, noe not so much as a Petty Constable's place'. Nicholas French, as Bishop of Ferns, would have much to say concerning Cromwell's reduction of Wexford later in 1649. Throughout the 1640s we find that there are many stories of cruelty to the Protestants of Wexford contained in the petitions of those surviving Protestants themselves. It is therefore important to consider that at the time of Cromwell's arrival before the walls of Wexford, the supreme commanding officer of the Confederate forces in Ireland, whose army would be required for the defence of Wexford, was the tenacious Protestant, James Butler, Earl of Ormond.

In 1641, agents of the Confederacy in Flanders were requested to look for 'able and honest men' who would control the Irish coastline and improve the chances of the success of the rebellion. It was considered that terrorising English vessels would seriously hamper communication between both countries and frustrate any plans that Parliament may have had for its ships to regulate these hazardous waters. As compensation for the expensive business of privateering, the participants were authorised to 'enrich themselves by the prizes taken upon our coast'. They were granted approval to accost all enemies of the 'Catholic cause' in Ireland and adversaries of Charles I in England as they patrolled the waters surrounding the island. There was a remarkably enthusiastic response from mariners of Flemish,

French, Irish and even English origins. As a result, by the mid-1640s, Wexford had become a notorious lair of international piracy. Now living within its walls were highly accomplished and vastly experienced pirates whose intimate knowledge of the treacherous Irish coastal seas made their profession extremely remunerative.

As Parliament tried to get to grips with the mercenary Wexford-based frigates in the Irish Sea, the local privateers simply extended their catchment area to include the western Isles of Scotland, the North Sea, the English Channel (which proved most fruitful), and the coastlines of Holland, Normandy and Brittany. Sometimes, Wexford pirates could be found in Baltic and even Mediterranean waters, such was their thirst for booty. Wexford soon became a tremendously prosperous area due to the occupations of many of its seafaring inhabitants. Even though the activity was illegal, it was after all a time of war, and most of the targets were English vessels, although other foreign ships of German, Spanish, French and Turkish origin also fell foul of the Wexford patrol frigates. In 1642 a Dublin business magnate, Daniel Hutchinson, had his ship with its £50 cargo taken by Wexford privateers. In the same year the *Hopewell* of London was taken off the Saltees by Wexford corsairs. In 1646 Wexford privateers took possession of the *Blessing* of Rotterdam, belonging to the burghers of Amsterdam and Rotterdam. In 1647 the 200-ton Dutch *Orange Tree,* while en route from Brill to Scotland, was taken by a Wexford frigate. Many local merchants and officials had investments in individual privateering frigates. In 1643 even the mayor of the town, Nicholas Hayes, had a share in the *Patrick,* since his brother Walter was a link in the chain of command of that ship. Other pillars of local society who had commercial interests in the privateering business were John Coffie, Nicholas Devereux, James Dillon, James Hay, William Keating, Patrick Lamport, Henry Roch, John Rooth, John and Michael Stafford, John Talbot and Michael Tooting. Aside from the mayor, three town officials are also documented as being patrons of the trade: Alderman Alexander Roch, Richard French (collector of customs) and Patrick Rooth (bailiff). The latter, Rooth, was part owner of the man-of-war called *Mary and John of Wexford,* whose captain, John Rosseter, was killed defending his ship. In 1644, Rosseter, who was described as 'an Irishman of warre' had 'pilladged much goods taken away from ye English and were brought into Wexford'. Symon Synnott, who was 'a Pyrat', was known to have sometimes sailed with Rosseter. James Welsh, a seaman of Wexford who lived in the town, was a 'Pyrat in the ffriggot called the Ffrancis and brought in much plunder'. John Rooth, a brother of Patrick and part owner of the *Mary and John,* was the beneficiary of the plunder of that vessel and would 'entertaine, harbour and relieve, in his house in Wexford, many seamen employed in the above and pyrats who robbed the English'.

The illicit bonanza of goods and commodities that was acquired, apart from the enormous value of the captured vessels themselves, comprised of cargoes of: beef, pork, various grains, beans, salt, vinegar, butter, malt, wine, oil, sugar, raisins, tobacco, goat and sheepskins, wood, tiles, tar, cloth, whiskey, silver and bullion.

These goods, with the entrepreneurial enterprise of the inhabitants of Wexford, dissolved into the local economy for a fraction of their market worth. At a time when the rest of the country was in a destitute condition, the population of the south-eastern corner of Ireland was experiencing a period of comparative affluence. The plundering of the town by the Roundheads would serve up a most worthwhile haul as a testament to the years of maritime expeditions. Significantly, even Cromwell himself would remark on the prizes that would ultimately fall into his soldiers' hands.

The assembling at Bristol of Cromwell's expeditionary army did not go unnoticed by the inhabitants of Wexford. On 6 August

1649, the mayor, Michael Boylan, wrote to Ormonde to tell him that a Captain Bradshaw, recently arrived from England, informed him that there were '20 ships in Milford Harbour and 26 more making for Milford to carry soldiers to Ireland; there are 15,000 men, 7,000 horse and 8,000 foot at Pembroke, ready to come for Ireland and the markets of Pembroke, Hereford and Milford are kept open'. No Royalist garrison was stationed in the town and the inhabitants were not keen to accept assistance from Ormond. On 19 September it was realised that after Drogheda, Wexford would now be Cromwell's target. The Supreme Council at Kilkenny ordered a general levy of men and arms in the area. In the county, 523 men were rallied, in Wexford town only fifty and in the nearby town of Ross, only twenty-five.

Following Drogheda, his army slightly reduced to approximately 9,000 men, Cromwell sat down in front of the walls of Wexford on 1 October 1649. Inside the town walls the defenders were riven with discord and indecision. They had only allowed Ormond's man, Col David Sinnott into the town a few days earlier to act as governor of the garrison. This is the backdrop to Wexford that is in stark contrast to the Pale town of Drogheda, where the Old English Catholic lords and their Anglo-Norman families prevailed. The native Catholic Irish were always at loggerheads with their co-religionists and the disparity between both towns is highlighted perfectly by this fact. Furthermore, the evidence that the townspeople of Wexford did not trust Ormond or his troops is clear. At the eleventh hour, with Cromwell's troops in the immediate area, Ormond somehow managed to convince the townspeople of Wexford to accept Sinnott as their governor and he garrisoned the place with 1,500 troops under his command.

Wrongly, Cromwell's sacking of Wexford is almost always treated the same as that of Drogheda. In *God's Executioner*, Micheál O'Siochrú fails to make any distinction between both sets of demographics, military and civilian. Most significantly, he fails to point out that there is very solid evidence to suggest that many of the Wexford townsmen took up arms in defence of their town. This is a hugely important point when it comes to the reports of the battle being written because there are contemporary accounts that mention the deaths of 'inhabitants' or 'townsmen'. Clearly local men in arms are not innocent civilians. But like many before him, O'Siochrú does not make the distinction between local townsmen in arms and non-military members of the local community, especially women and children. Indeed, he writes:

> Cromwell wrote that over 2,000 Irish soldiers and civilians, including Sinnott died, as the English "put to the sword all that came their way." According to a petition of the surviving inhabitants, all the men, women and children of the town, "to a very few" were killed during the assault, while a clerical account described how "the blood lust of the soldiers flooded the streets and the houses"...The deaths of large numbers of civilians at the hands of soldiers under his command further tarnished Cromwell's reputation with the Catholic Irish.

O'Siochrú clearly wants the world to think that women and children were indiscriminately massacred by Cromwell's troops at Wexford. Furthermore, he has no reservations about using post-Restoration evidence to suggest that the vast majority of the women and children of Wexford were slaughtered in cold blood, when there is not one contemporary eye witness account to support this. Maybe O'Siochrú is correct to cite this source in the context that he does. Maybe the petition of the people of Wexford to Charles II is historically correct and all of the popular eye witness source accounts (including the accounts reported in newsbooks) from those who were there on the day are suspect. But if we are to accept the words of the petitioners, then we must also accept what they say about Drogheda,

> Oliver Cromwell arriveing with a powerful army in Ireland in the year 1649 and having upon the taking of Drogheda put all the inhabitants and soldiers to the sword that the example thereof might strike terror into the hearts of the inhabitants of other townes.

We already know this not to be true, in as far as we can be sure about anything from this period of history. All of the inhabitants of Drogheda killed as well as the garrison is quite a claim. This allegation goes some way to explaining just how far the petitioners would go in order to try to regain their properties. This petition was in an effort to both curry favour with Charles II as soon as his royal seat had warmed the English throne again, and encourage him to restore the Catholics of Wexford to their properties. Sweeping post-Restoration statements from disgruntled parties with a clear vested interest is a poor example of evidence to support the innocent civilian atrocity theory. The petition of the people of Wexford is clearly at odds with the surviving contemporary evidence.

When it comes to Wexford, aside from the scurrilous words of Sir George Wharton again (*Mercurius Elencticus*, which for some reason O'Siochrú doesn't even use as evidence) the newsbooks of October/November 1649 do not mention the deliberate deaths of any unarmed men, women and children. Nor do Ormond, Inchiquin or any other writer whose written accounts date from 1649. To this writer it is obvious which evidence historians should prefer. It does not seem practicable to reach into the later post-Restoration minefield and pull out a phrase that smacks of disinformation and has no contemporary supporting evidence.

While the outcome of the siege of Wexford is similar to that of Drogheda, the events leading up to the storming of each town are markedly different. The townspeople of Wexford were keen to agree terms as Sinnott revealed, 'such impression they have of Drogheda' and Cromwell was equally inclined to take the town without a shot being fired. As we know the townsmen, perhaps eager to differentiate themselves from the garrison despatched a cartload of gifts addressed to Cromwell. This attempt to placate Cromwell and his officers clearly indicates that the atmosphere surrounding the deadlock was not like that of Drogheda where such a scheme would have been totally implausible. The two commanders exchanged letters from 3 to 10 October when Cromwell eventually gave the order to open fire to show that he meant business. Notwithstanding the ongoing negotiations, Cromwell proceeded with preparations for the storm, annoyed that Sinnott had the temerity to continue to ask for unrealistic terms, including continued free exercise of the Catholic religion. He snapped at Sinnott telling him that 'our tents are not so good a covering as your houses'.

Were it not for the actions of Captain Stafford, the officer in charge of the castle of Wexford, which was closely adjacent to the town walls, it is possible that terms could have been agreed. It seems that at the critical point when Cromwell was writing a reply to Sinnott, Stafford either abandoned or handed over the castle to the Parliamentarians and all hell broke loose. The New Model Army scaled the walls and suddenly found themselves on the streets of the town where a pitched battle took place. Cromwell had not given the order to storm, nor was quarter offered and withdrawn like at Drogheda. However, the attackers, more savvy in the art of hand-to-hand engagement, simply overwhelmed the defenders and a massacre ensued. Any hostile townsmen in arms were killed where they stood. Members of Sinnott's military garrison met with the same fate.

But what of the non-aggressive civilian community of Wexford: old men and old women, the cobblers, the inn-keepers, the merchants, their wives, their children and babies? We already know that on 9 October Ormond had ordered Sinnott to evacuate the 'unnecessary people such as old men, women and children' from the town. Since the attack took place on the 11th, the governor had two days to send whatever remaining civilians there were from the town. However, we know from a contemporary report that some women, at least didn't make it. As the town was being stormed it seems that some members of the garrison boarded boats alongside a number of women and the boats sank as they made their way across the estuary.

It is worth noting that when it comes down to the detail, there is just one eye-witness account that mentions the deaths of women, and it is equally worth noting that these deaths are not reported as being deliberate, but as the result of an unfortunate set of circumstances.

The reporting in London of the taking of Wexford by the New Model Army was similar to that of Drogheda in many ways. The 'master' account, the most detailed version of the events is from the pen of Cromwell himself who wrote to the Speaker of the House, William Lenthall on 14 October. While Wexford fell on 11 October news of the taking of the town had not hit London by the 23rd, but the correspondence between Cromwell and Sinnott was being published that week. For instance, Scobell's *Severall Proceedings in Parilament* was published on Tuesday 23 October and it carries a letter from Hugh Peters. The chaplain seems quite taken with the sunny south-east 'Here is a very good country, we want nothing but more men to possess it.'

The taking of

WEXFORD

A

LETTER

From an eminent Officer in the Army, under the command of the Lord Leiu-tenant of

IRELAND

Relateing the number put to the Sword, and the manner of the taking the said Town, with 71 peices of Ordnance, 40 Ships, 130.) Prisoners, with store of Arms, Ammunition, Mony, Plate and Iewells, and the advance of the Lord Leiutenants army to ROSSE.

And the engagement between Colonell MONROE and Colonell OCONELLY who was slain in the service.

LONDON Printed For *Francis Leach* 1649.

(3)

The Taking of VVexford,

a Letter from an emminent Officer in the Army under the command of the Lord Leiutenant of IRELAND

SIR,

I Doubt not but you have long ſince heard of the goodneſſe of God to our Army at *Wexford*, the ſecond of *October* we ſate downe with our Army before *Wexford*, and found from the Enemy a ſeeming Complement, Commiſsioners being oppointed to treat for ſurrender, but ſo ſoone as they had got reliefe of men from *Ormond*, they rejected all tearms, all this while we continued without attempting any thing, untill on the 9th. inſtant, we romoved to the South ſide of the towne, the 11th. we framed our Batteries againſt the Caſtle, which ſtands cloſe

A 2

(4)

close by the Works, & commands a great part of the Line; In this we made two good breaches; after which the Governour of the Castle and three more were sent forth to treat; the Governour We dealt with a part, who was sufficiently affrighted, that we easi'y perswaded him to march out with his men, and let ours enter, the *Commissioners* for the towne had in the interim delivered their Propositions to my *Lord Leiutenant*; who found them so unreasonable, that they were instantly by him rejected, and only a briefe returne made, offering security from the violence of the soldier to the lives and goods of all, they ingageing not to take up armes against the Parliament, but see our just *God* who will not let the wicked go unpunished.

No sooner had our men, that possest the Castle advanced our *Standard*, but instantly the Rogues generally deserted the Line, and left our Souldiers at liberty to use their scaling ladders without giuing the least opposition, nay, and before their Commissioners could returne into Towne to tell them of the offers of mercy the whole work was accomplished. In the

Town

(5)

towne were 1700. men at the leaſt, ſome ſay, three thouſand, of whom we have a generall beliefthat there eſcaped not above foure hundred at moſt: many were drowned endeavouring to get over the River, and two boates ſunke in which is ſaid the Governour to have bin,of ours not above 1 or two killed, in the town we found 51.peices of ſmall ordnance,& 10 aboard the ſhips, good ſtore of powder and ammunition, about forty good veſſells in the Harbour,3 or 4 whereof, will be fit for State-ſervice, money, plate, and Jewells was much removed out of town, but other plunder there was good ſtore: tallow, hydes, ſalt, and ſuch groſſe commodities are reſerved for the ſtate; but all other things at the ſouldiers devotion. *Ormond* is now joyned with *Inchequin*,both are about *Roſſe*, their number we compute to be about 2000. horſe and 3000 Foot, which is certainly the utmoſt they can make, their main expectation is upon a conjunction with *Owen Roe*; the Garriſon of *Youghall* under the command of Sir *Peircie Smith* lately declared for the Parliament, but for want of ſeaſonable reliefe it was againe reduced by *Inchequin*, We begin

our

our march to morrow to the Garrison of *Rosse* 12 miles hence, which we hope to obtein on composition; upon *Ormonds* advance towards *Wexford*, colonell Jones was sent with horse and dragoones to impede his march; *Ormond* hearing of it retreated, Jones pursued no farther then Enniscorthy, from thence he inclined to *Rosse*, and early in the morning lodged himselfe under the enemies works, sent out a party to enter the town under the notion of friendship, who past unsuspected, and had doubtlesse carried the businesse, but that one amongst them fell upon the sentinel, and so alarm'd the town.

We have lately had some losse in the North, Colonell *Oconelly* with a party of horse about 100. marching from *Belfast* to *Antrim*, was set upon by *George Monroe* with a bigger force, routed our men, Col. *Oconelly* and Capt. *Rooper* with about twenty others slaine, about the same number taken prisoners, the rest escaped; The report of the country people comming out of the Enemies quarters is, that they intend to give battle to our army within ten dayes, that all their Forces are drawing towards Rosse, or those parts joyned with *Owen Roe Oneale* for

that

(7)

that purpose,their forces besides his are reputed 6. or 7000. horse and foot, *Shirlock* the chiefe of the Tories with 80. horse is laid betwixt *Caturlaugh* and the *Liffe* to stop the running away of their men, who comes daily away from them to us by 30. 40. and sometime more together, *Inchequin* dare not trust the Irish, and is diffident of the English, they declaring their dislike of his actions every day more and more. *Yoghal* did declare for the Parliament & army,and had a plot to have secured *Inchequin*, and have sent him into safe custody to the *Generall*, but being discovered was prevented, stood upon their guard,three dayes against him and his forces,being not relieved was forced to submit upon promise of pardon.

we hope before this time my Lord is so neare them as to give them encouragement to try once more; since which Inchiquin hath dismounted all his Munster horse, & hath mounted Papists and Irish in their roome; it is reported *Owen Roe* is to have six moneths pay for his whole army, to be commander in chiefe of all the Irish Natives, to have liberty to burn & de-

stroy

It wasn't until 28 October that the news about the taking of Wexford hit the streets in newsbook format. The letter writer who went by the initials R.L. wrote his account from Ireland on the 20 October. The pamphlet was printed for Francis Leach, and it was licensed by the Secretary to the Army, John Rushworth now that Richard Hatter was out of the way. The document is entitled *The Taking of Wexford, A letter from an eminent officer in the army under the command of the Lord Lieutenant of Ireland.* The letter begins:

> Sir, I doubt not but you have long since heard of the goodnesse of God to our army at Wexford, the second of October we sate down with our Army before Wexford and found from the enemy a seeming complement, Commissioners being appointed to treat for surrender, but so soone as they had got reliefe of men from Ormond, they rejected all tearms, all this while we continued without attempting anything until on the 9th instant, we removed to the south side of the towne, the 11th we framed our batteries against the castle, which stands close by the works and commands a great part of the line. In this we made two good breaches, after which the governor of the castle, and three more were sent forth to treat. The governor we dealt with apart, who was sufficiently affrighted that we easily persuaded him to march out with his men and let ours enter. The Commissioners for the towne had in the interim delivered their Propositions to my Lord Lieutenant, who found them so unreasonable that they were instantly by him rejected, and only a brief returne made, offering security from the violence of the soldiers to the lives and goods of all, they ingaging not to take up armes against the Parliament, but see our just God, who will not let the wicked go unpunished.
>
> No sooner had our men, that possessed the castle advanced our standard, but instantly the rogues generally

> deserted the line, and left our soldiers at liberty to use their scaling ladders without giving the least opposition, nay, and before their commissioners could returne into Towne to tell them of the offers of mercy, the whole work was accomplished. In the towne were 1,700 men at the least, some say three thousand, of whom we have a general belief that there escaped not above foure hundred at most, many were drowned endeavouring to get over the river and two boats sunke in which is said the Governor to have bin, of ours not above 1 or two killed.

The 'eminent officer' succinctly explains what happened at Wexford in this missive. Stafford, the castle governor, sought terms for himself and his men in quite a separate deal, while the delegation from the town were still negotiating theirs. With the castle in Parliament's hands the opportunistic New Model simply attacked the adjacent town walls, the defenders, panicked, withdrew and ran for their lives.

The following day (29 October) '*A Perfect and Particuler Relation (of the severall marches and proceedings of the armie in Ireland from the taking of Drogheda to this present)*', a pamphlet also printed for Francis Leach and licensed by Rushworth, was published. It carried another anonymous letter that was written on 22 October and had just been received in London. The author writes:

> The Ordnance played their parts very handsomely, and by noone the battlements of the castle were beaten down and three great breaches were made in 2 of the said towers. Great feare and amazement fell upon the hearts of the inhabitants of the towne. The Governor sent a drum and beat a parley, the mayor and some of the aldermen came out with propositions for a surrender. The governor of the castle came out and submitted to my Lord's mercy and gave him the possession of the castle. My Lord being willing to save the inhabitants of the

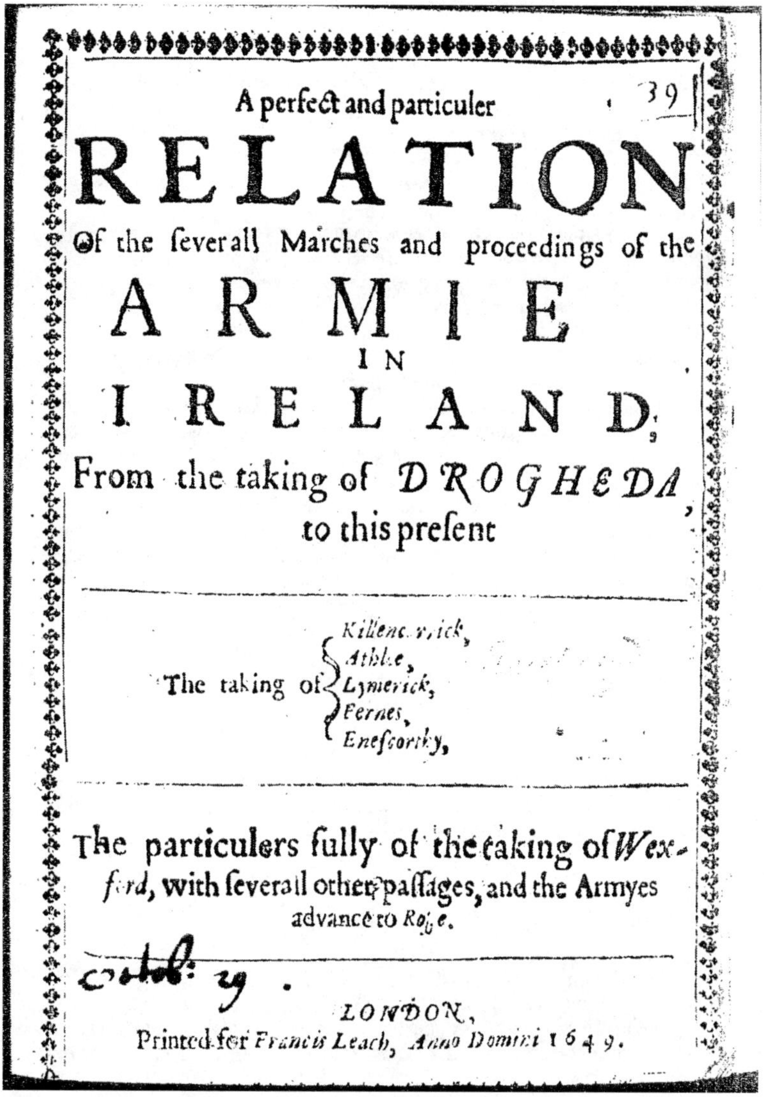

A perfect and particuler

RELATION

Of the feverall Marches and proceedings of the

ARMIE

IN

IRELAND;

From the taking of *DROGHEDA*, to this prefent

The taking of { *Killencarick*, *Athbie*, *Lymerick*, *Fernes*, *Enefcorthy*,

The particulers fully of the taking of *Wexford*, with feverall other paffages, and the Armyes advance to *Roffe*.

Octob: 29.

LONDON, Printed for *Francis Leach*, *Anno Domini* 1649.

town, and to preserve it from plunder condescended to let the soldiery repair everyone to their homes they engaging not to bear arms any more against the State of England. And the officers were to have their lives, but to render themselves prisoners. Just as my Lord was ready to sign this and send it into the town, such a fear fell upon them, that the soldiers left

(6)

better judgement, and my ſelfe to the aſſiſtance of the Almighty, and ſo conclude Your Servant

Wexford, October the 4th. 1649. *Da. Sinnot.*

For the Lord Generall Cromwell theſe.

My Lord return'd no anſwer to this Letter, but the Governour of *Wexford* the day following ſent this enſuing overture,

Sir, My Propoſitions being now prepared, I am ready to ſend my Agents with them unto you; and for their ſafe return, I pray you to ſend conduct by this bearer unto me, in hope an honourable agreement may thereupon ariſe between your Lordſhip, and My Lord,

Wexford, October the 5. Your Lordſhips ſervant,

1649. *Da. Sinnot.*

For the Lord Gen. Cromwell *theſe.*

According to the contents of this laſt Letter, my Lord ſent a permit unto him for his Agents to come, and return ſafely, but the Governours minde was altered before the morrow, and it was occaſioned by the comming in unto him of two freſh Regiments ſent by the Lord of *Caſtle-haven*; For on Saturday the 6. of this inſtant there came relief into the Town on the other ſide the water, which we had no notice of, neither if we had, could we have prevented it, and thereupon the Governour ſent out this excuſall, for the non ſending of his agents according to his promiſe and permit.

My Lord, Even as *I* was ready to ſend out my agents unto you, the L. Generall of the horſe came hither with releif, unto whom *I* communicated the proceedings between your Lordſhip and me, & delivered him the propoſitions, I intended to diſpatch unto your Lordſhip, who hath deſired a ſmall time to conſider of them, and to ſpeed them unto me; which, my Lord *I* could not deny, he having a commanding power over me. Pray my Lord, believe, that *I* do not doe this to trifle out time, but for his preſent content; and if *I* find any long delay in his Lordſhips returning them back unto me, *I* will proceed of my ſelf according to my firſt intention: To which *I* beſeech your Lordſhip give credit at the requeſt, My Lord, of

Wexford October 6. Your Lordſhips ready ſervant,

1649. *Da. Sinnot.*

For the Lord Gen. Cromwell theſe.

Hereunto my Lord gave this reply,

Sir, You might have ſpared your trouble in the account you give me of your tranſaction with the Lord Generall of your horſe, and of your reſolutions in caſe he anſwer not your expectations in point of time. Theſe are your own concernments, and it behooves you to improve them, and the relief

the wall, and all, both men and women, Officers and Soldiers endeavoured to break themselves to fly over the water in boats, for the safety of their lives. Our men saw this and presently scaled the walls to stop them in their intended flight. They did not find very much opposition, but in lesse than the

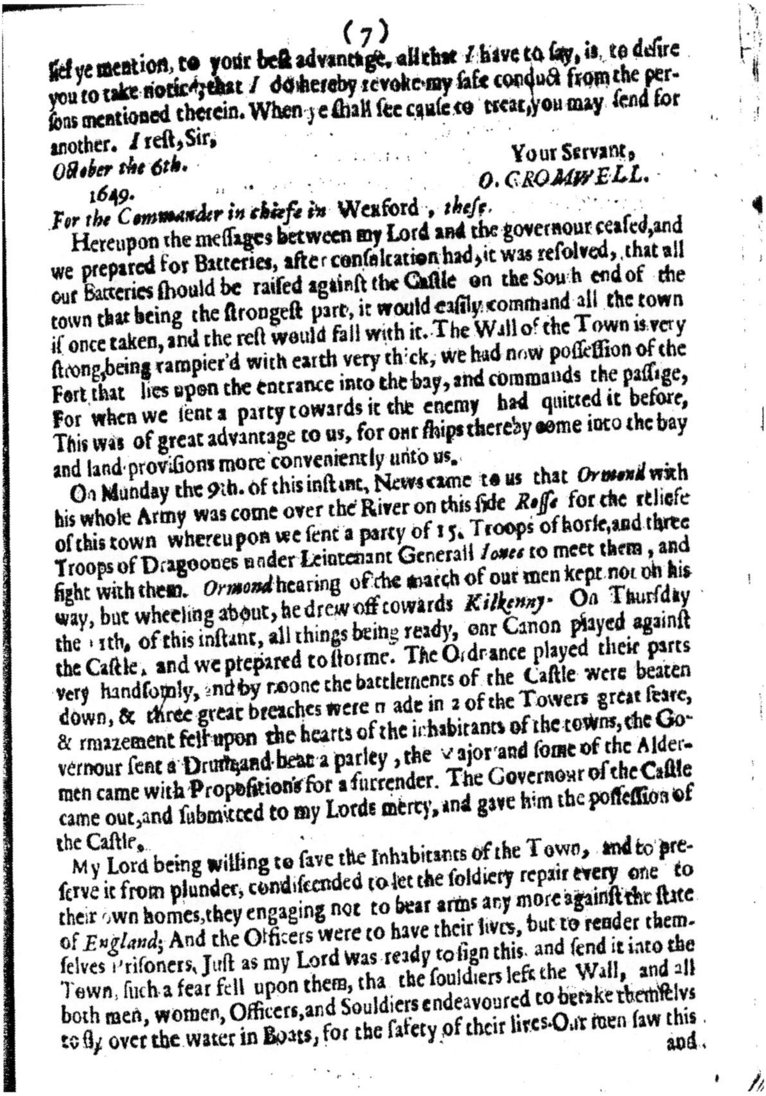

(7)

ſelf ye mention, to your beſt advantage, all that *I* have to ſay, is, to deſire you to take notice, that *I* do hereby revoke my ſafe conduct from the perſons mentioned therein. When ye ſhall ſee cauſe to treat, you may ſend for another. *I* reſt, Sir,

Your Servant,

October the 6th. 1649.

O. CROMWELL.

For the Commander in chiefe in Wexford, *theſe.*

Hereupon the meſſages between my Lord and the governour ceaſed, and we prepared for Batteries, after conſultation had, it was reſolved, that all our Batteries ſhould be raiſed againſt the Caſtle on the South end of the town that being the ſtrongeſt part, it would eaſily command all the town if once taken, and the reſt would fall with it. The Wall of the Town is very ſtrong, being rampier'd with earth very thick, we had now poſſeſſion of the Fort that lies upon the entrance into the bay, and commands the paſſage, For when we ſent a party towards it the enemy had quitted it before, This was of great advantage to us, for our ſhips thereby come into the bay and land proviſions more conveniently unto us.

On Munday the 9th. of this inſtant, News came to us that *Ormond* with his whole Army was come over the River on this ſide *Roſſe* for the reliefe of this town whereupon we ſent a party of 15. Troops of horſe, and three Troops of Dragoones under Leiutenant Generall *Jones* to meet them, and fight with them. *Ormond* hearing of the march of our men kept not on his way, but wheeling about, he drew off towards *Kilkenny*. On Thurſday the 11th, of this inſtant, all things being ready, our Canon played againſt the Caſtle, and we prepared to ſtorme. The Ordnance played their parts very handſomly, and by noone the battlements of the Caſtle were beaten down, & three great breaches were made in 2 of the Towers great feare, & amazement fell upon the hearts of the inhabitants of the towns, the Governour ſent a Drum, and beat a parley, the Major and ſome of the Aldermen came with Propoſitions for a ſurrender. The Governour of the Caſtle came out, and ſubmitted to my Lords mercy, and gave him the poſſeſſion of the Caſtle.

My Lord being willing to ſave the Inhabitants of the Town, and to preſerve it from plunder, condiſcended to let the ſouldiery repair every one to their own homes, they engaging not to bear arms any more againſt the ſtate of *England*; And the Officers were to have their lives, but to render themſelves Priſoners, Juſt as my Lord was ready to ſign this. and ſend it into the Town, ſuch a fear fell upon them, that the ſouldiers left the Wall, and all both men, women, Officers, and Souldiers endeavoured to betake themſelvs to fly over the water in Boats, for the ſafety of their lives. Our men ſaw this

and

space of an hour the whole town was cleared and gained. ...We lost not one man in the storm, and not above 3 or 4 wounded. Our soldiers killed many, both in the town and as they fled out of the town on the west side, a great slaughter was made, many were drowned as they thought to escape by boat over the water. Some were taken prisoners, one col, one

(8)

and presently scaled the walls to stop them in their intended flight; They did not find very much opposition; but in lesse then the space of an hour the whole town was cleer'd and gain'd. There was a wonderfull providence seen in it, That when they were even on the brink to have conditions, it should be so marvellously denyed them. The hand of *God* was mightily in it; this town which was a seate of pyracy, and the ruine of many familyes in England, was thus justly met with, we may read much of God in the whole carriage of this businesse; yea, even his righteous anger against this place, two things were very remarkable, The one was, That when the English in the beginning of this *Rebellion* fled hither out of the Countrys for protection they sent many of them to shipboard, and there they were drowned; even in the same waters many of these now through haste sank, and perished: The other was, That some preists and Friers were now killed in that Church, where they had caused many of the English to be famished to death, Thus the Lord has found out their wickednesse, and repayed it, many escaped over the water, and carried some goods along with them. Our souldiers had the plunder of the Town for the space of two hours, and then my Lord caused a Proclamation to be published, That all further violence, and plunder should cease upon perill. The rest of the goods that were saved together with the ships are to be valued for the State, wee lost not one man in the storm, and not above 3 or 4. were wounded, our *Souldiers* killed many, both in the town, and as they fled out of the Town on the West side, a great Slaughter was made, many were drowned, as they thought to escape by Boat over the water, Some are taken Prisoners; one Col. one Lieut. Col. five Captaines, six Leiutenants, four Ensignes, three Serjeants, One hundred fourescore and fifteen Soldiers, fourescore and fifteen whereof are taken to be Pioneers in our Army, thus has the Lord been pleased to give this strong place into our hands, *Blessed be his name for ever.*

Wee are now gone to *Rosse*, The Lord has done great things for us beyond our thoughts, great mercies in the North, very high successes there and now he has enlarged our borders towards the South, The Lord keep us humble, and his presence be with us still.

A present supply of more foot would be highly advantagious, for many garrisons do swallow up our infantry. Let us have your prayers, and blesse *God* for what he has already done.

October 22 1649

October 27. 1649.

Imprimatur, Jo. RUSHWORTH.

FINIS.

Lieut. Col, five captains, six Lieutenants, four ensigns, three serjeants, one hundred fourscore and fifteen soldiers, fourscore and fifteen whereof are taken to be Pioneers in our army. Thus has the Lord been pleased to give this strong place into our hands. Blessed be his name for ever.

A
LETTER
FROM
The Lord Lieutenant of *Ireland*,
To the Honorable *William Lenthal* Eſq; Speaker of the Parliament of *England*:
Giving an Account of the Proceedings of the Army there under his Lordſhips Command; and ſeveral Tranſactions between his Lordſhip and the Governor of *Wexford*.
Together with a Relation of the Taking in of
WEXFORD,
With the Fort, Haven and Shipping there; and of ſeveral other Gariſons of the Enemy.
As alſo the Propoſitions tendred for the Rendition of *Wexford*: And a Copy of a Cenſure, under the hand of *Nicholas* Biſhop of *Fernes*, againſt *Talbot* who dyed a Proteſtant.

ORdered by the Parliament, That theſe Letters and Tranſactions be forthwith printed and publiſhed.
Hen: Scobell, Cleric. Parliamenti.

London, Printed by *John Field* for *Edward Husband*, Printer to the Parliament of *England*. 1649.

This writer is the only writer who witnessed the events who mentions the word 'women'. He tells us very clearly that women were in the boats that sunk as they were filled to overcapacity

Die Martis, xxx. Octobr. 1649.

ORdered by the Parliament, That it be referred to the Lord Major of the City of *London*, to take care to diſperſe the ſaid Letters and Tranſactions to all the Miniſters within *London* and the Liberties, who are required reſpectively to Read the ſame in their reſpective Congregations on Thurſday next, and to take notice of this great and wonderful Mercy, in giving in the Fort and Town of *Wexford*, together with the Haven there, and the Shipping in it, as an addition unto the former Mercies, for which that day was ſet apart, and to return all humble Thanks to Almighty God for the ſame.

Hen: Scobell, Cleric. Parliamenti.

with panicking soldiers. It is worth noting here that Ormond suggested to Sinnott that he evacuates the civilians 'after' he had examined 'each inhabitant's provision'. It's not unreasonable to assume that women were still assisting their menfolk in the town right up to the last minute and were now hastily preparing to leave as mayhem ensued at the walls. Sinnott might well have been in the process of organising the evacuation of civilians. In that way the women might have drowned with the soldiers and other inhabitants that had jumped shipboard in an effort to escape the ferocity of the attackers. What is absolutely clear is that the writer does not imply that women were deliberately targeted by the attackers.

Cromwell, always the assiduous communicator to his superiors, wrote his own account of the taking of the town, which was read out in parliament and later printed and published in London on 30 October. Interestingly, like Cromwell's letter about Drogheda, *Letters from Ireland,* this pamphlet seems also to have been assembled by Henry Scobell and it too was printed by John Field for Edward Husband. Indeed Scobell also gives us an indication of how news was circulated in London when he inserted the following text on to page 2 of the pamphlet, *'Ordered by the Parliament, that it be referred to the Lord Mayor of the City of London, to take care to disperse the said letters and transactions to all the ministers within London and the Liberties, who are required respectively to Read the same in their respective congregations on Thursday next, and to take notice of this great and wonderful mercy, in giving in the Fort and the town of Wexford, together with the Haven there, and the Shipping in it, as an addition unto the former mercies, for which that day was set apart, and to return all humble thanks to Almighty God for the same.'*

(1)

For the Honorable William Lenthal *Eſquire,*
Speaker of the Parliament of England.

SIR,

THe Army marched from **Dublin** about
the 23 of *September*, into the Coun-
ty of *Wicklo*, where the enemy had
a gariſon about 14 miles from *Dub-
lin* called *Killingkerick*, which they
quitting, a Company of the Army
was put therein. From thence the Army marched
through almoſt a deſolated Countrey, until it came
to a paſſage over the River *Doro*, about a mile a-
bove the Caſtle of *Arcklo*, which was the firſt Seat
and Honor of the Marques of *Ormonds* family, which
he had ſtrongly fortified, but was upon the ap-
proach of the Army quitted, wherein we left another
company of foot. From thence the Army marched
towards *Wexford*, where in the way was a ſtrong
and large Caſtle, at a Town called *Limrick*, the
ancient Seat of the *Eſmonds*, where the enemy had
a ſtrong gariſon, which they burnt and quitted the
day before our coming thither. From thence we
marched towards *Ferns*, an Epiſcopal Seat, where
was a Caſtle, to which I ſent Colonel *Reynolds*
with a party to ſummon it, which accordingly he
did, and it was ſurrendred to him; where we ha-
ving put a company, advanced the Army to a paſ-
ſage

A 2

(4)

ſage over the River *Slane*, which runs down to *Wexford*, and that night marched into the fields of a Village called *Eniſcorſy*, belonging to Maſter *Robert Wallop*, where was a ſtrong Caſtle very well manned and provided for by the enemy, and cloſe under it in a very fair houſe belonging to the ſame worthy Perſon, A Monaſtery of *Franciſcan Fryers*, the conſiderables in all *Ireland*, they run away the night before we came; we ſummoned the Caſtle, and they refuſed to yield at the firſt, but upon better conſideration, they were willing to deliver the place to us, which accordingly they did, leaving their great Guns, Arms, Ammunition, and proviſions behinde them. Upon *Munday* the firſt of *October*, we came before *Wexford*, into which the enemy had put a gariſon conſiſting of their Army, this Town having until then been ſo confident of their own ſtrength, as that they would not at any time ſuffer a gariſon to be impoſed upon them; The commander that brought in thoſe forces was Colonel *David Synnot*, who took upon him the command of the place, to whom I ſent a ſummons, a Copy whereof is this incloſed, between whom and me there paſſed Anſwers and Replies; Copies whereof theſe alſo are. Whilſt theſe Papers were paſſing between us, I ſent the Lieut. General with a party of dragoons, horſe and foot, to indeavor to reduce their Fort, which lay at the mouth of their Harbor, about ten miles diſtant from us, to which he ſent a Troop of dragoons, but the enemy quit their Fort, leaving behinde them about ſeven great Guns, betook themſelves by the help of their boat to a fri-

got

(5)

got of 12 Guns, lying in the Harbor, within Canon-shot of the Fort: The dragoons possessed the Fort, and some Seamen belonging to your Fleet, coming happily in at the same time, they bent their Guns at the Frigot, and she immediately yielded to mercy, both her self, the soldiers that had been in the Fort, and the Seamen that manned her: And whilst our men were in her, the Town not knowing what had happed, sent another small Vessel to her, which our men also took: The Governor of the Town having obtained from me a safe conduct for the four persons mentioned in one of the Papers, to come and treat with me about the surrender of the Town, I expected they should have done so; but in stead thereof, the Earl of *Castlehaven* brought to their relief on the Northside of the River, about five hundred foot, which occasioned their refusal to send out any to treat, and caused me to revoke my safe conduct, not thinking it fit to leave it for them to make use of it when they pleased; our Canon being landed, and we having removed all our quarters to the South-east end of the Town, next the Castle, it was generally agreed that we should bend the whole strength of our Artillery upon the Castle, being perswaded that if we got the Castle, the Town would easily follow. Upon *Thursday* the 11. instant (our Batteries being finished the night before) we began to play betimes in the morning, and having spent neer a hundred shot, the Governors stomack came down, and he sent to me to give leave for four persons intrusted by him, to come unto me and offer terms of surrender, which I condescending

to,

(6)

to, two field Officers, with an Alderman of the Town, and the Captain of the Caſtle, brought out the Propoſitions incloſed, which for their abominableneſs, manifeſting alſo the impudency of the men, I thought fit to preſent to your view, together with my anſwer, which indeed had no effect; for whilſt I was preparing of it, ſtudying to preſerve the Town from plunder, that it might be of the more uſe to you and your Army, The Captain who was one of the Commiſſioners being fairly treated, yielded up the Caſtle to us: upon the top of which our men no ſooner appeared, but the enemy quitted the walls of the Town, which our men perceiving, ran violently upon the Town with their ladders and ſtormed it: And when they were come into the Market place, the enemy making a ſtiff reſiſtance, our forces brake them, and then put all to the ſword that came in their way: Two Boatfuls of the Enemy attempting to eſcape, being overpreſt with numbers, ſunk, whereby were drowned near Three hundred of them: I believe in all there was loſt of the Enemy not many leſs then two thouſand, and I believe not Twenty of yours killed, from firſt to laſt of the Siege. And indeed, it hath not without cauſe been deeply ſet upon our hearts, that we intending better to this place, then ſo great a ruine, hoping the Town might be of more uſe to you and your Army; yet God would not have it ſo, but by an unexpected Providence, in his Righteous Juſtice, brought a juſt Judgement upon them, cauſing them to become a prey to the Soldier, who in their Pyracies had made preys of ſo many families, and made

with

(7)

with their bloods to answer the cruelties which they had exercised upon the lives of divers poor Protestants; two of which I have been lately acquainted with: About seven or eight-score poor Protestants were by them put into an old Vessel, which being as some say bulged by them, the Vessel sunk, and they were all presently drowned in the Harbor: The other was thus, They put divers poor Protestants into a Chappel, which since they have used for a Mass house, and in which one or more of their Priests were now killed, where they were famished to death.

The Soldier got a very good Booty in this place, and had they not had opportunity to carry their goods over the River, whilest we besieged it, it would have been much more. I could have wished for their own good, and the good of the Garison, they had been more moderate. Some things which were not easily portable, we hope we shall make use of to your behoof: There are great quantities of Iron, Hides, Tallow, Salt, Pipe, and Barrel Staves, which are under Commissioners hands to be secured. We believe there are near a hundred Canon in the Fort, and elsewhere in and about the Town: Here is likewise some very good shipping; here are three Vessels, one of them of thirty four Guns, which a weeks time would fit to Sea; there is another of about 20 Guns, very near ready likewise; and one other frigot of 20 Guns, upon the stocks, made for sailing, which is built up to the uppermost Deck, for her handsomness sake I have appointed the workmen to finish her, here being materials to do it, if you or the Councel of State shall approve thereof. The Friggot also taken by the Fort, is a most excellent Vessel for sailing,

(8)

ing, besides divers other Ships and Vessels in the Harbor. This Town is now so in your power, that the former Inhabitants I believe scarce one in twenty can challenge any propriety in their houses, most of them are run away, and many of them killed in this service; and it were to be wished, that an honest people would come and plant here, where are very good houses, and other Accommodations fitted to their hands, and may by your favor be made of encouragement to them; as also a seat of good trade, both inward and outward, and of marvellous great advantage in the point of the Herring and other fishing. The Town is pleasantly seated, and strong, having a Rampert of Earth within the Wall, near fifteen foot thick. Thus it hath pleased God to give into your hands this other Mercy, for which, as for all, we pray God may have all the glory: Indeed your instruments are poor, and weak, and can do nothing but through Believing, and that is the gift of God also. I humbly take leave, and rest,

Your most humble Servant,

Wexford, Octob. 4. 1649.

O. CROMVVEL.

A day or two before our Battery was planted, Ormond, *the Earl of* Castlehaven, *the Lord of* Ardes *and* Clanneboys *were on the other side of the water, with about One thousand eight hundred Horse, One thousand five hundred Foot, and offered to put in four or five hundred Foot more into the Town, which the Town refusing, he marched away in all haste: I sent the Lieutenant General after him, with about One thousand four hundred Horse, but the Enemy made from him.*

For

(9)

For the Commnnder in Chief within the Town of Wexford.

SIR,

HAving brought the Army belonging to the Parliament of *England* before this place, to reduce it to its due obedience, to the end effusion of blood may be prevented, and the Town and Counrty about it preserved from ruine, I thought fit to Summon you to deliver the same to me, to the use of the State of *England*: By this offer I hope it will clearly appear where the guilt will lie, if innocent persons should come to suffer with the nocent. I expect your speedy Answer, and rest, Sir,

Your Servant,

October 3. 1649.

O. Cromwel.

For the Lord General Cromwel.

SIR,

I Have received your Letters of Summons for the delivery up of this Town into your hands, which standeth not with my Honor to do of my self, neither will I take it upon me, without the advice of the rest of the Officers and Major of this Corporation, this Town being of so great consequence to all *Ireland*, whom I will call together and confer with, and return my resolution unto you to morrow by Twelve of the Clock; in the mean time, if you be so pleased, I am content to forbear all acts of Hostility, so you permit no approach to be made: Expecting your Answer in that particular, I remain, My Lord,

Your Lordships Servant, *Da: Sinnot.*

B For

(44)

ville, or to Mr *de Avaux*; but though ſuch things have been mooved, yet there is nothing reſolved upon it as yet: And theſe changes are of ſuch nature, that they will admit an infinite number of Conteſtations and hinderances. The Propoſitions ſent by *Contarini* his Secretary to the Marquis of *Pignoranda* were, that this State did conſent, for an accomodation, to a truce of ſix moneths one Flanders ſide beginning at the firſt of *November* next: That *Catalonia, Porto, Longone*, and Lorraine doe remain in the poſſeſſion of this State; ſo that the two States for their mutuall commodity might reſtore one to another ſome of the places taken one from another during theſe Warres. It is obſervable that in theſe Propoſitions no mention is made of Portugall. The ſaid Marqueſs hath ſo deſpis'd them, that in his Letter (the Coppy whereof I have been promiſed) full of reproaches and mokerie, he ſaith to the ſaid Ambaſſador, that he needs not to ſend him Propoſitions for partiall, and as concerning the ſaid Truce of ſix Moneths, the King his Maſter would not be beholden to France for it, but to the Moneth of *November* which obleiged them both to ſuch a Truce.

There dyed at Rome and round about of the Malignant Feaver above 40000 Perſons ſince *May*.

Letters out of Germanie ſay that the Swedes doe give Benfeild to the Elector Palatine in recompence of Frankendale, and that it hath beene done without regarding the Inſtances of the French, who feare with reaſon that hereafter the ſaid Elector being little beholden to France ſhall cede the ſaid Benfeild to the King of Spaine for Frankendale, which will be a meanes to turne them out of *Alſatia*, ſo much the better that the People there will have a diſtaſt of the choice made of the Duke of *Eſpernon* for their Governour.

Paris the 30/20 *of October* 1649.

The Count of *Harcourt* came hither yeſterday night to his Towne: The great preſent care of this Court is to thinke upon the Winter Quarters, for their Souldiery. The change of charges, and Governments talked of the laſt Weeke ſeems to come to nothing. The Queene Regent hath yet beene ſo ſurpriſed by it, that ſhee complained that at laſt they would deveſt her and the King alſo, It was propounded laſt thurſday to diſpoſe of the Superintendence *des Finances*, Cardinall *Mazarin* would faigne have Mr *De Emery* to come into it again, to excerciſe the ſame under Mr *de Avaux*, to content the people in ſome ſort, who is ſtill ſo diſpleas'd with the ſaid *de Emery*, that ſeverall Papers were ſpread abroad of late againſt his comming, and re-eſtabliſhing: The Pariſians doe oppoſe the admiſſion of Marquis *de la Vieuville*, who (they feare would be their plague, and would preſſe for a Chamber of juſtice againſt them.) In a word they are not a little buſie how to hinder the diſorders of the ſaid Finances. Here happened laſt Saturday ſome rumour in the new Market, becauſe of the dearth of Bread: Some Fiſh-women complained to the Queene, as ſhee was paſſing through the ſame to goe to *Noſtre Dame*, ſome of them cryed out, *Madame Anne, Madame Anne*, make the Price of the Corne to fall, whereat her Guards taking exception, ſhee ſilenced them, ſaying to the ſaid Women, I will doe my beſt. Thoſe of *Joigny* upon the River of Yonne will not ſuffer their Corne to come to *Paris*, untill the ſaid Cardinall be firſt gone out of it. We ſhall ſee what the Parliament will doe thereupon, after St Martins day.

The Abbot *de la Riviere* hath ſent an expreſſe to Rome, their Majeſties the Duke of *Orleans*, the Prince of *Conde*, and the Prince of *Conti* have written by him to the Pope to procure the Cardinalls Cap to the ſaid Abbot.

Marſhall *de Ratzaw* hath been very ſicke in the *Bois, de Vincennes*. The Kings Councell

Nowhere in Cromwell's letter does he refer to the deaths of women at Wexford. Nor does he suggest that any of the

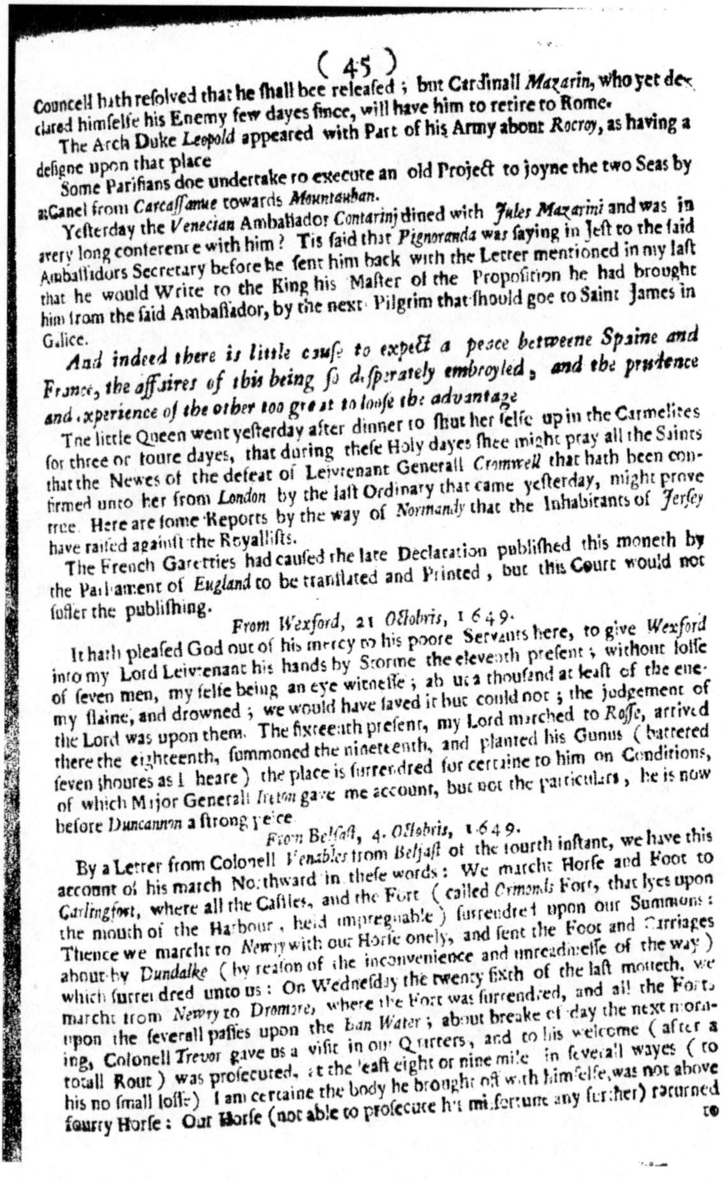
(45)
Councell hath reſolved that he ſhall bee releaſed ; but Cardinall *Mazarin*, who yet de-
clared himſelfe his Enemy few dayes ſince, will have him to retire to Rome.
The Arch Duke *Leopold* appeared with Part of his Army about *Rocroy*, as having a
deſigne upon that place
Some Pariſians doe undertake to execute an old Project to joyne the two Seas by
a Canel from *Carcaſſanue* towards *Mountauban*.
Yeſterday the *Venecian* Ambaſſador *Contarinj* dined with *Jules Mazarini* and was in
a very long conference with him ? Tis ſaid that *Pignoranda* was ſaying in Jeſt to the ſaid
Ambaſſadors Secretary before he ſent him back with the Letter mentioned in my laſt
that he would Write to the King his Maſter of the Propoſition he had brought
him from the ſaid Ambaſſador, by the next Pilgrim that ſhould goe to Saint James in
Galice.
And indeed there is little cauſe to expect a peace betweene Spaine and
France, the affaires of this being ſo deſperately embroyled, and the prudence
and experience of the other too great to looſe the advantage
The little Queen went yeſterday after dinner to ſhut her ſelfe up in the Carmelites
for three or foure dayes, that during theſe Holy dayes ſhee might pray all the Saints
that the Newes of the defeat of Leivtenant Generall *Cromwell* that hath been con-
firmed unto her from *London* by the laſt Ordinary that came yeſterday, might prove
true. Here are ſome Reports by the way of *Normandy* that the Inhabitants of *Jerſey*
have raiſed againſt the Royalliſts.
The French Garetties had cauſed the late Declaration publiſhed this moneth by
the Parliament of *England* to be tranſlated and Printed , but this Court would not
ſuffer the publiſhing.

From Wexford, 21 *Octobris*, 1649.

It hath pleaſed God out of his mercy to his poore Servants here, to give *Wexford*
into my Lord Leivtenant his hands by Storme the eleventh preſent ; without loſſe
of ſeven men, my ſelfe being an eye witneſſe ; about a thouſand at leaſt of the ene-
my ſlaine, and drowned ; we would have ſaved it but could not ; the judgement of
the Lord was upon them. The ſixteenth preſent, my Lord marched to *Roſſe*, arrived
there the eighteenth, ſummoned the nineteenth, and planted his Gunns (battered
ſeven ſhoures as I heare) the place is ſurrendred for certaine to him on Conditions,
of which Major Generall *Ireton* gave me account, but not the particulars , he is now
before *Duncannon* a ſtrong peice

From Belfaſt, 4. *Octobris*, 1649.

By a Letter from Colonell *Venables* from *Belfaſt* of the fourth inſtant, we have this
account of his march Northward in theſe words : We marcht Horſe and Foot to
Carlingfort, where all the Caſtles, and the Fort (called *Ormonds* Fort, that lyes upon
the mouth of the Harbour , held impregnable) ſurrendred upon our Summons :
Thence we marcht to *Newry* with our Horſe onely, and ſent the Foot and Carriages
about by *Dundalke* (by reaſon of the inconvenience and unreadineſſe of the way)
which ſurrendred unto us : On Wedneſday the twenty ſixth of the laſt moneth, we
marcht from *Newry* to *Dromore*, where the Fort was ſurrendred, and all the Forts
upon the ſeverall paſſes upon the *Ban Water* ; about breake of day the next morn-
ing, Colonell *Trevor* gave us a viſit in our Quarters , and to his welcome (after a
totall Rout) was proſecuted, at the leaſt eight or nine mile in ſeverall wayes (to
his no ſmall loſſe) I am certaine the body he brought off with himſelfe, was not above
fourty Horſe : Our Horſe (not able to proſecute his misfortune any further) returned
to

occupants of the boats were female, 'Two boatfuls of the enemy attempting to escape, being overprest with numbers sunk, whereby were drowned near three hundred of them. I believe in all there was lost of the enemy not many less than two thousand

and I believe not twenty of yours killed, from first to last of the siege.' The enemy, always the enemy. Cromwell always uses military terms. But unfortunately Cromwell left us some sentences in this letter (reputedly his own words) that some commentators have jumped all over, believing that they are an admission of his guilt in a wholesale indiscriminate massacre at Wexford. To William Lenthall he says, 'This town is now so in your power, that (of) the former inhabitants I believe, scarce one in twenty can challenge any propriety in their houses, most of them are run away and many of them killed in this service, and it were to be wished, that an honest people would come and plant here...'

Naturally by definition, he was talking about male inhabitants, since the context here is ownership of properties. It is also the case that he was talking about inhabitants that had been armed. All of the surviving evidence points in this direction, not to mention the sentiments he would later express in his declaration to the people of Ireland from Youghal. Many of the local men were involved in 'this service' as Cromwell puts it and for that, many of them paid with their lives. Some drowned accidentally; others were massacred by a rampant blood-thirsty New Model Army.

Wexford was ripe for transplantation. As soon as the peace talks ended so abruptly, and there was no hope of most locals retaining their properties (as Cromwell had indicated that they could if they had accepted his terms), there is talk about Wexford being colonised. Cromwell, however does tell us that at least some of the Wexfordians could still claim ownership of their properties when he says that 'one in twenty' could have had legitimate cause. In a population of 2,000 people, this would mean that about 100 local residents could have retained their properties in Wexford town. This suggests that maybe the entire town was not against Cromwell. Indeed, R.L. tells us that 'fourscore and fifteen' (95) men defected to Parliament immediately after the storm. These were most likely members of the garrison as opposed to armed townsmen, whose objectives were quite different.

Meanwhile back in London, the same day (30 Oct) Walter Frost, the Secretary to the Council of State, issued *A Briefe Relation of Some affaires and transactions, Civill and Military, both Forraigne and Domestique.* As a paid employee of Parliament Edward Husband was the printer/publisher of this particular edition. In the newsbook Frost also carries news of the fall of Wexford from a correspondent in Ireland, albeit a brief account:

> It hath pleased God out of his mercy to his poore servants here into my Lord Lieutenant's hands by storme, the eleventh present, without losse of seven men, myself being an eye-witnesse, a thousand of the enemy slaine or drowned. We could have saved it but could not; the judgement of the Lord was upon them.

(49) *Numb. 6.*

A very full and particular Relation

of the great progresse and happy proceedings of the Army of the Common-wealth of *England* *toward the reducing of* Ireland, *under the Command of his Excellency the Lord Lieutenant of* Ireland.

Oct: 31 1649

Licensed by Gualter Frost *Esquire, Secretary to the Councell of State, according to the direction of the late Act.*

WEE should not have doubled the labour of the Presse, or the trouble of the reader in one weeke, (being resolved not to *seeke* for *meanes* to *wast paper*, but to *make use* onely of *opportunities* for *necessary information* of the people,) were it not that the *impudency* of the *enemy* no longer able to *maintaine* their *Tyranny* by *Armes*, endeavour to *keepe up* their *reputation* by *lyes*, seeking to *impose* upon the *people* a *belief* of things at *distance*, as if they had *some where* a very powerfull party, and that the warre is not *ended*, nor they *overcome*, the *seat of it* is onely *transferr'd*, and where the place of *action* is, there they are *considerable*. This they spread among the people here, to *keepe them* in a *temper* for any *impression*, and from *closing cordially* with their *true Interest*, who still *too much* believe them, notwithstanding they have had so *many experiences* of these *impostures*. There having scarce *ever* been any *considerable Victory* given to our party from the good hand of God, who hath *wonderfully owned our cause*, which hath not had for a *Precursor* some *Malignant report* of our *losse*. Wee shall not now trouble the reader with what *rare reports* are come to us this weeke from *France*, *Holland*, and *Scotland*, of *losse*, *routs*, and *totall defeats*; of our Forces, *running away* of our *chief Commanders*, either to Sea, or to *Dublin* at best, where they will *have them besieged*. And that the good Catholique, and Scottish Presbyterian party have it all before them. *This refuge of lyes the hayle shall sweepe away.* And for the satisfaction of such as desire to know the truth of these affaires, wee have published this Relation from the Letters of two *worthy persons*, who wrote what they *saw*, and to all either *wise men* or *good men*, they carry their *evidence* with them.

Wexford

The next day Frost (via Husband) issued *A Very Full and Particular Relation (of the great progresse and happy proceedings of the Army of the common-wealth of England toward the reducing of*

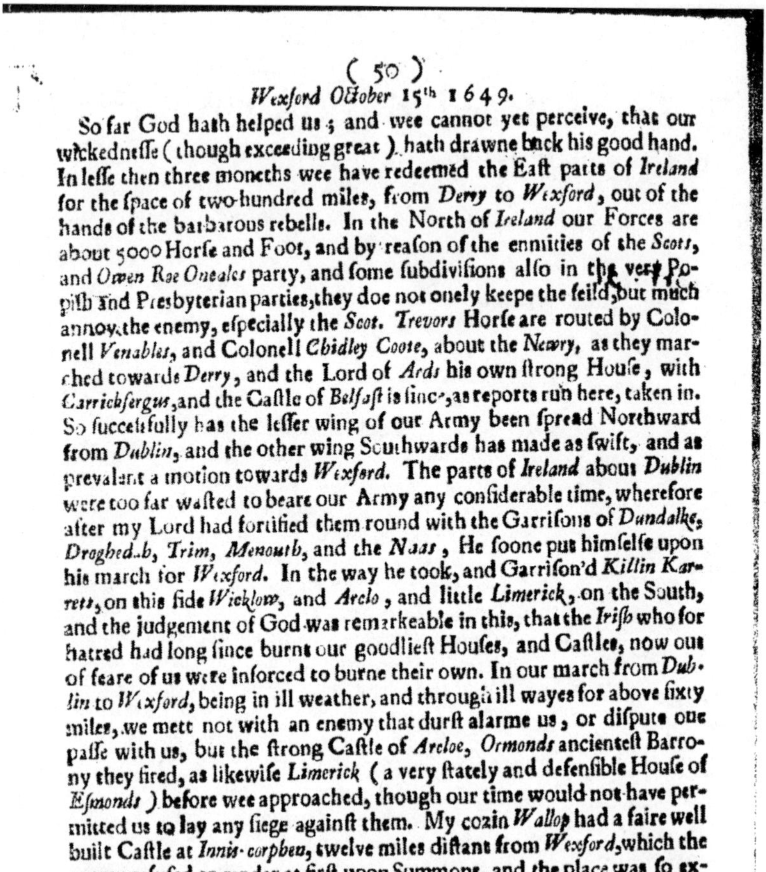

(50)

Wexford October 15th 1649.

So far God hath helped us; and wee cannot yet perceive, that our wickedneſſe (though exceeding great) hath drawne back his good hand. In leſſe then three moneths wee have redeemed the Eaſt parts of *Ireland* for the ſpace of two hundred miles, from *Derry* to *Wexford*, out of the hands of the barbarous rebells. In the North of *Ireland* our Forces are about 5000 Horſe and Foot, and by reaſon of the enmities of the *Scots*, and *Owen Roe Oneales* party, and ſome ſubdiviſions alſo in the very Popiſh and Presbyterian parties, they doe not onely keepe the feild, but much annoy the enemy, eſpecially the *Scot*. *Trevors* Horſe are routed by Colonell *Venables*, and Colonell *Chidley Coote*, about the *Newry*, as they marched towards *Derry*, and the Lord of *Ards* his own ſtrong Houſe, with *Carrickfergus*, and the Caſtle of *Belfaſt* is ſince, as reports run here, taken in. So ſuccesfully has the leſſer wing of our Army been ſpread Northward from *Dublin*, and the other wing Southwards has made as ſwift, and as prevalant a motion towards *Wexford*. The parts of *Ireland* about *Dublin* were too far waſted to beare our Army any conſiderable time, wherefore after my Lord had fortified them round with the Garriſons of *Dundalke*, *Drogheda*, *Trim*, *Menouth*, and the *Naas*, He ſoone put himſelfe upon his march for *Wexford*. In the way he took, and Garriſon'd *Killin Karrett*, on this ſide *Wicklow*, and *Arclo*, and little *Limerick*, on the South, and the judgement of God was remarkeable in this, that the *Iriſh* who for hatred had long ſince burnt our goodlieſt Houſes, and Caſtles, now out of feare of us were inforced to burne their own. In our march from *Dublin* to *Wexford*, being in ill weather, and through ill wayes for above ſixty miles, we mett not with an enemy that durſt alarme us, or diſpute one paſſe with us, but the ſtrong Caſtle of *Arcloe*, *Ormonds* ancienteſt Barrony they fired, as likewiſe *Limerick* (a very ſtately and defenſible Houſe of *Eſmonds*) before wee approached, though our time would not have permitted us to lay any ſiege againſt them. My cozin *Wallop* had a faire well built Caſtle at *Innis-corphen*, twelve miles diſtant from *Wexford*, which the enemy refuſed to render at firſt upon Summons, and the place was ſo exceeding knotty, that in that precious time wee durſt not make any ſtay upon it: yet upon drawing downe one peice of Cannon, and making onely ſome colour of an aſſault, the Enemy gave it up, with good ſtore of Armes, and Ammunition in it, conditioning onely for the Officers to march away with their ſwords. And herein appeared an extraordinary irreſolution, or infatuation amongſt the *Iriſh*, whilſt they were neither ſtout enough to hold that which might incommodate us, nor deſperate enough to deſtroy that which might accommodate us in ſo great a meaſure.

Ireland). In the pamphlet he transcribes two letters from the pens of two anonymous officers in the New Model Army. Both of the letters are quite detailed in their accounts and both illustrate the dire impression that the attacking army had of the town of Wexford. The writer of the second letter provides us with some interesting details in this regard:

> Seeing thus the righteous hand of God upon such a towne and people, we thought not good nor just to restraine off our souldiers from their right of pillage, nor from doing of execution upon the enemy (where the entrance was by force and a resistance endeavoured though too late). There was more sparing of lives (of the souldiery part of the enemy here, than at Drogheda) yet of their souldiery and townsmen here were about 1500 slaine or drowned (in boats sunk by the multitude and weight of people pressing into them). It was a place settled the most deepe in superstition and darkness that I have seene or heard of, and a people zealous against anything of better light. God visited both the deceivers and the deceived together. Of their priests (which deceived and led them) were many slaine. Some (I hearde) came holding forth crucifixes before them, and conjuring our souldiers (for his sake that saved us all) to save their lives. Yet our souldiers would not own their dead images for our living saviour but struck them dead with their idols, many of their priests (being got together in a church of the towne, where tis sayd, many poore Protestants were kept and killed together in the beginning of the Rebellion) were slaine together by our souldiers about their altar.

(51)

fure. From *Innis-corphen* wee marched in two dayes more to *Wexford*, in regard that the River was not fordable neere the Towne. The Towne runs North and South, bearing little breadth, having the Sea on the East for a mile to guard it, and on the West two Stone walls well lined with Earth, the maine difficulties to us were, that on the South end of the Towne there stood a little distance from the wall a strong Castle, high situated, and on the East (the Sea being open) no reliefe could be barred, besides the weather proved unreasonably wett, and windy, and want of bread, and other necessaries increased the discentery in our Leaguer, with many other sicknesses daily, so that discouragements thronged in upon us. Neverthelesse (according to our constant experience, and expectation) all discouragements were over-ballanced in due time by extraordinary mercies from above.

For our Fleet rid in sight without the barre, and received no mischief by the power of the windes; nay, the Fort at the mouth of the Bar ten miles from the Towne, which was by Art and nature very tenable, and stood most advantageously to lock up all that vast bosome of Sea, which secured the Towne on the East, was deserted by the Enemy, and left to us without any stroke at all. This shewed our Enemies to be voyd of all Councell, for neither had we Cannon to batter, nor provisions to subsist without our Navy, nor could our Navy force their passage by that Fort, and the two Frigots there riding, nor scarce any otherwise supply us.

The sudden gift therefore of such a Fort, and two such Frigots, at such a time was welcomed by us as the bounty of Heaven, and raised up our thoughts againe to their wonted pitch. Additionall to this grace also from above, newes came that two Regiments of *Inchiquines* had cast off their Officers, and possessed themselves of *Yougball* for the Parliaments use; and hereby *Inchiquin* was diverted, and by *Inchiquins* diversion *Ormond* was disabled, and *Clan Riccard* deterred from disturbing our Seige. The truth is, our Campe was without any intrenchment, almost drowned in rayne and durt, too obnoxious to the Enemies greater shot, and we knew the Irish about twelve miles of (for *Rosse* was their head Quarter) had vehement intentions to Camisadoe us; and we did not consist of above six thousand sound, effective men: Therefore the rumour of *Yougball* (and for ought we yet heare (though we six days agoe dispatcht away by Sea some Commissioners thereabout) the businesse of *Yougball* is more then a groundlesse rumour) did as much availe us, as if it had been true: Howsoever all things were ready now for a battery, and we having removed our Campe to the South end by the Castle

G 2

Caſtle for more ſafety, and conveniencies ſake, firſt playd with eight great Peices, and two Mortyr-peices upon the Caſtle, and finding the ſame batterable, courage began wonderfully to increaſe in us, and to quaile in the beſieged. The Towne within had two thouſand able men, moſt Marriners, and before our comming they had taken in from *Ormond* eight hundred Auxiliaries, and ſince our ſitting downe, they had received twenty Colours more from the other ſhore (not be by us interrupted) and they had gabled all their ſtreets, and had plenty of Artillery, Armes, and all manner of Proviſions; and till the tryall of the Cannon, they appeared very daring, but now on a ſudden, all ſpirit, councill, and manhood, cauſleſly forſook them.

The people within could not be reſtrained from boating away by Water, this made the Magiſtrates ſeek a party, which granted, my Lord proffered onely to the Souldier to depart home, renouncing bearing Armes againſt the Parliament of *England* for the future, and for the Towne, their perſons were to be ſecured from violence, and their goods from plunder.

This was accepted, and by my Lords hand ſigned; but before delivery, the Captaine of the Caſtle having ſome Trunks of value, belonging to Sir *Ralph Aſton*, it ſeemes out of hope to ſave the ſame, agrees by himſelfe for his owne Souldiery, and immediatly receives in a Garriſon of ours. The Towne therefore ſeeing their Commiſſioners not returned, but our Flag advanced upon the Caſtle, and our Gunns (for they were to play all the Treaty) traverſed from the Caſtle and bent againſt them, diſpaired preſently, and ſome of the Souldiers threw themſelves over the Wall amongſt our Horſe; but the greateſt part made eſcape by Water. This being ſeen by us made us fall on, and ſtorme with Ladders, and without reſiſtance, or loſſe of a man the Towne was entred, won, and ſackt. The ſpoyling of the Towne was extreamly incommodious to our ſelves, and we all deſired to reſerve it for our Winter accommodation, both parties were agreed about it, and the agreement was drawne and ſigned, but God had otherwiſe determined upon it.

Indeed the Towne, though of old Engliſh extraction, and retaining the old Engliſh Dialect ſtill without Iriſh mixture, and ſuch as had not been very obſtinate from the beginning from letting us in upon termes, had not *Ormonds* Military Faction overruled; yet were guilty of much Piracy, having been the receptacle of all the Princes roving Frigots for diverſe yeares paſt, and ſo we may conceive God had a further quarrell with them then we had, and by him the iſſue was otherwiſe ordered, then either we or the Iriſh had deſigned. Upon

(53)

Upon entring the Towne, about men were put to the Sword, and about more drowned by overcharging Vessels in the fight, and great spoyle and havock was made of many rich commodities, so that now we are inforced to seek further for a Winter retirement, and want that refreshment which else the place might have afforded in the declining of the yeare; but for my part, I am strong in my confidence. that this is so directed by God for our good; and that though our Army be now very sick and impaired, and likely to be further weakened by accesse of Winter, and more gusty weather, yet God crosses us here, that we may onely be better provided for and entertained elsewhere. My Lord accordingly is now advancing to *Rosse*, the most invincible refuge and Rendezvouz of the Irish, and if the same felicity attend us herein, which hath hitherto been faithfull to us, this will be a strange criticall day betwixt us, especially when their greatest strength is to encounter with our greatest weaknes: All our disadvantage is, that we fight not with men armed with steele, but with Walls lined with men; and that our Enemies doe not onely lye in Ambuscadoe behind Walls, but (as I may say) behind diseases, tempests, wants, and difficult ways; for nothing is more obvious to sense then this, that a Lyon-like heart is inspired into our men, whilst all that is Manlike is taken from our Enemy.

I cannot but beleive that the time is now come, or neare at hand, which the soules of the Saints have so long cryed out for from under the Altar, and that God is now rouzing himselfe to returne unto *Babylon*, that which shee hath so cruelly inflicted for so many yeares upon us. And for the cheife Instrument in this businesse chosen by God, I doubt not but he knows; he has in his hands the Arrows of Gods deliverance against *Assyria*; and therefore he will not smite the ground with them twice or thrice as the King of *Israel* did, but he will discharge six or seven times, till the Enemy be wholly consumed. I wish mens minds in *England* were better setled, and prepared for such dispensations of God; tis fearefull that such graces should be better accepted, and finde more gratitude in *Israel* then in *Judah*; but tis most fearefull, that the Clergy (upon I know not what principles of Prelacy in Classes and Generall Assemblies) should be more averse from acknowledging Gods wonderfull deliverances then the Laity.

Wexford, 16. of *October*, 1649.

Upon our returne to Dublin from Droghedah (where the Lord had blest us) I Writ to you some account what he had done for us, which I hope ere this time you have received. Since then we Marcht from Dublin

(54)

lin hither (beeing above Threescore Miles Southward upon the Sea Coast) wee were nine or ten dayes upon our March, and had five Garrisons of the Enemy either surrendered, or quitted, or left to us upon our March, so as we cleared all our way as we came, and setled small Garrisons for our selves at every ten or twelve Miles distance along the Sea Coast, we lay before this Citty eight dayes, and the ninth day which was the eleaventh of this Month, God delivered it, and the strong Castle thereof into our hands, having got the Fort six Miles off, upon the mouth of the Haven; the next day after we came, the Enemy that kept it (their hearts being taken away) run out of the Fort upon the first appearance of our Men, and betooke themselvs to a Pyrat Frigot, belonging to this Town) which Road within the mouth of the Haven is within shot of the Fort) and our Men playing upon them but three or foure shoots with their owne Guns (which they left in the Fort) they presently sent a shoare and surrendred both themselves (Prisoners) and also the Frigot with sixteene or eighteene peices of Ordnance in her. This gave us opportunitie for our ships and Vessells, that attended us along the Coast from Dublin with Provisions, Ordnance, and Ammunition, to be brought into the Haven, and so up to the Campe neer the Towne, where the Army lay, within Foure or Five dayes, so soone as the Winds and spring Tide served. But in this time our Men endured great extremity for want of bread, and other necessaries, wee had a strong Enemy within the Towne, and Feild Army greater then ours hovering about us, (for most part within a dayes March) but keeping themselves upon the advantage, of Rivers, Hills, and Woods, and not having confidence to come out to fight us. On Wedensday last having made our approaches, and prepared our Batterys, we made two breaches into the Castle. They had upon our first Summons (when wee came before the Towne) seemed willing to Treat, and upon good tearmes to surrender. But making some trifling delayes for three or foure dayes, till they had got more strength into the Towne from the other side of the River (which we could not prevent) they then slightly broke off, and we heard no more from them, till we had made the breaches into the Castle, and then they sent out againe desireing to Treat. We received their Propositions (which conteyned large demands, concerning the free Toleration of their Religion, and their Bishops, and Priests to injoy their Offices, power, and Revenues hereabouts, and the Townesmen their Liberties, and Estates free) We rejected their Propositions with disdaine, and without Answer. But beeing desirous, if it had appeared the will of God, to save blood, and prevent the spoyling of so Rich a Towne, which

(55)

which we thought might be a place of receipt for many honeſt Families out of England, we offered them in ſhort (if they would immediately ſurrender) to let the common Souldiers goe to their homes (upon engagement to ſerve no more againſt the Parliament, to give the Officers Quarter for life (but to be Priſoners) and to ſecure the Towne from Pillage, or Plunder of the Souldiers, but their eſtates to be at the States mercy to diſpoſe of. But though thus wee (then not knowing otherwiſe of the mind of God towards them) were mercifully inclined, God ſhewed that he had a further controverſy againſt ſuch a Place, and People, who had inriche themſelves with the ſpoyle of the Innocent (by Robbing and pillaging at Sea all Engliſh Merchants they could light on ſince the Warr began, and making a Trade of that Pyracy) and where (as we better underſtand ſince) there hath been ſo great cruelties exerciſed towards Engliſh Proteſtants, that were many in theſe Parts at the beginning of the Warre, and now none left but, either killed, or driven away.

And therefore God ſo ordered it, as to make them vomit up againe their ſtolne riches in one houre, and pay dearly for the innocent blood here ſpilt, for when we had ſet downe our aforeſaid offer, and delivered it to their Commiſſioners to convey into the Towne, our men being ready to aſſault the breaches of the Caſtle; the Governour thereof for feare and haſt accepted our termes for himſelfe and his, and admitted our men into the Caſtle (and thereupon though it ſtood cleare without the Walls of the Towne) yet ſo ſoone as ever the Garriſon within the Towne ſaw our Colours upon the Caſtle, they had not confidence to ſtand to their Armes, or maintaine their Walls ſo long as to receive their Commiſſioners back with our offer. When we (although wee would grant no Ceſſation of Armes for a minute yet) had no thoughts of attempting any more at that time then the Caſtle: But they ran away from their Walls (on that ſide that was towards the Caſtle, quitted their Guards, and betooke themſelves towards their Boats (whereof they had abundance belonging to their Ships at their Keyes within the Haven) which many of our Souldiers from the Caſtle and ſome higher grounds perceiving, they fell on of their owne accords, firſt without Ladders, lifting and helping one another with their Pikes or any other way over the Walls, and after with Ladders, till they were got in a good number into the Towne, and then (the Enemy made head and got heart againe, and attempting to have returned to their Guards and Wals) we ſoon beat and diſperſt them, and poſſeſt the Towne (their Commiſſioners this while, not having hearts to put themſelves into the

Towne

(56)

Towne againe with our offer:) Seeing thus the righteous hand of God upon such a Towne and People, we thought not good nor just to restraine off our Souldiers from their right of Pillage, nor from doing of execution upon the Enemy (where the entrance was by force, and a resistance endeavoured though too late.) There was more sparing of lives (of the Souldiery part of the Enemy here, then at *Drogheda*) yet of their Souldiery and Townsmen here were about 1500 slaine or drowned (in boats sunk by the multitude and weight of people pressing into them.) It was a place setled the most deepe in superstition and darknesse that I have seene or heard of; and a people zealous against any thing of better light. God visited both the deceivers and deceived together. Of their Priests (which deceived and led them) were many slaine. Some (I heare of) came holding forth Crucifixes before them, and conjuring our Souldiers (for his sake that saved us all) to save their lives; yet our Souldiers would not owne their dead Images for our living Saviour; but struck them dead with their Idols; many of their Priests (being got together in a Church of the Towne, where tis sayd, many poore Protestants were kept and killed together in the beginning of the Rebellion) were slaine together by our Souldiers about their Altar.

The riches of the Towne, (wherein as to Houshold Furniture, Merchandise, and Tradeing Commodities, it did abound) being so ill gained as I have said, was (most part) taken or rent, and torne a peices, or wasted and spoyled by the Souldiery in one hower or two. The grosser sorts, and stores of Merchandise which our Souldiers minded not in the hower of Plunder as Hides, Tallow, Salt, Pipe staves, Iron, &c. With all their Ships and Boates fall into the States hands, and we have appoynted Commissioners to collect and improove them for the Publique, as also to preserve, and buy back from the Souldiery (as they may for small Prices) all Houshould Furniture, to be kept for such honest Families as shall hereafter come out of England to Inhabit this Towne, we being desirous by any such encouragements to draw over a Generation and Seed of good people (if God see it good) to possesse such places, and to plant the Countreyes. Thus I thought good as my time will admit, to give some hints of those remarkable dispensations of God in righteous judgements upon the adversaries of his peace and glory, and mercies towards his People, whom he has wrought to a denyall of themselves, and dependance on his good will. He suffers us to undergoe much hardships, by wet and cold Seasons, without habitation or shelter, and many extremeties even for want of Bread (while in the Feild) but recompenceth all with the comforts of his presence, and the beholding of his wisdome, power, justice, and goodnesse in all his dealings. Our Army is much weakned with sicknesse (especially among the Regiments that came fresh with us out of England) we have above a third part of them sicke of the Fluxe, or Feavers left at Dublin and here, and many small Garrisons in the way. The Army advanced hence Yesterday, against the Garrisons of Rosse and Duncannon.

London, Printed by Matthew Simmons, *for* J. O. 1649.

(214)

that, bloody and perfidious Faction.

Yet all this moves not the Grandees at *Edenburgh*, whether it be out of the confidence they have of concluding fairely with the King, and conſequently to ſhake hands and bee friends with *Montroſſe*; or out of the diffidence they have of the affections of their *Army*, I know not: But as yet they have not ſent any Force to ſuppreſſe them; for, although two Regiments (Commanded by *Carre* and *Straughan*) were appointed to March towards them, yet were they contrary to all expectation remanded, the Reaſon hitherto not knowne; ſince which no mention hath beene made of ſending them or any other, which is ſubject to ſeverall Interpretations; but that which ſwayes moſt is, That they Deſpaire of warring againſt the *Kings-Intereſt*, and are therefore loath to provoke him, eſpecially at this time, when the poore People of that Nation are ſo much burthened with Taxes, and extorted Loanes; and the hearts of the People ſo fixed upon *Monarchy*, and utterly averſe to all Overtures made them for withſtanding the *King* (though under the faireſt of all their pretences;) themſelves ſo divided upon their owne Principles, and the Land in a generall diſtraction, that there is no hopes of removing their diſcontents, without eaſing them of their Burthens (and that will disband the Army;) nor of any Concord or quietneſſe, without including the *Royalliſts*, and bringing in the King, which yet they would not doe, but that they ſee they ſhall be compelled to it, *Nolens, Volens*.

However *Argile* (whoſe hands are ſo deeply dy'd in the Kings blood) expects no benefit by any Peace that can be concluded, much leſſe by his owne Atchievements (for *Mars* was under the Hatches at his Nativity) and therefore hath he made Addreſſes to the King, depending more on the Kings Mercy, then eyther his owne Innocency or Valour; yet ſtrives by all meanes to waſh his hands of his Fathers blood, and if any Circumſtances or preſumptions ſhall render him contrary, that he will be pleaſed to impute it to his ill-adviſedneſſe, or weakeneſſe in Judgement, and grant him his Pardon; which obtained, he will live and die his Majeſties moſt Humble and Faithfull Subject and Servant, *Argile*.

Now what Anſwere he hath received, I heare not as yet; nor will I trouble the Reader with conjectures, much leſſe Sentence him before he be heard, as is the Cuſtome of the Saints.

But that which fills up the remainder of the Squires ſheete, is the news they have received from *Ireland*, of the Treacherous ſurprizall of *Wexford* (*alias Waſhford*) even during the time of Ceſſation and Treaty, as himſelfe in a manner confeſſeth, and the Barbarous murther of moſt part of the Inhabitants and Souldiers, their blood-thirſty hands not diſtinguiſhing

Interestingly, this writer tells us that more lives were spared here than at Drogheda. This piece of information makes a wholesale civilian massacre even more unlikely. If the attackers were

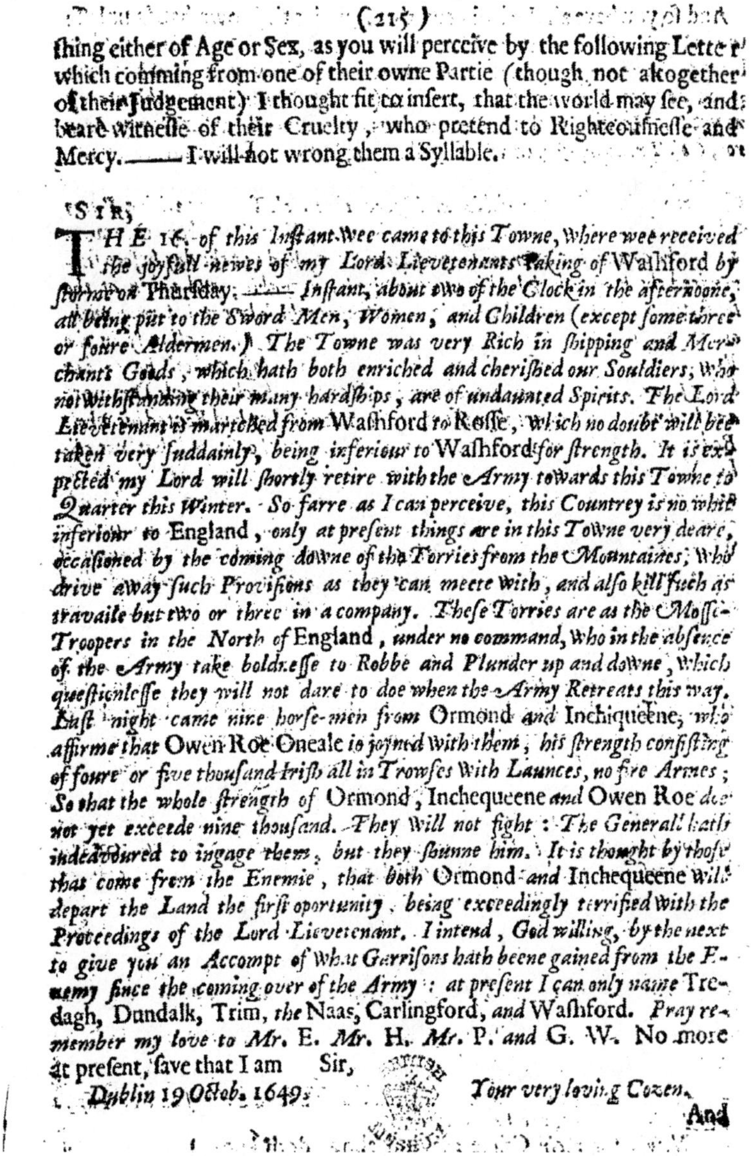

(215)

ſhing either of Age or Sex, as you will perceive by the following Letter which comming from one of their owne Partie (though not altogether of their Judgement) I thought fit to inſert, that the world may ſee, and beare witneſſe of their Cruelty, who pretend to Righteouſneſſe and Mercy. —— I will not wrong them a Syllable.

SIR,

THE 16. of this Inſtant Wee came to this Towne, where wee received the joyfull newes of my Lord Lieveтenants Taking of Waſhford by ſtorme on Thurſday. —— Inſtant, about two of the Clock in the afternoone, all being put to the Sword Men, Women, and Children (except ſome three or foure Aldermen.) The Towne was very Rich in ſhipping and Merchants Goods, which hath both enriched and cheriſhed our Souldiers, who notwithſtanding their many hardſhips, are of undaunted Spirits. The Lord Lievetenant is marched from Waſhford to Roſſe, which no doubt will bee taken very ſuddainly, being inferiour to Waſhford for ſtrength. It is expected my Lord will ſhortly retire with the Army towards this Towne to Quarter this Winter. So farre as I can perceive, this Countrey is no whit inferiour to England, only at preſent things are in this Towne very deare, occaſioned by the coming downe of the Torries from the Mountaines, who drive away ſuch Proviſions as they can meete with, and alſo kill ſuch as travaile but two or three in a company. Theſe Torries are as the Moſſe-Troopers in the North of England, under no command, who in the abſence of the Army take boldneſſe to Robbe and Plunder up and downe, which queſtionleſſe they will not dare to doe when the Army Retreats this way. Laſt night came nine horſe-men from Ormond and Inchiqueene, who affirme that Owen Roe Oneale is joyned with them, his ſtrength conſiſting of foure or five thouſand Iriſh all in Trowſes with Launces, no fire Armes; So that the whole ſtrength of Ormond, Inchequeene and Owen Roe doe not yet exceede nine thouſand. They will not fight: The Generall hath indeavoured to ingage them, but they ſhunne him. It is thought by thoſe that come from the Enemie, that both Ormond and Inchequeene will depart the Land the firſt oportunity, being exceedingly terrified with the Proceedings of the Lord Lievetenant. I intend, God willing, by the next to give you an Accompt of what Garriſons hath beene gained from the Enemy ſince the coming over of the Army: at preſent I can only name Tredagh, Dundalk, Trim, the Naas, Carlingford, and Waſhford. Pray remember my love to Mr. E. Mr. H. Mr. P. and G. W. No more at preſent, ſave that I am Sir,

Dublin 19 Octob. 1649.

Your very loving Cozen.

And

prepared to save the lives of their sworn enemy, why then would they arbitrarily engage in war crimes against the local community? The anonymous letter writer concludes that 1,500 soldiers and townsmen were killed, either in the battle or by drowning. Coincidentally, this is the same figure that is in the petition of the people of Wexford except that now the 1,500 are described as 'man, woman and child to a very few'. Something doesn't add up.

On 2 November Henry Scobell (or Henry Walker) published the fifth edition of *Severall Proceedings in Parliament* (Friday 26 October – Friday 2 November) in which is transcribed Cromwell's letter to Lenthall and the correspondence between Cromwell and Sinnott that in the end was superfluous but it served to highlight the fact that Cromwell was keen to offer lenient terms.

Predictably, after the flurry of official publications to emerge in the last week of October and the first week of November reporting the news about Wexford came the newsbooks of royalists George Wharton (*Mercurius Elencticus*) and John Crouch (*The Man in the Moon*) on 5 and 7 November respectively. Before reviewing these newsbooks, it is worth noting again that seventeenth century print industry expert Jason McElligott revealed that Wharton was one of a few royalist writers who 'met once a week in a tavern in Oxford to muster up whole regiments of lies, slanders and ridiculous quibbles against the Parliament and the city of London'. So it is with a mindset influenced by this information that Wharton's publication must be viewed. Indeed on close examination, it could easily be construed that Wharton's 'testimony' regarding Wexford is nothing but a tissue of lies:

> But that which fills up the remainder of the squire's (Walter Frost) sheete is the news they have received from Ireland, of the treacherous surprizall of Wexford (alias Washford) even during the time of cessation and treaty, as himself in a manner confesseth, and the barbarous murder of most part of the inhabitants and souldiers, their blood-thirsty hands not distinguishing either of age or sex, as you will perceive by the following letter, which coming from their owne partie (though not altogether of their judgement) I thought fit to insert that

the world may see and bear witnesse of their cruelty, who pretend to righteousness and mercy – I will not wrong them a syllable.

Sir, The 10th of this instant wee came to this towne, where we received the joyfull newes of my Lord Lieutenant's taking of Washford by storme on Thursday about two of the clock in the afternoon, all being put to the sword, men, women and children (except some three or foure aldermen).

(227) (Numb. 28.) 9

The Man in the Moon.

Discovering a World of

KNAVERY

Under the

SUNNE;

Both in the *Parliament*, the *Councel* of *State*, the *Army*, the *City* and the COUNTRY.

With *Intelligence* from all Parts of *England*, *Scotland*, and *IRELAND*.

Die Lunæ, From *Octob.* 31. to *Wednesday Novemb.* 7. 1649.

Now *Pryde* must unto *Ireland* go,
with a new *Regiment*;
For *Noll* (alack and alas for wo)
has lost *Lusts Instrument*.

Which makes his *Wife* to *wail* and *sob*,
in *tears* of briny *grief*;
And *curse* the *Cavees* that would *rob*
her *Puss-ship* of *relief*.

Two *Geldings* now there are to draw
the *Juncto* into *Hell*,
For judging *Charls* without the *Law*,
Skippon and *Cromwel*.

Jack Lilburn now is brisk and merry,
in hopes to RULE the *Land*;
And ferrit the *States* Conny-berry,
and then the *Cause* will *stand*.

NOw must Mistris *Juncto* dispair of her Royal *Issue*, since *Cromwel* has lost his *instrument* of *Generation*, and his *Standard-bearer* of *Lust* is shott quite off; which makes the

Ee Shee-

(228)

She-*Saints* in a *back-ſliding* condition for fear of want of *increaſe* of that holy *breed* of *Regicides* & *Cromwelians* to Reign over them : and his Lady (ſirreverence) to howl and make direful complaints to the *Councel* of *State* for ſpeedy Supplies for *Ireland*; telling them it was a Plot of them and the Juncto to ſend her Husband thither to be kill'd and Murdered : (it ſeems ſhe thinks he ſhall ſcape the Gallows) and that ſhe would require his *bloud* at their hands : whereupon they conſidered which way new Forces ſhould be drawn to go over; at laſt they agreed to beat up Drums for Volunteers to go over; and in caſe none would go, to Raiſe *Auxiliaries* to encreaſe their Army here, and to draw out of their own main Army 10000 to go over, and to make a ſhew of Colonel *Prydes* going over with them, the better to get them a Ship-board; and then that *Pryde* ſhould Return back,and *Peters* Regiment,and the broken Regiments of *Hewſon* and *Venable*, and the reſt of their ſhattered Forces, ſhould be made up the Number they were at firſt : by which it appears, that ſetting *Peters* his Regiment aſide, 9000 will but make up their loſſes ; which for verity I beleeve, the rather becauſe I ſay the Copy of a *Letter* written to an eminent Member of Parliament by *CromWels* own hand, (which for a Servants ſake in that houſe that ſhewed me the *Letter*, I muſt not diſcover the name) but the very words of the Letter were theſe ;

Sir,

T*He hand of God, and his providence , hath been mightily ſeen working for Us by his poWerful arm, ſince Our Armies arrival in* Ireland , *to the great terror and amazemant of Our enemies ; yet not without great Loſſes on Our ſide : We having taken* Drogheda, Killencarick, Athloe, Lymrick, Fernes, Eneſcorthy, Wexford, *and are noW going to* Roſs, *Which We hope to gain: But Sir, the taking theſe ToWns and Garriſons hath not a little Weakned Our Army ; as neer as We can count We have loſt* 9000 *men in all ; And Sir, unleſs you haſten on Supplies to be in* Ireland *before November the* 12. *We ſhall go neer (after all theſe Mercies) not only to looſe what the Lord hath given Us , but Our Selves to become a prey to the cruel Enemies ; who now are Muſtering their main Forces to fight Us, When We are at weakeſt : Sir, as you tender*

Close examination of the entire letter shows an inordinate lack of detail. It could easily be concluded that the 'news' in the letter actually consists of snippets of information from the licensed newsbooks, all cobbled together in a cohesive narrative to make the letter look authentic. We know that Wharton and Crouch were certainly capable of making up stories and publishing them to make Parliament look bad. When it comes to Crouch's *The Man in the Moon* that week we see a perfect example of this type of propaganda in action. Introducing the transcription of a letter on page 2 of his newsletter, that Crouch purports to be from the pen of Cromwell himself, Crouch gleefully exaggerating the losses of the New Model Army in Ireland writes:

> ...And the rest of their shattered forces should be made up of the number they were at first, by which it appears that setting Peters his regiment aside, 9,000 will but make up their losses, which for verity I believe the rather because I say the copy of a letter written to an eminent member of parliament by Cromwell's own hand, (which for a servant's sake in that house that showed me the letter, I must not discover the name) but the very words of the letter were these;
>
> Sir, The hand of God and his providence, hath been mightily seen working for us by his powerful arm, since our Armies arriving in Ireland, to the great terror and amazement of our enemies, yet not without great losses on our side, we having taken Drogheda, Killencarick, Athloe, Lymrick, Fernes, Enescorthy, Wexford and are now going to Ross which we hope to gain. But Sir, the taking of these towns an garrisons hath not a little weakened our army as neer as we can count we have lost 9000 men in all. And sir, unless you hasten on supplies to be in Ireland before November the 12 we shall go neer (after all these mercies) not only to loose what the Lord hath given us but ourselves to become a prey to the cruel enemies, who are now mustering their main forces to fight us when we are at weakest. Sir, as you render the work of the Lord, hasten the forces over, least by delay we loose the advantage with ourselves. We want foot most by reason of the maning of our garrisons, the horse may be sent after. Let us

have your prayers, and bless God for what he hath wrought for us.

Wexford October 29 1649. Your Servant
O Cromwel.

This letter is obviously fabricated. Throughout history it has never been taken to be the words of Cromwell by any historian, including those who transcribed all of Cromwell's letters, writings and speeches, Thomas Carlyle and Wilbur Cortez Abbott. Cromwell's army did not lose 9,000 men by that stage.

der the Work of *the Lord: hasten the Forces over, least by Delay We loose these advantages With Our Selves: We want Foot most by reason of the maning of Our Garrisons; the Horse may be sent after: Let Us have your Prayers, and bless God for what he hath Wrought for Us.*

Wexford, Octob. 29. 1649. *Your Servant,* O. CROMWEL.

By this Letter you may judge in what need he stands for Men, and whether he hath lost but 500 as the Round-heads would make us beleeve in their Licensed sheets; but since this Letter was writ, we have more certain Intelligence of the worsting of *Venables* Regiment between *Dromore* and *Dondrem* in the North, and by Col. *Trevor*, and Sir *George Monroes* Rowting *Oconelly* at *Carrogh*, where they lost 500 men, and killed *Oconelly*; not six of two whole Regiments escapeing: but worse then all this, *Noll* himself hath got a *pockey clap* with a brace of Bullets in his *Gennitals*; being shot-free, it is by some thought incredible that a Bullet should enter him: but a Chyrurgion gave me this Reason; for quoth he, That place (being formerly impaired by an accident of a malignant fire called *Morbus*) was corrupt, and a breach formerly made by a *State-pinnace* that carried *Wild-fire* in her *Poop*, that in the discharging Recoyled, and did execution on *Nolls* Gun-stick; else quoth he, they could never have shot off his *Main-yard*, and missed the rest of his *Tacklings*; but sure he is preserved for some other end: Also one Captain *Lebunt*, being of his Life-guard, was run thorow his jawes with a Halbert, and Col. R*oe* run thorow that mouth which formerly had vented so much Blasphemy in his zealous Babblements in *White-hall* to his crop-ear'd bloudy Auditory.

A just *revenge* at length will seaze them all;
Bloud must have *bloud*, *Murder* make *Murderers* fall.

His Majesty King *Charles* the Second is yet in the Island of *Jersey*, His Counsel sit close, and are very Reserv'd: The Lord *Libberton* is Arrived there with some accomodations from the *Scots*, and hath had good Audience: Whether His Majesty intends for *Scotland*, or *Ireland*, is not yet certainly known;

Ee 2 some

at their perrill: And laftly, Ordaines thefe prefents to be Printed and Publifhed at all the ordinary places of Publication throughout the feverall Shires of the Kingdome. *Th: Henderfon.*

How welcome this will be at *Jerfey*, and what a preparation to the entertainment of the Leird of Libbertoun, may be eafily gueffed. They fend to invite their King, and in the meane time proclaim his beft friends Rebels. It is well knowne, thofe in *Orkney* are *Montroffe* his party, as it is alfo, that their King doth principally rely upon him, and that Party to carry on his defignes in *Scotland*, by whofe affiftance he refolves to come in upon them with an high hand, what ever flam; *Libertoun* may receive for anfwer, to keepe thofe men afleepe till they can be deftroyed, for whom, there fcearfe remains any vifible help, they have fo abfurdly deferted their owne true intereft. And what they may expect from their King is of eafie conjecture, by what he was heard to fay, within 14. dayes before the publifhing hereof, when a Gentleman who had been ever on that fide waited on him in *Jerfey*, and told him his refolution was for *England*, and defired to receive his commands to his friends here, adding that though as things now ftood, they did not fhew themfelves upon any good occafion; they would be ready to declare. To which Gentleman, his reply was, he could not account any of thofe to be his friends, who were content to fit ftill and enjoy their owne quiet, and not appeare for him till others had opened the way, and that when he fhould recover his right he would put no difference between fuch Neuters and his declared Enemies, but would ufe them both alike.

An Account of what was taken in the Towne of *Wexford*.

1. *The fhipping and their appurtenances being about* 100. *faile, I tooke an Inventory of, and are all preferved to be fold, when by command.*

2. *The fifhing trade wholly managed to the advantage of the Army, the falt and caske being all our owne, which was no fmall quantity, and the Boats alfo, which was about* 100. *wherof* 80. *fitted well; I thought it my duty to defire of my Lord the lives of all the fifher men.*

3. *The Pipeftaves, Barrell, and Hogfhead ftaves, wher of there were ftore, are fhipt for* London *in foure or five fhips, that elfe muft goe empty home, and were in our pay.*

4. *The Iron whereof we had a great quantity, we referved to be made out*

into

(85)

into work for the Countrey and Army.

5. *Tanned Hides which were ſome thouſands, we keepe to worke out alſo for our owne uſe and the Countries.*

6. *The Neat Hides being about foure thouſand, we ſold at ſix pound a ſcore, cuſtome paid, and Tag and Rag gathered up by the buyer.*

7. *Tallow worth* 3. *or* 400 li. *we ſend to* London, *the reſt not plundered we reſerve for the Garriſons.*

8. *A great deale of other goods of all kindes, we fild divers Warehouſes with, and them we ſell at an open Market, for the good of the place; what we could keepe after the Proclamation of my Lord againſt plunder; for never did I ſee more, or richer plunder any where.*

9. *Every houſe in the Towne we inventoried, with the yearly value of it, and the goods in them, ſo that the Town & Houſes lye open, to any good* Engliſh *Inhabitants, my Lord offering me, that if a godly congregation would come over, they ſhould pay but two ſhillings of the pound of that Houſes and Lands went for.*

10. *I procured* 3. *or* 4. *honeſt men to take charge of the Cuſtom houſe, who carry things very well, and will give a good accompt.*

11. *There are fifteen Mils continually grinding, and are ours: The Sequeſtraons within and about the Towne left to my Lords diſpoſing; the county of* Wexford *paid the Enemy* 30000. li. per annum.

12. *For the government of the Towne, it muſt yet be purely under the ſword, there being for preſent, a godly Governour, Colonell* Cooke: *In truth, that Towne and others, gape for good Engliſh to poſſeſſe them, where they may live richly and well.*

There I ſaw the Spoyler ſpoyled, the Drowner drowned, they that have made naked, were themſelves made naked, and which was ſtrangeſt, I ſaw the *Hoggs* gnaw their fleſh, and ſuck their bloud, and had divers other witneſſes of it; and their ill gotten goods ſo ſcattered into ſtrange and ſeverall hands, that we know not who hath them, or who will be mended by their torne condition.

Roſſe, 29. Octobris. 1649.

Through the goodneſſe of God, my Letters come thick upon you, a new occaſion miniſtred this day, cauſeth me to ſpeed this unto you. It hath pleaſed the Lord to move the hearts of divers of *Inchiquins* men to deſert him, the enemy lying ſome ſeven or eight miles from us, where is *Ormond*, *Inchiquin*, the Lord of *Ardes*, *Caſtlehaven*, *Clanbrazell*, the Lord *Moore*, and *Trevor*. *Inchiquines* men are many of them gone back into Munſter; The Towne of *Corke* and the Fort, have declared for England, and ſent to me for ſupplys of men, and money, and ſome ſhipping

In fact it *consisted* of 9,000 men at that point of the campaign. The losses that Cromwell himself incurred during his nine month campaign would not have been in excess of 2,500 men. The biggest losses that the New Model Army ever incurred were at

Clonmel where the death toll is estimated to be around 2,000. Crouch simply pretends that he got hold of a letter written by Cromwell to an MP from a servant, and like all good hacks, of course, he couldn't reveal his source. If Crouch was prepared to publish a fictitious letter purporting to be written by Cromwell himself, then we can easily assume that the royalist writers were happy to make up anything, pretending it was from 'an eminent officer' in order to help bring down the new regime.

Curiously, in the same edition of *The Man in the Moon,* John Crouch decides to start a rumour that Cromwell's penis was shot off at Drogheda. His front-page news, usually being in the form of a rhyme reads:

> Now Pryde must unto Ireland go,
> With a new regiment,
> For Noll (alack and alas for wo)
> Has lost Lust's instrument
> Which makes his wife to wail and sob
> In tears of briny grief
> And curse the Cavees that would rob
> The puss-ship of relief

Crouch was predicting that Colonel Pride was now set to go to Ireland to assist Cromwell in his time of need. Like all Royalist newsbooks he calls Parliament the 'Juncto'. The ensuing article opens with the lines:

> Now must Mistris Juncto despair of her royal issue, since Cromwel has lost his instrument of generation, and his standard-bearer of lust is shott quite off...Noll himself hath got a pockey clap with a brace of bullets in his gennitals, being shot-free, it is by some thought incredible that a bullet should enter him, but a chyrurgion gave me this reason; for quoth he, that place (being formerly impaired by an accident

> of a malignant fire called morbus) was corrupt, and a breach formerly made by a State-pinnace [a type of sailing boat] that carried wild-fire in her poop, that in the discharging recoyled, and did execution on Noll's gun-flick; else quoth he, they could never have shot off his main-yard and missed the rest of his tacklings, but sure he is preserved for some other end.

This is fairly typical of the type of lurid and obscene stories of which the Royalist newsbook writers were capable. Perusing some of these publications, it is quite clear that they are simply the opinions of one man, the author, who simply wrote what he wanted to write with impunity. What they lack in facts, they make up for in invective.

Continuing the chronology of the appearance of newsbooks concerning the reporting of the fall of Wexford, in his edition of 5 – 12 November, Samuel Pecke's *Perfect Diurnall* simply reports that 'It is certified that Sir Robert Steward is come unto the Hague from Ireland where he has made a very partial relation of the taking of the town of Tredagh and Wexford in Ireland by the forces of Lord General Cromwell and the present condition of his army'. A week later on 20 November, Walter Frost, who was empowered by Parliament to produce an official weekly intelligence publication, after the new act had taken effect, released issue No. 9 of *A Briefe Relation of Some affaires and Transactions, Civill and military, both Forrainge and Domestique* where he prints a full account of the plundering of Wexford. After outlining the comprehensive list of commodities the Parliamentarian army commandeered, Frost's correspondent couldn't help but add his own feelings about the Wexfordians to the list, augmenting the already grim assessment of the town that his comrades had made:

> There I saw the spoiler spoyled, the drowner drowned, they that have made naked were themselves made naked, and which was strangest, I saw the hogs gnaw their flesh and suck

their blood and had divers other witnesses of it.

By the third week in November Wexford was no longer news. The newsbook writers moved on and Cromwell moved on. It is fair to say that we have now examined all of the well-known contemporary accounts of the taking of Wexford. As we have discovered, there are no wild allegations from the defending army about unarmed civilians being killed at Wexford, which, had it happened, one would have expected. Neither Ormond, Castlehaven, Taffe, nor Inchiquin accuse Cromwell of civilian atrocities at Wexford, which is quite a crucial point when it comes to this issue.

The following is the popular primary source evidence concerning Wexford in date order:

11 October: Wexford was stormed

28 October:

The pamphlet *The Taking of Wexford* is published and it contains a letter from an eminent officer in the army called R.L.

29 October:

A Perfect and Particuler Relation is printed by Francis Leach where the writer mentions the accidental drowning of some women.

30 October:

Cromwell's letter to Lenthall about the capture of Wexford has arrived in London and is published by Parliament

Walter Frost issues *A Briefe Relation of Some Affaires and Transactions, Civill and Military, both forraigne and domestique*. It mentions the taking of Wexford briefly.

31 October:

A Very Full and Particular Relation is published by Walter Frost (printed by Edward Husband) and it carries two anonymous letters concerning the storming of Wexford

2 November:

Henry Scobel (or Henry Walker) published the 5th edition of

Severall Proceedings in Parliament that includes Cromwell's letter to Lenthall and his correspondence with Sinnott

5 November:

George Wharton publishes *Mercurius Elencticus* and says that Cromwell put 'all to the sword, men, women and children, except three or foure aldermen.'

7 November:

John Crouch published *The Man in the Moon* wherein he prints a completely fictitious letter he claims to be written by Cromwell and he also reports that Cromwell's penis had been shot off at Drogheda.

12 November:

Samuel Pecke publishes his *Perfect Diurnall* and mentions briefly that Wexford has been taken.

20 November:

Walter Frost publishes a full account of the taking of Wexford in *A Brief Relation* where his correspondent outlines the plunder captured by the Roundheads and he concludes that there he saw 'the spoiler spoyled.'

And so, for the next eleven years no other document, that we are aware of, entered the public domain that implicated Cromwell in war crimes; no newsbooks, no military accounts, no private letters, no ecclesiastical documents, nothing - until a full two years after his death when the royalists resumed power. Yes, Parliament held sway over the official printing presses during the 1650s, but it is futile to say that there was a unilateral control mechanism in place that would have prevented such documents/sentiments being promulgated when we have already seen that any act of Parliament could be circumvented quite easily in the shape of unlicensed newsbooks or pamphlets by those with the will to do so. Of course, they could do nothing about private correspondence and there is none of that existing that will point the finger at Cromwell either. In 1641 the printing presses had clicked profusely for weeks on end producing stories of dead Protestant civilians, satiating the morbid fascination of those early newspaper readers. Allegations from those same printing presses of thousands of dead men, women and children at Drogheda and Wexford might have had the potential to topple Cromwell's Protectorate government before it even got up and running. By 1653 Cromwell was installed as Protector and still neither the royalists nor the (Old English and native Irish) Catholics slung any mud about Drogheda or Wexford. Surely we must conclude that this is because there was no mud to sling. There was nothing but a deafening silence about this issue for eleven long years.

Twelve years after the events at Wexford, on 21 May 1661, the petition of the people of Wexford to Charles II was read out in parliament. This document has made a considerable impact on our interpretation of what exactly happened at both Drogheda and Wexford. It is, therefore, prudent to set out the entire text here in order to appraise the words of the petitioners. It is this document that historians will point to as irrefutable proof of a civilian massacre at Wexford, and indeed at Drogheda. As Muddiman has said, 'Surely the words of those whose relatives and friends died are worth listening to.' A simplistic assertion, but nonetheless one with which it is difficult to argue.

TO THE KING'S MOST EXCELLENT MAJESTY

The humble petition of the Ancient natives, inhabitants of the town of Wexford, and of the heires, orphanes and widowes of such of them as are dead.

Humbly Sheweth That the Petitioners in the beginning of the Rebellion in Ireland helde firme to their ancient loyalty, and never acted anything relating to the said troubles till they observed that some of his late Majestie's shipping revolted against him; and finding their trade was interrupted by those in England that stood in opposition to his late Majestie's authority, then and not sooner did the said inhabitants begin to stand upon their defence; and having fitted and armed some shipps for the support of their trade in the year 1643, the Earle of Castlehaven and the Lord Viscount Taffe being sent by advice of the Lord Marquess Ormonde then your majestie's Lord Lieutenant of Ireland to demand assistance of shipping from the petitioners for his late Majestie's Service, they having imparted the contents of their employment to the said inhabitants, they chearfully and freely agreed to supply the said Lieutenant with the number of tenne shipps, and to have them in readynes in 15 days, and had not failed so to doe but that the occasion was diverted; yet the petitioners zeal and readynesse did sufficiently appeare if there were cause. And as the said inhabitants have been always a people adhearing to the interest of the Crowne and ancient Collonies continued there since the reigne of King Henry the second, soe did they on all occasions expresse their chief loyalty in his Majestie's Service and particularly in embracing the peace concluded by your Majestie's authority 1648, as was manifested afterwards in the time of greatest danger; for the late Usurper Oliver Cromwell, arriveing with a powerful army in Ireland in the year 1649 and having upon the taking of Drogheda put all the inhabitants and soldiers to the sword, that the example thereof might strike a terror into the hearts of the inhabitants of other townes which hee was soone after to besiege, he writt to the petitioners of Wexford being his next designe, and courted them to submitt to his authority and to quitt the royal interest, and that they should injoy all their possessions and fortunes, and be used as well as any others under his power; whose proposall the petitioners did reject, and sent to the Lord Marquess of Ormond, then your Majestie's Lord Lieutenant, praying his Lordship to take care of that place of consequence, and to garrison it as hee should thinke fitt, and that they were ready to expose their lives and fortunes for the defence thereof against the said Usurper, the said Lord Lieutenant did garrison the said towne accordingly and sent thither an able and resolute Commander, Sir Edmund Butler, to whose government and care the inhabitants submitted the whole towne and fortifications, with their lives and fortunes. Yet soe it is, may it please your Majestie, that after all the resistance they could make, the said Usurper having a great Army by sea and land before the said towne, did, on the nynth of October 1649, soe powerfully assault them, that hee entered the towne, and put man, woman and child, to a very few, to the sword, where among the rest the said Governor lost his life and others of the souldiers and inhabitants to the number of 1500 persons; and besides the whole stock and fortune of the inhabitants, to an inestimable value, became pillage and booty to the said Usurper and his souldiers.

The petitioners therefore in the behalfe of themselves who escaped the sword of the said Usurper, and in the behalfe of the children, heires, and widowes of those who soe sacrificed their lives in your Majestie's Service, doe most humbly beseech your Majestie, to be graciously pleased to looke on them as deserved objects of your favour and justice, soe farr as to give order for their restitution to their former habitations, possessions, and interests in the said towne and country; and that the rather, that such of them as were capable to serve your Majestie went first to Silly and Jerzey then in your Majestie's hands and afterwards followed your fortune into forraigne parts, still acting by your Commission in all occasions untill that after your Majestie's happy restauration their Commissions were called in. To which they readily submitted; and now to the number of 30 Captains of them are expecting your Majestie's favour and justice for restoring their former possessions aforesaid, having noe other livlyhood or subsistance at present: which being granted they will ever pray.

A List of such of the inhabitants of Wexford which were captains at sea, Owners and adventurers in the Frigots employed in his majestie's service from the several coasts of Britany and Biscay, since the yeare 1651

Captain William O'Doran.
Captain James Dillon.
Captain Nicholas Jordan.

Captain Richard Dillon.
Captain Christopher Turnor.
Captain Michael Kelly.
(Kild in the service)
Captain Nicholas French.
Captain William Dake.
(Dyed in this service)
Captain Ignatius Brett.
Captain Jasper Hurleston.
Captain Nicholas Hay.

Captain George Codd.
Captain Nicholas Moraugh.
Captain Robert Jordan.
Captain Patrick Dillon.
Captain George Dowdall.
Captain James Long.
Captain Peter Chivers.
Captain Edward Sinnott.

Captain Martin Brice.
Captain Hugh Kelly.
Captain Harman Hendrikson.
Fitzgerald.

Master Thomas Griffin.
Master James Walsh.
Master Bartholomew Dillon.
Master Philip Dillon.
Master Christopher Bath.
Master James French.

Master Mark Furlong.
John Keating

James Keating.
Edward Keating.
Barnaby Stafford.
(kild in the service)
Master Henry Dillon.
Master Leonard Bolan.
Master Francis Beling.
Master James Dalton.
Master John Farrel.
Richard Roch.
Matthew Roch.
Arlonder More.
(kild in the service)
Patrick Kelly.
James Esmond.
Captain James

Captain Christopher Dowdal.
(kild in the service)
Captain Thomas Turnor.
Captain Garret Hay.
(kild in the service)
Captain Laurence Sutton.
Captain Patrick Tayler.
Captain Paul Roch.

All which persons named, (amongst others of the same place), being well knowne to his majestie's Court of Admiralty in forraigne parts to have been severally interested and imployed in his majestie's maritime service, the judge and register of the said court, in testimony of the truth thereof, have hereunto subscribed at St Sebastian's, this fourth day of July 1660.
Signed Tho. Holder
Ben Johnson, Registrar.

In the early twentieth century (1905) historian Robert Pentland Mahaffy published the *Calendar of State Papers relating to Ireland 1660-62* in which he reproduces (most of) the actual petition on page 336. However, concerning the sentence that relates the number of dead, Mahaffy prints the following sentence 'The governor and 1500 men lost their lives, and the property of the inhabitants became pillage to the usurper's soldiers'. Mahaffy worked on the State Papers for 18 years, from 1896 to 1914. On the face of it, his assiduous transcription of the State Papers does not facilitate bias, so it is interesting to note that while paraphrasing the petition, his interpretation of the petition is that 1500 was the total killed, and that they were all 'men'.

Samuel Rawson Gardiner in his *History of the Commonwealth and Protectorate* says:

> After asserting that 'Cromwell put man, woman and child, to a very few to the sword' the petitioners estimate the loss of 'the soldiers and inhabitants' at 1500. It is obvious that if this figure is correct, the whole population, 'man, woman and child' cannot have been killed.

Conversely, Muddiman in his *Cromwell's Massacre at Wexford,* an article he published in *The Irish Ecclesiastical Record* in 1915 says:

> The most important part of this petition, as regards the fate of the inhabitants of the town, is in the phrases I have italicised – 'where, among the rest the said governor lost his life and others of the soldiers, and inhabitants to the number of fifteen hundred persons'. This can only mean that 1500 inhabitants were killed and the number of soldiers slain is, naturally, not specified, since it has nothing to do with the prayer of the petition.

Muddiman's assertion that the petition implies there were 1500 inhabitants killed by the New Model Army and that the petitioners did not specify the number of soldiers slain typifies the man and his campaign to find Cromwell complicit in civilian atrocities. If there is anything to be gleaned from Muddiman's contention it lies in the ability of the petitioners to embroider the facts.

The actual document itself is signed by Judge Thomas Holder and Ben Johnson, Registrar of the Court. In order to evaluate the document fully it is necessary to put it into context. Firstly, it is not contemporary with the events since it is dated from twelve years afterwards. Secondly, it is a desperate plea for clemency and as such could be seen to both exaggerate the civilian death toll to make the petitioners' circumstances appear more dire and at the same time to castigate Cromwell at a time when he was posthumously hung at Tyburn, decapitated and his body thrown in a ditch. Thirdly, and most significantly, we know that Holder and Johnson grossly exaggerated the circumstances at Drogheda, again painting the 'usurper' Cromwell in as bad a light as possible.

It is difficult to concur with Muddiman because none of the firsthand accounts on either side imply that 3,000 were killed at Wexford (1500 civilians plus 1500 soldiers). In many articles throughout his life Muddiman trenchantly accused Cromwell of civilian atrocities. He implicitly believed the story that 300 women were killed at the cross in the marketplace at Wexford, but could not find any eye witness account. Instead he cited later references for the story, firstly clinging to an account from 1758, then discovering an earlier one from 1682. In fact James Heath's *Flagellum, The Life and Death, Birth, Burial of O Cromwell, the Late Usurper* (1660) first carries the story. Relating a very brief account of Cromwell's Irish campaign, starting at the events at Drogheda, page 85 of Heath's book reads:

> The town was stormed resolutely thrice, and as well defended; Sir Arthur Aston being so confident, that he advised the Lord Lieutenant not to precipitate anything, for he should hold them play a while; but in the third assault Colonel Wall being unfortunately killed, his dismayed soldiers listened to the offer of quarter before they had need of it, and admitted them upon those terms. Cromwel having notice that the Flower of the Irish army was in his hands, gave order to put all in arms to the sword, where were killed, Sir Arthur Aston, Sir Edmund Verney, Coll warren, Coll Dun, Finglass, Tempest, &c. With 3,000 soldiers, the best in that kingdome.
>
> He came next before Wexford, which having refused to accept of a garrison, now the enemy was under their walls, was content to admit of 500 men under the command of Sir

Edmund Butler, and the Lord Lieutenant came also in sight of the town; before whose face Stafford the governor of the castle basely betrayed it to Cromwel; together with the town who there treacherously murthered 2000 more.

Most abominably and barbarously cruel he was in this place; for near 200 of the better sort, and the beautifullest women of the city, having (upon the town being entered) fled to the cross, and with the command of their charming eyes, and those melting tears, prevailed upon the souldiers for quarter, now at his coming thither, and after a laughing jeering enquiry what they did there, and other mocking insultations, were commanded to be knocked on the head, which those that promised them life nobly refusing, He commanded another regiment to encompass them, and there most horribly massacred them all.

Flagellum:

OR

The LIFE and DEATH,
BIRTH and BURIAL
OF

O. Cromwell

The late USURPER:
Faithfully Described.

WITH

An Exact Account of His Policies
and Successes:
Not heretofore Published or Discovered.

The Fcurth EDITION *with Additions.*

—Furto *lætatus* inani
Distulit in seram commissa piacula mortem.
Virg. Æneid.

LONDON,
Printed by *E. C.* for *Randall Taylor*, and are to be
sold at his Shop at the Crown in
Little Britain. 1669.

Leads of the Church, and were saluted with a Message of Decimation; but that *Cromwel* might ingratiate with the Army, for his sake, and at his instance they were all pardoned, and sent home to their own houses. The great Chieftain of them, being pursued as he was marching towards the party, took into *Willingborough-wood*, where couragiously defending himself, he was killed by Carbine shot, refusing to take quarter at such perfidious peoples hands. This Hurly Burly being over, and ended like a flash, the General came to *Oxford*, where he was highly treated, and he and *Oliver* made Doctors of the Civil Law.

This proved the utter Suppression of that faction, and rendred the Army entirely at his command, without any farther dispute of their Leading; so that they presently submitted to the Lot which Regiments should be sent to *Ireland* (then almost reduced to the Kings obedience by the Marquiss of *Ormond*) which thus decreed it, *viz.* 11. Regiments, *Iretons*, *Scroops*, *Hortons*, and *Lamberts*. Of Horse, One of Dragoons under Coll. *Abbot*. Of Foot, *Eures*, *Cooks*, *Hewsons*, and *Deans*. And three new ones, *viz.* *Cromwels*, *Venables*, and *Phayrs*.

Cromwel was ordained Commander in Chief, and tituladoed with the Style of Lord Governor of *Ireland*; while *Fairfax* was left here to attend the Parliament, and pass away his time in the Dotages of his Success, giving him the Honour of subduing that Realm, and preparing it to his Usurpation.

He, with a very potent Army was now landed at *Dublin*. Whereupon a strong Garrison of 2500. Foot and 300 Horse, resolved men under the charge of Sir *Arthur Aston*, was put into *Drogheda*, the nea-

rest

rest Carrison to the late defeat of the Marquiss of *Ormond*; which *Cromwel* (having refreshed his Army a while at *Dublin*) came to besiege. The Town was stormed resolutely thrice, and as well defended; Sir *Arthur Aston* being so confident, that he advised the Lord Lieutenant not to precipitate any thing, for he should hold them play a while; but in the third assault Colonel *Wall* being unfortunately killed, his dismaied Soldiers listened to the offer of quarter before they had need of it, and admitted them upon those terms. *Cromwel* having notice that the Flower of the *Irish* Army was in his hands, gave order to put all in Arms to the Sword, where were killed Sir *Arthur Aston*, Sir *Edmund Verney*, Coll. *Warren*, Coll. *Dun*, *Finglass*, *Tempest*, &c. with 3000 Soldiers the best in that Kingdome.

He came next before *Wexford*, which having refused to accept of a Garrison, now the Enemy was under their Walls, was content to admit of 500 men under the command of Sir *Edmund Butler*, and the Lord Lieutenant came also in sight of the Town; before whose face *Stafford* the Governour of the Castle basely betrayed it to *Cromwel*, together with the Town who there treacherously murthered 2000 more.

Most abominably and barbarously cruel he was in this place; for near 200 of the better sort, and the beautifullest Women of the City, having (upon the Town being entred) fled to the Cross, and with the command of their charming eyes, and those melting tears, prevailed upon the Souldiers for quarter; now at his coming thither, and after a laughing jeering enquiry what they did there, and other mocking insultations, were commanded to be knock'd on the head;

F 3 which

which thofe that promifed them life nobly refufing, He commanded another Regiment to encompafs them,and there moft horribly maffacred them all.

Roffe was the next place whither a Garrifon was fent under the command of *Luke Taaff*, with order (the Town not being tenable) to render upon Conditions, which accordingly (a breach being made) they did, and marched away with their Arms. His next attempt was upon *Duncannon*, but the noble *Wogan* and the *English* Cavaliers gave him a foyle; hence he retreated to *Rofs*, where he made a floating-bridge,that fo, having a paffage to the other fide, he might compel *Ormond* either to divide his Army to obferve his motions, or otherwife to get a paffage into *Munfter*, where he held intelligence with the feveral places that would then Revolt; and accordingly for all my Lord *Taaff* was fent thither before hand to fecure them, yet *Yonghall*, *Corke*, and all the *Englifh* Towns of *Munfter* openly Revolted, and many of my Lord *Inchiqueens* men, allured by Money and Commands in *Cromwel*'s Army, ran over to the Enemy; and his Excellency the Lord Lieutenant having loft the opportunity of Fighting *Cromwel*, by his diflodging from *Duncannon* by night when the *Irifh* were cheerful and earneft to engage, was never after in a condition fit to venture a Battel. He therefore paffes over this Bridge and fo into the County of *Kilkenny* facing his enemy and moving up and down after him, while his Lieut. G. *Jones* with parties took in the Caftles, and *Carrick* was wretchedly betrayed to him by *Martin*, that commanded there; whence *Cromwel* paffes his Army into *Munfter*, and takes feveral Caftles by the appearance only of his Horfe: only at *Kilteran* he received a repulfe, but

Had Muddiman discovered Heath's account, no doubt he would have used it to attempt to copper-fasten Cromwell's complicity in atrocious deeds. According to Heath (whose scurrilous tome is generally disregarded by most historians) Cromwell arrived on the scene at the cross, jeered the women, ordered his men to kill them and when they refused, he called a different regiment up to carry out his terrible orders. It goes without saying that this is not in keeping with Cromwell's Irish campaign. Nor is it in keeping with Cromwell the man. Indeed it has a ring of the Thomas á Wood story about it, fanciful, dramatic and designed to shock. It is certainly in keeping, however, with the Restoration picture of Cromwell and capricious propaganda methods. It dates from the same time that the Wexford petitioners were writing their plea. Parliament's time in power was over; indeed the republic had failed when the second Protector, Richard Cromwell, Oliver's eldest surviving son, did not measure up to his father, clearing the way for the return of the king. And now many who were associated with Parliament's usurpation were being hunted down and punished at this time, particularly the regicides themselves. The printing presses were producing anti-Cromwell stories by the bucket-load, and it is into this atmosphere that the petitioners' appeal appears.

Interestingly in his scandalous biography of Cromwell (although he is notoriously unreliable) Heath does not mention the deaths of any inhabitants at Drogheda – armed or unarmed. A ferocious royalist, Heath had no credentials to be an authority on the events in Ireland but strangely he did not embellish either Wharton's or Crouch's allegations of civilian atrocities at Drogheda, both of which had been in the public domain for eleven years. Perhaps the reason is that there were no other accounts published in the interim period for Heath to draw from and the controversial editions (*Mercurius Elencticus* and *The Man in the Moon*) were already cast to the mists of time. We certainly do not know of any. Heath's ignoring of Drogheda, later to become the biggest blot on his subject's career, just emphasises the inconsistencies in the civilian atrocity stories.

We have now analysed the sum total of contemporary documents that provide us with primary source information of Drogheda and Wexford. Others may yet surface in years to come, but those that are consulted here are the popular sources, and one or two that are not often used (like Heath). As already mentioned, the historians (McElligott, O'Siochrú and Morrill) have made no real use of post-Restoration accounts of Drogheda and Wexford to support their belief in civilian atrocities, aside from the ones already cited here. As experts, they know only too well the further away in time from the events one gets, the less reliable accounts become, since they can be influenced by a multitude of factors in the intervening period. Few periods of history can be as volatile as this one when it comes to misinformation and half-truths, all of which makes drawing conclusions a pretty precarious pastime. But it is the vitriolic way that Cromwell is perceived in Ireland that demands our attention. If this is a cataclysmic historical miscarriage of justice, then the world should know. If he is innocent of war crimes, then history should record this. This study is not just a robust defence of Cromwell's reputation; it is also a challenge. It is a challenge to those historians (some mentioned here) whose period of expertise this is, to set the records straight.

If the facts are inconclusive then at the very least balance should be introduced. If the case here is a good one, and there is no solid evidence to convict Cromwell of civilian atrocities, then we, the Irish nation owe Cromwell an apology for destroying his reputation over the last 365 years. Therefore, I would like this book to serve as a challenge to historians everywhere to justify the statement in the children's school textbook *Timeline* 'He (Cromwell) first laid siege to Drogheda. He was determined to make an example of the town. When he captured it he slaughtered the entire population'. If it cannot be justified then we need to stop teaching children lies. If it can, then please produce the solid evidence.

In conclusion, it seems appropriate to use the words of Cromwell himself in this challenge to those who espouse the traditional version of events. In a letter to the general assembly of the Church of Scotland on 3 August 1650, he said, 'I beseech you, in the bowels of Christ, think it possible that you might be mistaken.'

CHRONOS BOOKS

Chronos Books is a historical non-fiction imprint. Chronos publishes real history for real people; bringing to life historical people, places and events in an imaginative, easy-to-digest and accessible way. We want writers of historical books, from ancient times to the Second World War, that will add to our understanding of people and events rather than being a dry textbook; history that passes on its stories to a generation of new readers.